Programming with
Miranda™

D1766761

Programming with Miranda™

Chris Clack
Colin Myers
Ellen Poon

Prentice Hall
New York   London   Toronto   Sydney   Tokyo   Singapore

WITHDRAWN
LIBRARY
COLLEGE

First published 1995 by
Prentice Hall International (UK) Ltd
Campus 400, Maylands Avenue
Hemel Hempstead
Hertfordshire, HP2 7EZ
A division of
Simon & Schuster International Group

© Prentice Hall International (UK) Ltd, 1995

All rights reserved. No part of this publication may be
reproduced, stored in a retrieval system or transmitted,
in any form, or by any means, electronic, mechanical,
photocopying, recording or otherwise, without prior
permission, in writing, from the publisher.
For permission within the United States of America
contact Prentice Hall Inc., Englewood Cliffs, NJ 07632

Typeset by Chris Clack and Colin Myers

Miranda™ is a trademark of Research Software Limited

Printed and bound in Great Britain by
Redwood Books Ltd, Trowbridge, Wiltshire

Library of Congress Cataloging-in-Publication Data

Clack, Chris.
Programming with Miranda / Chris Clack, Colin Myers, Ellen Poon.
    p. cm.
   Includes bibliographical references and index.
   ISBN 0–13–192592–X
   1. Functional programming languages. 2. Miranda (Computer program language)
   I. Myers, Colin. II. Poon, Ellen. III. Title.
QA76.62.C55 1994
005.13′3—dc20   94–30689 CIP

British Library Cataloguing in Publication Data

A catalogue record for this book is available from the British Library

ISBN 0–13–192592–X

---

  2   3   4   5   98 97 96 95

Contents

Preface

The purpose of this book is to teach structured programming skills using the functional programming language Miranda. It may be used as an introductory textbook for people with little programming experience or as an intermediate textbook for more advanced programmers who wish to learn a functional programming language. Both novice and advanced programmers will learn how to use a functional language to develop sound software design and code management techniques. Additionally, advanced programmers will find that knowledge of a functional language provides a foundation for further studies in the theory and implementation of programming languages and formal specification.

Miranda is one of the most popular functional languages employed in education and research, used in over 500 sites, and it is also increasingly having an impact on industry. Miranda has evolved from earlier languages such as SASL and KRC, which were developed in 1976 (Turner, 1976) and 1982 (Turner, 1982), respectively. It is a general-purpose programming environment, with a compiler embedded in an interactive system (implemented under UNIX[1]) providing access to a screen editor, an on-line reference manual and an interface to UNIX. Separate compilation is supported (to an intermediate code, which is subsequently interpreted), with automatic recompilation of altered source files. The Miranda programming system is a product of Research Software Limited; this textbook is based on Miranda *release two*.[2]

This is a practical programming book. Theoretical issues are avoided unless they are essential for a proper understanding of the use of the language. However, some formal definitions are introduced in order to aid the reader when referring to other texts. The boundary between those theoretical matters that are discussed and those that are not is, unavoidably, somewhat arbitrary. For example, Chapter 3 discusses the use of inductive reasoning to help with software design; however, we

---

[1]UNIX is a trademark of AT&T Bell Laboratories.

[2]The Miranda system can be obtained directly from Research Software Ltd of 23 St Augustines Road, Canterbury, Kent, CT1 1XP, UK. email: mira-request@ukc.ac.uk.

do not extend this to the use of denotational semantics to reason about a program. Similarly, we provide a gentle introduction to the theory of strong typing, but we do not discuss type inference mechanisms. We do not discuss the lambda calculus, formal program transformation, numerical analysis, efficiency or any implementation methods.

The approach we adopt in this book is to show good software engineering principles by discussion of both correct and incorrect design decisions, using realistic examples. There is no Ackermann function and there are no miracles.

Acknowledgements

This book was developed during the teaching of functional programming courses to undergraduate and postgraduate classes at University College London and the University of Westminster. We thank our students for their many helpful recommendations and corrections.

Many thanks also to Don Clack, Simon Courtenage, Michael Fourman, Mark Hardie, Neil Harris, Hessam Khoshnevisan, Dave Pitt, Mike Poon, Mark Priestley, Will Richardson and David N. Turner for their positive suggestions concerning the companion volume to this book, *Programming with Standard ML*. These comments have proven equally valuable in the writing of this book.

We also thank Anthony Davie, Mark d'Inverno and Dr John Sharpe for their many helpful suggestions and corrections. Finally, thanks to David Turner for his many constructive comments and to Research Software Limited for permission to include information about the Miranda system in this book, and for allowing us to quote from the Miranda on-line reference manual.

Chris Clack
Colin Myers
Ellen Poon

Introduction

Programming languages may be grouped into several "families" with similar characteristics. Two of the most important families are the *imperative* languages (also
known as "procedural" languages) and the *functional* languages. The imperative
family includes such languages as BASIC, Pascal, C, Fortran, Ada, Modula-2 and
COBOL. The functional family includes Miranda,[1] SML, Lispkit,[2] FP and Haskell;
a good survey is provided in (Hudak, 1989).

The basic difference between functional and imperative languages is that functional languages are concerned with *describing a solution to a problem*, whereas
imperative languages are concerned with *giving instructions to a computer*. Rather
than attempt an explanation in isolation, this introduction *compares* the functional
and imperative styles of programming. A number of claims will be made for the
functional style and these will be substantiated in the main body of the text.

The reader should notice that this chapter compares *styles* and not *languages*:
it is often possible to use a functional style when programming in an imperative
language. Readers with no previous programming experience may safely skip this
chapter on first reading.

Implications of the imperative style of programming

A program written in an imperative language describes in detail a sequence of
actions that the computer must execute (these are sometimes called commands—
hence the name "imperative"). This means that the imperative programmer must
be familiar with the way the computer works. In general, a programmer must
think in terms of the computer hardware—the conceptual model is one of memory
locations containing values which may change during the execution of a program.

---

[1] Miranda is a trademark of Research Software Limited.

[2] Lispkit is a pure functional subset of the well-known language LISP which was the first
important language with functional features.

1

The major consequence of this conceptual model is that a programmer is forced to muddle together the three separate activities of:

1. Describing the solution to a problem.
2. Organizing that solution into a set of instructions for a computer.
3. Administering low-level storage allocation.

A programmer should only be concerned with the first of these.

To a great extent this complexity derives from one particular feature—the assignment statement (Backus, 1978). The dangers inherent in the assignment statement include ambiguous pointer assignment, forgetting to initialize variables or incorrectly changing loop control variables (possibly causing an infinite loop). The availability of global variables also offers the opportunity of bad programming style, since it becomes very difficult to keep track of what value the variable is meant to have at any time and which parts of the program are changing the value of the variable. Assignment to pointers serves to compound these problems.

Consider the following Modula-2 solution to select all the items in an integer array that are less than 10:

```
j := 1;
FOR i := 1 TO LineLength DO
    IF line[i] < 10 THEN
        newline[j] := line[i];
        j := j + 1;
    END
END
```

The code has a relatively difficult interpretation; it is not easy to read compared with the simplicity of the natural language specification. Even in this small program extract, the major concern has been with the assignment to storage and maintaining indexes; that is, making the solution fit the hardware model.[3] This intellectual overhead is magnified if the problem were to select all the items less than 10 in a dynamic linked list. The emphasis would be even more towards the manipulation of memory rather than the representation of the data structure or the selection of items from it.

In general, the following observations hold for most existing imperative languages:

1. They have a limited set of control structures for expressing iteration and for combining subcalculations and hence it is often difficult to take advantage of a high-level modular design.
2. They have a limited set of built-in data structures. Although it is possible to model other data structures, the process often involves complex manipulation of pointers and a lot of code.

---

[3] To keep this example simple, the problem of retaining knowledge of the array newline's size has been ignored.

3. They have complex semantics, which makes it difficult to apply formal reasoning and hence more difficult to arrive at a correct solution.

Benefits of the functional programming style

Functional languages are an example of the *declarative* style of programming, whereby a program gives a description (or "declaration") of a problem to be solved together with various relationships that hold for it. It is the responsibility of the language implementation (perhaps a compiler or an interpreter) to convert this description into a list of instructions for a computer to run.[4] There are a number of implications of this alternative computational model:

1. A programmer does not have to worry about storage allocation. There is no assignment statement—a functional programmer does not assign values to storage locations, but instead has the ability to give names to the values of expressions; these names may then be used in other expressions or passed as parameters to functions.

2. The fact that in a functional language a name or an expression has a unique value that will never change is known as *referential transparency*. As a consequence of referential transparency, subcomputations always give the same result for the same arguments. This means that the code is safer and may often be reused in similar contexts; the nett result is a higher level of quality assurance and faster programming.

3. Functions and values are treated as mathematical objects which obey well-established mathematical rules and are therefore *well suited to formal reasoning*. This allows the programmer a high level of abstraction and so greater flexibility in defining control structures and data structures.

4. The syntax and semantics of functional languages tend to be simple and so they are relatively easy to learn. Furthermore, the resultant programs tend to be more concise and have fewer mistakes. Brooks (Brooks, 1975) observes that *"productivity seems constant in terms of elementary statements"*; if this applies equally to functional programmers then the conciseness of functional programs should lead to greater programmer efficiency.

It is not possible to justify all of these assertions in this brief introduction but, as a sample of the functional style, a typical solution to the problem discussed in the previous section (of selecting items from a sequence of numbers) would be:

```
filter (lessthan 10) number_sequence
```

---

[4]Many functional languages are based on a mathematical theory known as the "lambda calculus" (Revesz, 1988). At advanced levels, it may be useful for a programmer to understand this theory but, in general, it is not necessary for the novice or intermediate programmer.

There is no need to manage storage, no danger of forgetting to initialize or increment variables and no need to worry about where the results are kept! The code is clearly much nearer to the specification—indeed sometimes functional programs are considered as "executable specifications" (Turner, 1985a).

The functional style is also more flexible. For example, changing the Modula-2 code to select all items not equal to `"fred"` from a sequence of strings requires writing a new function—even though the structure of the solution is identical. Changing the functional code is straightforward:[5]

```
filter (notequal "fred") string_sequence
```

Finally, there is the question of efficiency. It is claimed that the higher the level of the programming language (that is, the further away from the hardware model), the less efficient the language is in terms of speed and memory utilization. To a certain extent this may be true,[6] however two very important points are worth making:

1. The first concern of a programmer is that a a program is written on time and is *correct*: performance is generally a secondary concern.
2. Functional languages are not tied to the von Neuman architecture (Backus 1978). This facilitates implementations on other hardware configurations such as multi-processors.

Consider the following:

```
sumofsquares := square (x) + square (y)
```

In an imperative language it is necessary to have an ordering of instructions; typically **square (x)** is executed before **square (y)**. Logically, however, it does not matter whether **square (x)** is executed first or second; actually both **square (x)** and **square (y)** could be calculated simultaneously. The very fact that functional languages are not based on any particular hardware conceptual model helps them to take advantage of parallel and multi-processor hardware (Peyton Jones, 1987; Kelley, 1989). In summary, the programmer is freed from the burden of implementation.[7]

However, the above discussion should not lead the reader to the idea that functional languages are the cure for all programming evils. There is still the need to

---

[5] In Miranda the function `filter` is built into the system, but could actually be written by the programmer with just three short statements. The reason why the code is so flexible derives directly from the ability to treat functions as parameters to other functions; `filter` takes any function which returns a Boolean value.

[6] Although modern implementations of functional languages rival the speed of compiled imperative languages such as Pascal and C.

[7] Because of this freedom, functional languages are also well suited to program transformation techniques. These allow programs to be mathematically derived from their specifications, or an inefficient algorithm to be converted to an efficient one by the compiler (Darlington *et al.*, 1982). Program transformation techniques also guarantee that new errors are not introduced into the code. However, such optimization techniques are outside the scope of this book.

recognize problems and find sensible solutions! There are also a number of software engineering issues that arise from large-scale programming tasks; in the main these are beyond the scope of this book.

Miranda in context

Miranda is not an acronym but a woman's name possibly first used by Shakespeare in *The Tempest*, and is the Latin for "to be admired". It has evolved from earlier languages such as SASL and KRC, which were developed by David Turner at (respectively) St. Andrews University in the late seventies and the University of Kent in the early eighties. An overview of Miranda's conceptual framework and key features is given in (Turner, 1985b).

Miranda is a purely functional language, with no imperative features of any kind. Following the style of SASL and KRC, Miranda has *lazy* semantics; this permits the use of potentially infinite data structures and supports an elegant style of problem decomposition. Miranda is now a general purpose programming language and is used for a wide variety of activities, especially in the areas of proof systems and specification.

Miranda shares with most other functional languages the notion that functions and data values have "equal citizenship"; that is, they can be manipulated in the same manner (Landin, 1966). Other Miranda characteristics of note include polymorphism (which gives flexibility to the strong type system), pattern matching (to provide an elegant selection control structure), list comprehension, partial function application and new type construction. These topics are dealt with in depth in the main text.

Miranda is an example of a *lazy* functional language, which means that a function's parameters are normally evaluated only if they are needed. This is in contrast to the alternative *strict* style of evaluation, whereby a function's parameters are normally evaluated before the function body itself. (A good example of the latter style is Standard ML (Myers, Clack and Poon, 1993)). The Bibliography contains references which will provide further discussion of strict and lazy implementations.

How to use the book

The first two chapters of this book provide a simple introduction to Miranda syntax and the functional approach to programming, whilst also serving to reorientate the imperative programmer. Some of the features shown will be quite familiar to anyone with imperative programming experience; these include the standard mathematical operators, the clear distinction made between different types of data and the idea of function definition and application. Novel features are dealt with in greater depth; these include pattern matching, polymorphism and the use of recursion for program control.

The third and fourth chapters explore in depth the heart of the functional style. They are core to Miranda (and functional) programming and will probably appear quite new to a programmer only familiar with an imperative programming language. In Chapter 3, the list aggregate type is introduced as the most fundamental Miranda data structure and various styles of recursive programming using lists are investigated. The chapter ends with the design of a program similar to the UNIX utility *grep*, which is used in subsequent chapters to highlight the expressive power of new features. Chapter 4 introduces the important concept of partial application and demonstrates that functions can be treated as data. It also shows how recursive solutions to programming tasks can be generalized to facilitate control structure abstraction.

Chapter 5 explores two important concepts: controlling the availability of identifiers and functions; and lazy evaluation. The former is essential for any production programming since it gives the ability to make blocks of code private to other blocks of code—thereby facilitating safer and more reusable software. The latter provides an important mechanism for combining functions and structuring programs.

The next two chapters explore the relationship between data and process by showing Miranda's powerful facilities to create new types and data structures, and to encapsulate a type and its associated operations into a single abstraction.

Chapter 8 introduces the programmer to file handling and interactive programming, and Chapter 9 provides tools for medium to large-scale program construction.

It is recommended that the main body of the book is studied sequentially, and that the reader should attempt the exercises as they are encountered. The exercises serve both as a review of the student's current knowledge and also as a commentary on the text; sample solutions are given at the end of the book.

Chapter 1

Operators, Identifiers and Types

This chapter starts by showing some elementary Miranda programs, where only simple expressions involving built-in arithmetic and relational operators are used. Since these simple expressions can only make simple programs, more enhanced features are needed in order to create real-life applications. These include the access to built-in functions, such as those to calculate the sine or square root of a number, and more importantly, the ability to associate names either with immediate data values or with expressions which are evaluated to some data value. Once a name is defined, it can be recalled in all subsequent expressions within a program. This makes programs more readable and makes it easier to create more complex expressions.

In order to promote good programming, Miranda has a strong type system whereby a function can only be applied to an argument of the expected type. Any attempt to give an argument of a type other than the one it expects will result in a "type error". In practice, the strong type system is a useful debugging tool.

Good style is further encouraged by the use of comments in order to document the code.

1.1 A Miranda session

Typically, the Miranda system will be entered from the host system by typing the command `mira`. Miranda responds by displaying an initial message, such as:

```
The   Miranda   System

version 2.009 last revised 13 November 1989

Copyright Research Software Ltd, 1989
```

7

This message may be surrounded by site and version specific details and may be followed by the Miranda system prompt, `Miranda`.

Exit from Miranda systems is achieved by typing `/quit` or `/q`, to which Miranda responds: `Miranda logout` and then returns control to the UNIX shell.

Using the Miranda system

The Miranda interactive system issues a prompt and waits for the programmer to type something. The programmer may type either an expression to be evaluated or an instruction to the Miranda system; all instructions start with a slash (for example, `/q` to quit from Miranda, or `/e` to ask Miranda to edit a file). Miranda will either evaluate the expression or obey the instruction; it then issues a fresh prompt and waits for the programmer to type something else.

The simplest use of Miranda is to type in an expression to be evaluated; in this way, Miranda acts rather like a desk calculator.

All Miranda expressions and instructions, when entered at the prompt, must be terminated by a newline. The following is an example of an expression with the Miranda system response:

```
Miranda 3 + 4
7
```

Miranda responds to the expression by simply displaying the result: 7.

An expression cannot be split across more than one line; if it seems incomplete then the system will give an error message, such as:

```
Miranda 3 +
syntax error - unexpected newline
```

Standard operators

Miranda provides built-in functions for the standard arithmetical and relational operations. The rest of this section discusses their general characteristics, more specific detail being provided in subsequent sections.

Examples:

```
Miranda 34 + 56
90

Miranda 2.0 * 3.5
7.0
```

```
Miranda 3 > 4
False
```

```
Miranda 3 = 3
True
```

All of the arithmetic operations can be used several times in an expression or in combination with other operators. For example:

```
Miranda 2 + 3 + 5
10
```

```
Miranda 2 + 3 * 5
17
```

```
Miranda (2 + 3) * 5
25
```

The above behave as expected, with brackets being used to enforce the order of evaluation.

An interesting, although perhaps surprising, feature of Miranda is that the relational operators >, >=, etc., can also be chained together to form "continued relations". For example, the expression (2 < 3 < 4) evaluates to True. However, the expression ((2 < 3) < 4) would give an error, as explained later in this chapter.

Simple function application

Miranda provides a number of useful functions, full details of which are given in Section 28 of the On-line Manual (see below). To use one of these functions, it must be applied to an argument. Function application is denoted by giving the name of the function, followed by the argument enclosed in brackets. If the argument is a single value then the brackets may be omitted.

Examples:

```
Miranda sqrt (4.0 + 12.0)
4.0
```

```
Miranda sqrt (25.0)
5.0
```

```
Miranda sqrt 9.0
3.0
```

```
Miranda (sqrt 9.0) + (sqrt 25.0)
8.0


Miranda sqrt (sqrt 81.0)
3.0
```

1.1.1   On-line help

Miranda offers a brief *help* screen and a more detailed on-line *manual*. By typing /help or /h the help screen appears with a short explanation of Miranda's interactive features. The on-line manual can be accessed by typing /man or /m. This gives rise to the help menu as shown in Figure 1.1. Notice that the on-line manual is extensive and contains detailed information for experienced users as well as novices; furthermore, the manual is well structured for on-line browsing and it is consequently neither necessary nor advisable to print a hard copy.

```
Miranda System Manual    Copyright Research Software Limited 1989

 1. How to use the manual system   20. Algebraic types
 2. About the name "Miranda"       21. Abstract types
 3. About this release             22. Placeholder types
 4. The Miranda command interpreter 23. The special function {\bf show}
 5. Brief summary of main commands  24. Formal syntax of Miranda scripts
 6. List of remaining commands     25. Comments on syntax
 7. Expressions                    26. Miranda lexical syntax
 8. Operators                      27. The library mechanism
 9. Operator sections              28. The standard environment
10. Identifiers                    29. Literate scripts
11. Literals                       30. Some hints on Miranda style
12. Tokenisation and layout        31. UNIX/Miranda system interface
13. Iterative expressions          32. -->> CHANGES <<--
14. Scripts, overview              33. Licensing information
15. Definitions                    34. Known bugs and deficiencies
16. Pattern matching               35. Notice
17. Compiler directives
18. Basic type structure           99. Create a printout of the manual
19. Type synonyms                  100. An Overview of Miranda (paper)

::please type selection number (or return to exit):
```

Figure 1.1 The menu for the Miranda on-line manual.

1.2   Identifiers

In Miranda it is possible to give a name or *identifier* to the value of an expression. This is achieved by typing /e or /edit to enter the editor and then modifying the default *script file* (which has the name script.m). An expression may then be given a name, using the format:

   identifier = *expression*

The simplest kind of expression is a basic data value, examples of this being:[1]

```
hours   = 24
message = "Hello World"
```

The value associated with the name hours is now 24 and the value associated with the name message is "Hello World".

Once the editor has been exited, the system checks the syntax of the script file and, if it is valid, then the value given to a name can readily be recalled by entering the name as an expression to be evaluated:

```
Miranda hours
24
```

Similarly, the value returned by the expression ((4 * 30) + (7 * 31) + 28) may be given a name, within the script file, as follows:

```
days = ((4 * 30) + (7 * 31) + 28)
```

and recalled by entering days at the system prompt:

```
Miranda days
365
```

In general, any name may appear on the left-hand side of the equals sign and any expression may appear on the right-hand side. Note that a name is a kind of expression, but an expression is not a name, so twentyfour = hours is a legal definition but (3 + 4) = hours is not. Giving a name to a value is useful because that name can then be used in subsequent expressions; the choice of meaningful names will make a program easier to read.

The following is a simple example of an expression that itself involves names that have been previously defined:

```
hours_in_year     = (days * hours)

hours_in_leapyear = ((days + 1) * hours)
```

---

[1]In the rest of this book, script files are presented within a box.

The values of these two identifiers can be recalled as follows:

```
Miranda hours_in_year
8760
```

```
Miranda hours_in_leapyear
8784
```

Legal and sensible identifiers

In practice there is a limitation to the choice of names. There are three restrictions:

1. Certain words are reserved by the Miranda system and therefore *cannot* be used:[2]

   abstype div if mod otherwise
   readvals show type where with

2. Certain words have already been defined within the Miranda *Standard Environment* and should similarly be avoided. Appendix A contains a list of those definitions provided by the Miranda system.
3. An identifier must begin with an alphabetic character and may be followed by zero or more characters, which may be alphabetic, digits or underscores (_) or single quotes ('). For names of simple expressions such as described in this chapter, the first character *must be in lower case*.

1.2.1   Referential transparency and reusing names

The functional programming style is that a name is given to a value rather than giving a name to a memory location. In an imperative programming language, the memory location referred to by a name is constant, but the value stored in that location may change; in a functional programming language, the value itself is constant and the programmer is not concerned with how or where this value is stored in memory.

The functional style has the important consequence that the values of names do not change and therefore the result of a given expression will be the same wherever it appears in a program. Any program written in this style is said to have the property of *referential transparency*.

Programs exhibiting referential transparency have many benefits, including the fact that it is easier to reason about these programs and hence easier to debug them. For example, one part of a program may be tested independently of the rest.

---

[2]Throughout this book, the use of a **bold** font indicates a reserved name.

Miranda adopts this style and hence it is not possible to use the same name more than once.[3] Thus constructing the following definition sequence within the script file is illegal:

```
message = "Hello World"

message = "Goodbye Cruel World"
```

On exit from the editor, the Miranda system will report a syntax error and abandon compilation.

1.3   Types

Types are a way of classifying data values according to their intended use. A data type may be specified either by enumerating the values that data items of that type may have, or by the operations that may be performed upon data items of that type. Conscientious use of a type classification system aids the construction of clear, reliable, well-structured programs.

Miranda has a number of built-in data types, including the simple types—integers, fractional (or real) numbers, strings, characters and Booleans—together with fixed-length aggregate types which are discussed in this chapter. Chapter 3 introduces the variable-length list aggregate type, whereas the facility to define new data types is presented in Chapter 6.

Miranda is a *strongly typed* language. This means that the system uses information about the types of data values to ensure that they are used in the correct way. For example, the predefined function **sqrt** expects to be applied to an argument that is a number. In Miranda, numbers are not surrounded by quotation marks and so the following is detected as an error (the error message, itself, will be explained in the next subsection):

```
Miranda sqrt '4'
type error in expression
cannot unify char with num
```

This principle extends to the infix arithmetic operators, in that an error will arise if the wrong type of value is used. For example, in the following session Miranda expects the function **div** to be used with two numbers and gives an error if used with a number and a Boolean value:

```
Miranda 2 div True
type error in expression
cannot unify bool with num
```

---

[3]See, however, Chapter 5.

1.3.1 Error messages

On exit from the editor, Miranda checks the script file (assuming that it has changed) and, if the script file is an error-free Miranda program, then the following message will be printed:

```
compiling script.m
checking types in script.m
Miranda
```

By contrast, if the program contains errors then Miranda will issue one or more error messages and will refuse to accept *any* of the definitions in the program.

Error messages highlight two kinds of error; syntax errors and type errors. Here is an example of a syntax error, where the value `"hello"` has been wrongly entered as `"hello`:

```
wrong_message = "hello
```

On exit from the editor, Miranda gives the following report, including the line number where the syntax error was found (which is useful in large programs):

```
compiling script.m
syntax error: non-escaped newline encountered inside string quotes
error found near line 1 of file "script.m"
compilation abandoned
```

Note that the error message assumes that the fault is the newline occurring immediately after the word `"hello`; this is because a newline is not allowed unless the terminating quote character has been given.

Here is an example of a type error:

```
wrong_value = sqrt 'A'
```

On exit from the editor, Miranda gives the following report, including the line number where the error was found (which is useful in large programs):

```
compiling script.m
checking types in script.m
type error in definition of wrong_value
(line   1 of "script.m") cannot unify char with num
Miranda
```

The last line of the error message states that Miranda "cannot unify char with num". This means that Miranda realizes that the built-in function **sqrt** expects to be applied to a number (a "num") and not to a character (a "char"). In general, type error messages may include obscure information for advanced programmers as well as information that is useful for relative beginners. These type error messages will become clearer in later chapters.

1.3.2   Numbers

Miranda recognizes two sorts of number: integers and fractional (or real) numbers, and is generally happy for these two subtypes to mix. Notice that fractional numbers are indicated by decimal points (trailing zeros are required) or by using exponential format. The precision cannot be specified by the programmer; it is determined by the machine in use, but it is guaranteed to be at least the equivalent of 16 decimal places.

Data values of both sorts of number are indicated by the type name **num** and may be manipulated by the operators shown in Table 1.1. Notice that whenever a fractional number appears as one of the operands to these operators then the result will be a fractional number. The only exceptions are **div** and **mod** which expect two integer operands, and will produce an error message otherwise.

Table 1.1 Operations on numbers.

+	addition
−	subtraction
*	multiplication
/	real number division
div	integer division
mod	integer remainder
^	exponentiation

For example:

```
Miranda 365.0 / 7.0
52.142857142857

Miranda 365 / 7.0
52.142857142857

Miranda 365 / 7
52.142857142857

Miranda 365 div 7
52

Miranda 365 mod 7
1

Miranda (1 / 3) * 3
1.0
```

```
Miranda 3 ^ 3
9
```

```
Miranda 4.0 ^ -1
0.25
```

```
Miranda days div 7
52
```

where **days** has already been defined as having the value 365.

Notice, that the fractional number divide operator, /, allows integers and fractional numbers to mix but that the **div** operator expects *both* of its operands to be integers:

```
Miranda 365 div 7.0
program error: fractional number where integer expected (div)
```

Negative numbers

It is possible to denote negative numbers by prefixing them with a minus sign: -. For example:

```
x = -33
```

However, the - character is actually a built-in prefix operator that takes a single argument and negates the value:

```
Miranda - (-33.0)
33.0
```

```
Miranda - (- (33.0))
33.0
```

```
Miranda -x
33
```

The last of the above examples shows that there need not be a space between the - and a name.

The fact that - can be used in this prefix manner is important, as illustrated by the following session which uses the built-in function **abs** (which takes a positive or negative number, and returns its absolute or unsigned, value):

```
Miranda abs -33
type error in expression
cannot unify num->num with num
```

```
Miranda abs -x
type error in expression
cannot unify num->num with num
```

Neither expression succeeds because the – appears as the first object after the function name **abs** and therefore Miranda believes that – is the argument for **abs** (which obviously gives an error). The intended meaning can be enforced by bracketing the -x or the -33 thus forcing Miranda to interpret the whole subexpression as the argument to the function **abs** :

```
Miranda abs (-x)
33
```

```
Miranda abs (- 33)
33
```

To avoid confusion, the Miranda Standard Environment also provides the function **neg**:

```
Miranda abs (neg 33)
33
```

Integers and fractional numbers

Miranda generally treats integers and fractional numbers in the same manner. However, it is sometimes necessary to distinguish between integers and fractional numbers. Miranda provides the built-in predicate **integer** in its Standard Environment to test whether a number is a whole number:

```
Miranda integer 3
True
```

```
Miranda integer 3.0
False
```

It may also be necessary to convert from fractional numbers to integers. This can be achieved by the Standard Environment function **entier**, which returns the largest whole number which is less than the given fractional number:

```
Miranda entier 3.2
3
```

```
Miranda entier 3.7
3
```

```
Miranda entier (-3.2)
-4

Miranda entier (-3.7)
-4
```

1.3.3   Characters and strings

Miranda differentiates between single characters and strings of characters. As will be seen in Chapter 3, strings of characters are special instances of the type `list`.

Characters

A character is a single token, denoted by the type name **char**. For example:

```
Miranda 'a'
'a'

Miranda '1'
'1'
```

However, there is no "empty character":

```
Miranda ''
syntax error: badly formed char const
```

Notice also that characters and numbers do not mix. For example:

```
Miranda '1' + 1
type error in expression
cannot unify char with num
```

Special characters

Miranda follows the C language philosophy of implementing "special characters" by a two-character sequence (the first character of which is a backslash). The special characters include the newline character (`'\n'`), the tab character (`'\t'`), backslash itself (`'\\'` (**backslash**) and quotes (`'\''`). It is also possible to use the ASCII decimal codes for characters; for example \065 for the character **A** (in this format, a three-digit sequence is used after the backslash character).

Character to number type conversion

Miranda assumes an underlying character set of 256 characters, numbered from 0
to 255, where the first 128 characters correspond to the ASCII character set. The
built-in function `code` returns the ASCII number of its character argument, whilst
`decode` decodes its integer argument to produce a single character. For example:

```
Miranda code 'A'
65

Miranda decode 65
'A'
```

It is to be noted that an attempt to apply `decode` to a number not in the range 0
to 255 will result in an error:

```
Miranda decode 256
CHARACTER OUT-OF-RANGE decode(256)
```

Strings

Character strings are represented by any sequence of characters surrounded by
double quotations marks and are denoted by the type `[char]`. Hence there is a
difference between the character `'a'` and the string `"a"`. Strings may be operated
on by the functions given in Table 1.2.

Table 1.2 Operations on strings.

++	concatenation
--	subtraction
#	length
!	indexing

The following examples show that Miranda responds by representing an input
string *without* the quotation marks:

```
Miranda "functional programming is fun"
functional programming is fun

Miranda "aaa" ++ "rgh" ++ "!!!!!"
aaargh!!!!

Miranda # "a"
1
```

```
Miranda # "a string"
8

Miranda "abc" ! 0
'a'

Miranda "abc" ! 1
'b'

Miranda "abc" ! 999
program error: subscript out of range
```

Notice that the index operator ! considers the first position in the string as position 0.

Concatenation treats the empty string in the same way as addition treats the constant value zero, as illustrated below:

```
Miranda "" ++ ""


Miranda "1" ++ ""
1

Miranda "" ++ "anything"
anything
```

The string difference operator -- returns a value which is derived from its first operand with some characters removed. The deleted characters are all of those which appear in the second operand (the actual sequence of characters being irrelevant):

```
Miranda "abc" -- "ab"
c

Miranda "abc" -- "ccar"
b

Miranda "abc" -- "def"
abc

Miranda "aa" -- "a"
a

Miranda "miranda" -- "mira"
nda
```

Special characters and strings

The convention for special characters also extends to strings, with "\"" representing a string containing the double quotes single character. Similarly, the string
"\"Buy us a drink\"" will appear as the characters "Buy us a drink". Notice
that the two-character sequence is considered to be a single character, hence:

```
Miranda # "\"Buy us a drink\""
16
```

Number to string type conversion

It is possible to represent a number as a string of characters using the general
purpose **show** keyword or by the more specific **shownum** function. For example:

```
Miranda "mir" ++ (show 123) ++ "anda"
mir123anda

Miranda "mir" ++ (shownum 123) ++ "anda"
mir123anda

Miranda (shownum (12 * 3)) ++ "anda"
36anda
```

1.3.4 Booleans

Boolean values are truth values, denoted by the type name **bool**. Data values of
type **bool** are represented by one of the two constant values **True** and **False**.
    Data values of type **bool** may be operated on by special logical operators shown
in Table 1.3 or be produced as a result of the relational operators (>,>=,<,<=,=, ~=).

Table 1.3 Logical operations on Booleans.

~	logical negation
&	logical conjunction
\/	logical disjunction

The following presents some simple examples of their use. Especial notice should
be taken of the fact that the sign = is used both as a way of giving an identifier to
a value, within a script file, and to check if two values are equal. This is shown in
the following sample session (where x already has the value 3):

```
Miranda 3 = 4
False
```

```
Miranda 7.8 < 9.2
True
```

```
Miranda x <= 7
True
```

```
Miranda ~ True
False
```

```
Miranda (2 < 3) = (~ (~ True))
True
```

```
Miranda 2 < 3 < 4
True
```

The last example recalls that it is not necessary to bracket the relational operators to form more extended expressions. Indeed, if brackets were to be used, such as ((1 < 2) < 3), then this would give rise to an error because (1 < 2) evaluates to the Boolean value **True**, which cannot legally be compared to the number 3.

There is no built-in conditional expression—the ability to denote alternatives is provided by conditional guards on the right-hand side of function definitions, which will be discussed in Chapter 2. These conditional guards will return Boolean values.

Boolean to string type conversion

As with values of type **num**, it is possible to convert values of type **bool** to their string representation, using the **show** keyword. For example:

```
Miranda "mir" ++ (show True) ++ "anda"
mirTrueanda
```

Lexicographic ordering

The relational operators will work with numbers and also with characters, Booleans and strings: Booleans are ordered such that **False** is less than **True**; characters take the ASCII ordering; and strings take the normal lexicographic ordering:

```
Miranda 'a' < 'b'
True
```

```
Miranda "A" < "a"
True
```

```
Miranda "A" < "A1"
True
```

```
Miranda "B" < "A1"
False
```

As expected, different types cannot be compared, hence it is meaningless to attempt to compare a character with a string:

```
Miranda 'a' < "ab"
type error in expression
cannot unify [char] with char
```

Fractional numbers and equality tests

Note that comparing two fractional numbers for *equality* is highly suspect, since many real numbers do not have a terminating decimal representation. Miranda allows fractional numbers to be tested for equality, but it is assumed that the programmer understands the limitations of fractional representations. Using the built-in function **abs** (which gives the absolute value of a number, regardless of its sign), it is possible to determine whether two fractional numbers x and y (which have been defined in the script file) are the same to within a given precision (say 0.1):

```
Miranda abs(x - y) < 0.1
True
Miranda
```

Conjunction and disjunction

The Miranda operators for both conjunction & (logical and) and disjunction \/ (logical or) are sometimes known as "lazy" operators because they do not strictly need to evaluate their second operand. The left operand is always evaluated, but sometimes it is not necessary to evaluate the right operand in order to determine the overall truth value.[4]

The special operator & evaluates to **True** when both of its operands evaluate to **True**, otherwise it evaluates to **False**. Similarly, the special operator \/ evaluates

---

[4]In this respect they are similar to the LISP conditional "cond" and the C operators "&&" and "||" but dissimilar to the Pascal "and" and "or" functions (which always evaluate each subexpression in a compound Boolean expression before deciding the overall truth value).

to **False** when both of its operands evaluate to **False**, otherwise it evaluates to **True**. Thus, in the expression **False & (x = y)** it is not necessary to evaluate the right operand because, regardless of the value of the right operand, the overall result will always be **False**. The current implementation of Miranda takes advantage of this fact and *does not* evaluate the right operand if the result can be determined from the left operand alone.

Example session, given x has the value 0 and y has the value 42:

```
Miranda (y = 42) & (x = 0) & (y = x)
False
```

```
Miranda (y = 42) & ((x = 0) & (y = x))
False
```

```
Miranda (x = 0) \/ ((y div x) > 23)
True
```

The last of these examples shows that the lazy evaluation of the right operand is quite useful when it is not desirable for it to be evaluated. In this case a divide by zero error has been avoided.[5]

1.3.5   Determining the type of an expression

The type of any expression may be determined by typing either the expression or its name followed by *two colons*. This invokes Miranda's type checker and reports the type. For example:

```
Miranda (3 + 4) ::
num
```

```
Miranda 'A' ::
char
```

```
Miranda x ::
num
```

```
Miranda True \/ True ::
bool
```

If the name is undefined, Miranda returns the answer *, which indicates that the value could have any type.

---

[5]Notice that the lazy evaluation means that \/ and & are not the precise equivalent of logical disjunction and conjunction.

1.4   Tuples

This section introduces the *tuple* which combines values to create an *aggregate type*. As an example, it is possible to give a name to the combination of an integer, string and integer that represents a given date:

```
date = (13, "March", 1066)
```

Formally, the tuple represents the *Cartesian product* (or *cross product*) of the underlying components.

Domains and Cartesian products

In order to understand the type information in error messages (and to create new types as will be shown in Chapter 6), it is useful to understand the concept of *type domains*. The following is an informal introduction to this topic. The reader is referred to (Gordon, 1979) and (Thompson, 1991) for more details.

   The collection of values that a type can have is known as its *domain*. For example, the domain of type `bool` is the collection of built-in values `True` and `False`. Similarly, the collection of values of the type `int` is the theoretically infinite range of whole numbers from *minus infinity* to *plus infinity*.[6]

   During evaluation, it is possible for an error to occur: either an error message will be produced, or the program will enter an infinite loop. The formal treatment of type domains treats such an error as a valid ("undefined") result and a special "Error" value (representing both kinds of error) is added to the domain of every type. This error value is often given the special symbol $\perp$ and called "bottom". Thus, the formal expression of the type domain `bool` will contain the values {`True`, `False`, $\perp$}.

   Some programming languages allow the program to recognize an error value as the result of a calculation and to take action accordingly (although it is normally impossible for the program to detect an infinite loop!). However, Miranda does not do this—for example, there is no special pattern which can be used in pattern-matching to detect an error value[7]—and so this informal presentation of type domains does not include $\perp$ as a domain value.

   The type (`bool`,`bool`) contains the Cartesian product operator ",". This indicates that the domain contains all possible combinations which combine one value from the first domain (for type `bool`) with one value from the second domain (for type `bool`). Therefore the domain for the type (`bool`,`bool`) is fully represented by the four tuples:

---

[6]Of course, in practice, there is a machine-dependent restriction on this range.

[7]Although the programmer can express such behaviour with user-defined types—see Chapter 6.

```
(False, False)
(True,  False)
(False, True)
(True,  True)
```

Similarly, the infinite domain (num, [char], bool) contains all the tuples (n,s,b) where n is any value drawn from the number domain, s is any value drawn from the string domain and b is any value drawn from the Boolean domain.

Tuple equality

Any simple type has at least two operations defined upon its elements; that of equality (=) and inequality (~=). Thus any two tuples of the same type (whose elements are simple types) may be tested for equality, as is shown in the following session (a script followed by an interaction with the Miranda command interpreter):

```
date = (13, "March", 1066)
```

```
Miranda date = (13, "March", 1066)
True
```

```
Miranda (3,4) = (4,3)
False
```

```
Miranda date = (abs (-13), "March", 1065 + 8 mod 7)
True
```

As might be expected, tuples with different types cannot be compared:

```
Miranda (1,2) = (1, True)
type error in expression
cannot unify (num,bool) with (num,num)
```

```
Miranda (3,4,5) = (3,4)
type error in expression
cannot unify (num,num) with (num,num,num)
```

Tuple composite format

The *composite format* of a tuple can be used on the left-hand side of an identifier definition, thereby providing a convenient shorthand for multiple definitions:

```
(day, month, year) = (13, "March", 1066)
```

The names **day**, **month** and **year** can now be used as single identifiers:

```
Miranda day
13

Miranda month
March

Miranda year
1066
```

This shorthand notation is in fact a simple example of the powerful mechanism known as *pattern matching*, which will be discussed in Section 2.5. This general mechanism extends to complex patterns:

```
((day, month, year), wine, price)
        = ((13, "May", 1966), "Margaux", 60)
```

1.5   Properties of operators

An understanding of the properties of operators may significantly assist debugging and may aid the design of better functions, as will be seen in Chapter 4. This section explains the following key concepts:

1. *Precedence* and *order of association* determine the correct meaning of any expression which includes multiple occurrences of operators and/or function applications.
2. *Associative* and *commutative* functions and operators present an opportunity for the programmer to reorganize an expression without changing its meaning.
3. *Overloading* refers to the fact that some operators may manipulate values of different types.

1.5.1   Precedence

In an expression such as (3 + 4 * 5), there is an inherent ambiguity as to whether the expression means ((3 + 4) * 5) or (3 + (4 * 5)). This ambiguity is resolved by a set of simple rules for arithmetic operators; in the above example it is clear that the expression really means (3 + (4 * 5)) because the rule is that multiplication should be done before addition. This is known as a rule of *precedence*; multiplication has a higher precedence than addition and therefore the subexpression 4 * 5 should be treated as the right operand of the addition operator. If it is necessary to override the precedence rules then brackets are used to indicate priority.

For example:

```
((3 + 4) * (5 + 6))
```

All Miranda operators are given a precedence level—a table of precedence levels (referred to as "binding powers") is given in Section 8 of the Miranda On-line Manual. However, it is important to remember that function application has a very high precedence, so that:

```
(sqrt 3.0 + 4.0)
```

is interpreted as:

```
((sqrt 3.0) + 4.0)
```

In general, the use of brackets is encouraged for reasons of safety and good documentation.

1.5.2   Order of association

Some operators (for example, * and /) have the same level of precedence; this means that there is still ambiguity in the meaning of some expressions. For example, the expression (4.0 / 5.0 * 6.0) is ambiguous—it might mean either ((4.0 / 5.0) * 6.0) or (4.0 / (5.0 * 6.0)). Furthermore, repeated use of the same operator leads to similar ambiguity, as with the expression (4.0 / 5.0 / 6.0). This ambiguity may be resolved by determining the *order of association*. In Miranda, all operators (except for ++ -- and :, as will be seen in Chapter 3) associate to the *left*. That is, (4.0 / 5.0 * 6.0) is interpreted as ((4.0 / 5.0) * 6.0) and (4.0 / 5.0 / 6.0 / 7.0) is interpreted as (((4.0 / 5.0) / 6.0) / 7.0). This left-associating behaviour also extends to function application so that (sqrt abs 1) is interpreted as ((sqrt abs) 1) and gives an error—the programmer should therefore take particular care to bracket function applications correctly. To summarize:

1. Precedence is always considered first; the rules for association are only applied when ambiguity cannot be resolved through precedence.
2. The rules governing the order of association only apply to operators at the same level of precedence; this may be two or more different operators, or perhaps two or more occurrences of the same operator (such as (5 - 6 - 7)).
3. Brackets are used for priority, to override precedence and the order of association. For example, although it is now clear that the expression (4.0 / 5.0 * 6.0) means ((4.0 / 5.0) * 6.0), it is possible to bracket the multiplication, to ensure that it happens first: (4.0 / (5.0 * 6.0)).

Associativity

For some operators, it makes no difference whether they associate to the right or to the left. These are called *associative* operators, for example multiplication:

```
Miranda ((4.0 * 5.0) * 6.0) = (4.0 * (5.0 * 6.0))
True
```

However, some operators are *not* associative:

```
Miranda ((4.0 / 5.0) / 6.0) = (4.0 / (5.0 / 6.0))
False
```

This property of *associativity* only refers to repeated use of the same operator in an expression; notice that an operator can only be associative if its result type is the same as its argument type(s).

Commutativity

Some operators are *commutative*; that is, it makes no difference in what order their parameters appear. For example:

```
Miranda (4 * 5) = (5 * 4)
True
```

However, some operators are *not* commutative:

```
Miranda (4 - 5) = (5 - 4)
False
```

Sometimes the non-commutativity of an operator is due to it being lazy in one of its operands:

```
Miranda True \/ ((3 div 0) = 3)
True
```

```
Miranda ((3 div 0) = 3) \/ True

program error: attempt to divide by zero
```

The recognition of non-associative and non-commutative operators often assists debugging. The associativity of operators is given in Section 8 of the On-line Manual.

1.5.3   Operator overloading

The idea of an *overloaded* operator such as > or < is that the same symbol may be used for two operations or functions that are internally dissimilar but semantically similar. For example, the internal representation of real numbers and strings on most computers is different and thus the implementation of comparison operators is also quite different; it would perhaps be logical to have two operators *num<* and *string<* to mirror this. However, the behaviour of the two operations appears to the programmer as identical and Miranda supports this semantic congruence by using the single operator symbols <, <=, >, >= for both number and string comparison. When an overloaded operator is used incorrectly, the resulting error message reports that it cannot unify the type of the right operand with that of the left. It is not legal to mix numbers, characters and strings:

```
Miranda 3 < "hello"
type error in expression
cannot unify [char] with num

Miranda True >= 0
type error in expression
cannot unify num with bool
```

1.6   Programs, layout and comments

Direct interaction with the Miranda command interpreter may be used for simple desk calculator operations. However, the inability to define names means that even for relatively small programs it is necessary to use the /e or /edit commands which allow definitions to be edited in the script file and automatically read by the system on exit from the editor. If no filename is given, Miranda assumes that the program file is called *script.m*. Miranda's notion of the current program can be changed by using the /f or /file command followed by the name of the new file. For example, given a file called "spending_money.m", typing /f spending_money.m will cause the system to read this new file from the current directory. The new file is automatically compiled; if it contains syntax errors then Miranda will abandon compilation and not incorporate any of the definitions into the current environment (consequently no previous script file definitions will be available).

1.6.1   Program layout

It is not legal to enter more than one expression at the Miranda prompt. By contrast, it is permitted to have several definitions on one line within a script file, provided that each is terminated by a semicolon. However, this generally results in code that is cramped and difficult to read or to modify, and is not recommended.

Similarly, whilst it is not legal to enter a long expression over more than one line at the Miranda prompt, this is permitted within a script file (with a restriction, known as the *offside rule*, discussed in Chapter 2.1.1). Rather than present a long expression all on one line, it is recommended to layout the program by using spaces, tabs and newlines (as illustrated by the examples in this book).

1.6.2   Program documentation

To enhance readability, all programs in a file should be documented; in Miranda this is achieved by using *comments* or by using a *literate script*.

Comments

Within a Miranda script file, commented text is anything to the right of two parallel bars || and before the end of the line (the end of the line terminates the comment). Figure 1.2 provides an example of this style of commenting.

```
|| Program "spending_money.sml".
|| Calculates the amount of holiday spending money.
|| Only deals with three different currencies.

amount_of_sterling = 200.0     || amount of money available

|| different exchange rates
uk_to_us = 1.70
uk_to_dm = 2.93
uk_to_fr = 10.94

|| amount of spending money in different currencies
us_spending_money = amount_of_sterling * uk_to_us
dm_spending_money = amount_of_sterling * uk_to_dm
fr_spending_money = amount_of_sterling * uk_to_fr
```

Figure 1.2 Simple commenting style.

Literate scripts

Miranda recognizes that it is often the case that the comments to a program are more extensive than the actual program code and offers a *literate script* facility— whereby the default text is comment and code must be emphasized. Within a literate script, the *first line* and *all code lines* must commence with a > sign. Additionally, blank lines (that is lines without text) must separate text and code.

Reworking the program in Figure 1.2 as a literate script gives the program in Figure 1.3. Notice that the || comment convention is also allowed.

```
>|| literate script version of above program

Program "spending_money.m".
Calculates the amount of holiday spending money.
Only deals with three different currencies.

> amount_of_sterling = 200.0  || amount of money available

different exchange rates

> uk_to_us = 1.70
> uk_to_dm = 2.93
> uk_to_fr = 10.94

amount of spending money in different currencies

> us_spending_money = amount_of_sterling * uk_to_us
> dm_spending_money = amount_of_sterling * uk_to_dm
> fr_spending_money = amount_of_sterling * uk_to_fr
```

Figure 1.3 A literate script.

1.7   Summary

It is possible to treat the Miranda command interpreter as a simple desk calculator which evaluates expressions entered by the programmer. However, for the purposes of real programming, four additional features have been introduced:

1. The provision of built-in functions; user-defined functions will be introduced in Chapter 2.
2. The classification of data values into different types; the ability to create new types is discussed in Chapter 6.
3. The ability to give names to expressions and thereby use their values in other expressions; Chapter 5 shows how a programmer can specify where a name can and cannot be used.
4. The ability to combine built-in types to form tuples; another important aggregate type is introduced in Chapter 3.

It is worth emphasizing that the classification of data values ensures that they are used correctly and therefore that many common programming errors are detected early in the software development process.

Chapter 2

Functions

Miranda functions may either be built-in (for example `show`), predefined in the Standard Environment (for example `sqrt`) or they may be defined by the programmer. This chapter explains how to define new functions and then use these functions by applying them to values. Functions can be defined in terms of built-in functions (and operators) and/or other user-defined functions. The result of a function application may either be saved (by giving it an identifier) or it may be used immediately in a bigger expression (for example as an argument to another function).

Tuples may be used to package more than one argument to a function. Functions that only operate on the structure of the tuple and not on its components belong to the class of *polymorphic* functions. An example is a function to select the first component of a tuple, regardless of the values of its other components.

Two powerful tools, *pattern matching* and *recursion*, are introduced in this chapter. Pattern matching allows programmers to give alternative definitions for functions for different values of input data. This forces consideration of all inputs to functions and thus eliminates many potential errors at the design stage. Recursion is used to provide iteration and is an essential mechanism for flow control in programs.

Functions are important because they provide a basic component from which to build modular programs. This facilitates the technique of *top-down design* for problem solving; that is, a problem may be broken down into smaller problems which can easily be translated into Miranda functions. Programs structured in this way are easier to read and easier to maintain.

This chapter ends with a slightly larger example, which shows the use of top-down design to solve a problem.

2.1   Simple functions

This section introduces the simplest form of function definition and discusses how functions may be applied to arguments (or "parameters"[1]) and how Miranda evaluates such function applications.

2.1.1   Function definition

In Miranda, functions are defined within the script file. The simplest function definitions have the following template:

function_name parameter_name = function_body

Miranda knows that this is a function definition because the left-hand side of the expression consists of more than one name. Both the *parameter_name* and the *function_name* may be any legal identifier as described in Chapter 1 (Section 1.2) of this book (and must similarly start with a lower case character). The *parameter_name* is known as the *formal parameter* to the function; it obtains an actual value when the function is applied. This name is local to the function body and bears no relationship to any other value, function or formal parameter of the same name in the rest of the program. The function body may contain any valid expression, including constants, value identifiers and applications of built-in functions and user-defined functions.

In the following example `twice` is the function name, `x` is the parameter name and `x * 2` is the function body:

```
twice x = x * 2
```

At the Miranda prompt `twice` can be used in three ways:

1. Most importantly, as a function applied to an actual argument, for example:

    ```
    Miranda twice 2
    4
    ```

    This will be discussed further in the next section.

2. In conjunction with the special type indicator keyword `::`

    ```
    Miranda twice ::
    num->num
    ```

    The arrow in the system response indicates that the name `twice` is a function. The type preceding the arrow is known as the *source type* of the function and states the expected type of the argument to which the function will be applied. The type following the arrow is known as the *target type* and states the type of the value returned by the function. This is further illustrated in Figure 2.1 for the function `isodd`.

---

[1]In the rest of this book the words "argument" and "parameter" will be used interchangeably.

3. As an expression:

```
Miranda twice
<function>
```

This gives the information that `twice` is a function rather than a value identifier or something not yet defined.

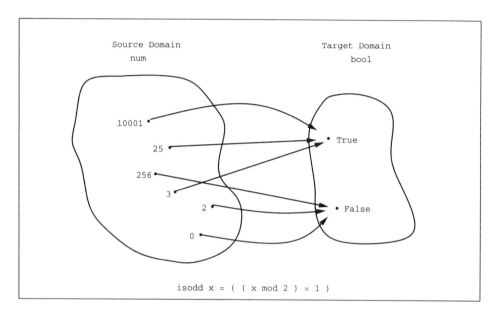

Source Domain
num

Target Domain
bool

isodd x = ((x mod 2) = 1)

Figure 2.1 Function source domain and target domain.

In general, a function *translates* (or "maps") a value from a source type (or "argument type") to another value from a target type (or "result type"). Though many values from the source type can have the same target value, normally each value from the source type will have just one target result. The source and target types need not be the same. Both of these points are illustrated in the next example, which checks if a character is upper case:

```
isupper c = (c >= 'A') & (c <= 'Z')
```

```
Miranda isupper ::
char->bool
```

The following example makes use of the built-in functions **code** and **decode** to convert a lower case alphabetic into its upper case equivalent; all other characters being left unaltered. The calculation relies upon three facts:

1. Subtracting the ASCII code for lower case 'a' from the ASCII code for a lower case alphabetic character will give a number within the range 0 to 25.
2. Adding the ASCII code for upper case 'A' to a number within the range 0 to 25 will give the ASCII code for an upper case alphabetic character.
3. It is assumed that the argument c will be a character in the range 'a' to 'z'.

```
toupper c = decode ((code c) - (code 'a') + (code 'A'))
```

```
Miranda toupper ::
char->char
```

The offside rule

The "offside rule" is a syntactic constraint for actions that cannot be written on one line; its template is of the form:

> *function parameter =*   *start of action on first line*
> *next line of action must NOT be to the left*
> *of the start of the action on the first line*

For example:

```
wrong_timestamp (time, message) =
        message ++ " at "
    ++ (show time) ++ " o'clock"

correct_timestamp1 (time, message) =
        message ++
        " at " ++ (show time) ++ " o'clock"

correct_timestamp2 (time, message)
        = message ++ " at " ++
        (show time) ++ " o'clock"
```

2.1.2   Function application

The function **twice** can be applied to an actual value, in exactly the same manner as system-defined functions:

```
Miranda twice 3
6
```

Here, the formal parameter x has obtained the actual value 3.

The integer value returned by the above application may also be used as the actual parameter for another function application. There is no restriction on the number of the times this principle may be employed, as long as the types match. However, it is important to remember that function application associates to the left; for example, the application:

        abs twice 3

is interpreted by Miranda to mean:

        ((abs twice) 3)

which is clearly an error because abs expects an integer as an argument rather than the name of another function. It is therefore essential to use brackets to give the intended meaning, as shown in the following sample session:

        Miranda abs (twice (-3))
        6

        Miranda twice (twice 3)
        12

        Miranda (sqrt (abs (twice 8)))
        4.0

An application of a previously user-defined function, such as twice, may also appear inside a function body:

        quad x = twice (twice x)

        Miranda quad ::
        num->num

        Miranda quad 5
        20

        islower c = ~(isupper c)

        Miranda islower ::
        char->bool

Exercise 2.1
    Provide a function to check if a character is alphanumeric, that is lower case, upper case or numeric.

2.1.3   Function evaluation

The example below presents a model of how the application of the function quad to an argument may be evaluated by a Miranda system. The example is interesting in that the argument is itself an expression involving an application of a function (the built-in function sqrt). Note that the ==> sign is used to indicate the result of a conceptual evaluation step and has no special meaning in Miranda; this device is used in the rest of the book to indicate a "hand evaluation" of an expression.

```
quad (sqrt (22 + 42))

==> twice (twice (sqrt (22 + 42)))
==> (twice (sqrt (22 + 42))) * 2
==> ((sqrt (22 + 42)) * 2) * 2
==> ((sqrt 64) * 2) * 2
==> (8.0 * 2) * 2
==> 16.0 * 2
==> 32.0
```

The above example illustrates several important points about function evaluation and about evaluation in general:

1. In order to evaluate the function body, effectively a new copy of the function body is created with each occurrence of the formal parameter replaced by a copy of the actual parameter.

2. It is impossible for any function application to affect the value of its actual parameters.

3. The argument to a function is only evaluated when it is required (this is sometimes known as "call-by-name"). Furthermore, if an argument is used more than once inside the function body then it is only evaluated *at most once*—all occurrences of the formal argument name benefit from a single evaluation of the actual argument (this is sometimes known as "call-by-need" or "lazy evaluation").

4. In general, the evaluation of function applications (and indeed evaluation of any expression) may be viewed as a sequence of substitutions and simplifications, until a stage is reached where the expression can no longer be simplified.

It should be noted that in the above discussion there has been no mention of *how* the evaluation mechanism is implemented. Indeed, functional languages offer the considerable advantage that programmers need not pay any attention to the underlying implementation.

2.2   Functions as values

Perhaps surprisingly, a new name may also be given to a function. The name then has the same properties as the function:

```
tw = twice
```

```
Miranda tw ::
num->num
```

```
Miranda tw 4
8
```

This shows that functions are not only "black boxes" that translate values to other values, but are values in themselves. They may also be passed as parameters to other functions, as will be shown in Chapter 4.

Thus, entering a function's name without parameters is the equivalent of entering a constant value. However, because the function has no meaningful value (it would not generally be useful for the system to print out the code definition for the function), the system responds with an indication that the value of a function has been requested:

```
Miranda twice
<function>
```

This principle explains the error message for the following incorrect attempt to apply `twice`:

```
Miranda twice twice 3
type error in expression
cannot unify num->num with num
```

The error arises because the argument to `twice` is a function, which contradicts the expected type of `num`. The above error message highlights the fact that `twice` is a value itself, of type `(num->num)`.

The major difference between a function and other values is that two functions may not be tested for equality—even if they have precisely the same code, or always result in the same value. For example, the expression `(tw = twice)` will give rise to an error. This difference is reflected in that the **show** keyword merely reports that a function is a function rather than echoes its code.

```
Miranda show twice
<function>
```

Redefining functions

It is important to remember that Miranda does not allow identifiers, and hence functions, to be given more than one value within a script file.[2]

2.3   Function parameters and results

Normally, functions translate from a single argument into a single result. However, it is often necessary to translate from more than one input argument or even to have functions that do not require any input value to produce a result. This section shows how Miranda caters for these types of function and also for functions that produce an aggregate result.

2.3.1   Functions with more than one parameter

At first sight, the notion of a function having more than one parameter seems to violate the constraint that all functions are translations from a source type to a target type (and so a function to evaluate the greater of two values would be impossible). Miranda has two ways of coping with this apparent problem—currying and tuples. The currying approach is introduced in Chapter 4, whereas the tuple approach is presented below.

   Employing tuples to represent the formal parameter of functions with more than one argument is a natural consequence of the fact that a tuple will have a value drawn from an aggregate type (as discussed in Chapter 1). The formal parameter can either use a single name to represent the entire tuple or the tuple composite form to give names to each of the tuple's values.

   The following example shows a simple function that checks the entire parameter and therefore uses a single formal parameter name (**date**) for the tuple:

```
ismybirthday date = (date = (1, "April", 1900))
```

```
Miranda ismybirthday ::
(num, [char] ,num)->bool
```

The system response makes explicit the fact that the formal parameter **date** has an aggregate type with three components.

   In the next example, which embellishes an input message, it is necessary to extract the individual elements of the tuple and so the composite form is used for the function parameter; the corresponding domains are shown in Figure 2.2.

```
timestamp (time, message)
        = message ++ " at " ++ (show time) ++ " o'clock"
```

---

[2]See, however, Chapter 5 for a discussion of the Miranda rules of scope.

```
Miranda timestamp ::
(num,[char])->[char]
```

```
Miranda timestamp (8, "important meeting today")
important meeting today at 8 o'clock
```

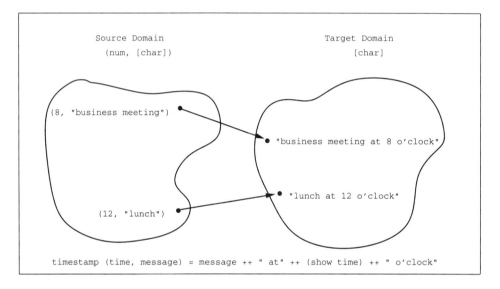

Figure 2.2 Source and target domains for `timestamp`.

2.3.2   Functions with more than one result

It is possible for a function to return more than one result because a tuple may also be the target type of a function. This is demonstrated in the following function `quotrem` (and in Figure 2.3) whose result holds both the quotient and remainder of dividing the source tuple's first component by its second component:

```
quotrem (x, y) = ((x div y), (x mod y))
```

```
Miranda quotrem ::
(num,num)->(num,num)
```

```
Miranda quotrem (7, 3)
(2,1)
```

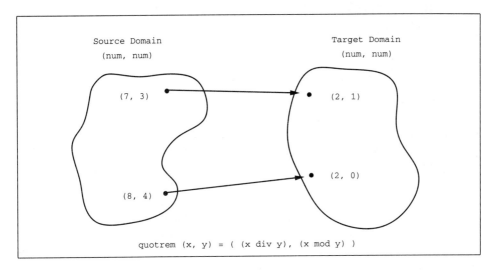

Figure 2.3 Source and target domains for `quotrem`.

2.3.3   Functions without parameters

Sometimes functions do not need any parameters. As such, they have no obvious source type—which unfortunately violates the constraint that all functions are translations from a source type to a target type!

In general, a function can only return differing results if it is applied to differing arguments. Thus, by definition a parameterless function must always return the same result. Normally, it is adequate to cater for such a requirement by means of a constant value definition, as described in Chapter 1. An alternative is to use the explicit "null" parameter, (), which is the only value of the special empty tuple type:

```
message () = "Buy us several drinks"
```

2.4   Polymorphic functions

It can be useful to define functions that provide general operations on tuples regardless of their component types. For example, the functions `myfst` and `mysnd`, respectively, extract the first item and second item from a pair:

```
myfst (x,y) = x
mysnd (x,y) = y
```

```
Miranda myfst ::
(*,**)->*
```

```
Miranda mysnd ::
(*,**)->**
```

These two functions mimic the action of the built-in functions `fst` and `snd`, which are defined in exactly the same way (see Section 28 of the on-line manual).[3]

The type of `myfst` is different to previously defined functions in that it takes a pair of values of *any* two types and returns a value of the first type. It does not operate on the elements in the pair but on the shape or construction of the pair itself; therefore `myfst` does not care about the type of x nor about the type of y. This is indicated by the system response which gives the general purpose type names * and **, which are known as *polytypes*. It should be noted that the actual values of the tuple could be of different types, which is indicated by the two different polytype names (a single star and a double star). However, because * and ** can stand for *any* type, the actual components could also be of the same type.

```
Miranda myfst (3,4)
3
```

```
Miranda myfst (3,("a",True))
3
```

```
Miranda mysnd (3,("a",True))
("a",True)
```

The above are examples of *polymorphic* functions. In general, a function is said to be polymorphic in the parts of its input which it does not evaluate.[4] Thus, in the above example `myfst` is polymorphic in both x and y, whereas in the following example g is only polymorphic in x:

```
g (x,y) = (-y,x)
```

```
Miranda g ::
(*,num)->(num,*)
```

Polymorphic functions need not take a tuple argument. For example, both of the following functions are polymorphic in their argument x:

---

[3]Remember that it is not possible to reuse names which are already defined in the Standard Environment. However, since it is recommended that the reader tries out these example definitions for themselves, this book adopts the practice of prefixing the names of Standard Environment functions with the letters my.

[4]There is, in theory, no restriction on the number of polytypes in the tuple parameter to a function.

```
id x = x
three x = 3
```

```
Miranda id ::
*->*
```

```
Miranda three ::
*->num
```

Exercise 2.2

What happens in the following application and why?

```
myfst (3, 4 div 0)
```

Exercise 2.3

Define a function **dup** which takes a single element of any type and returns a tuple with the element duplicated.

2.5   Pattern matching

One of the more powerful features of Miranda is *pattern matching*, which allows the format of one value to be compared with a template format (known as a "pattern"). For example, the appearance of a tuple composite form as the formal parameter to a function is an instance of pattern matching. Pattern matching is used both in constant definitions and in function definitions; the former has already been introduced in Section 1.4. In this section, the principle of pattern matching is extended to enable alternative definitions for a function depending on the format of the actual parameter. This facility has several advantages:

1. As a means of taking different actions according to the actual input.
2. As a design aid to help the programmer to consider all possible inputs to a function.
3. As an aid to the deconstruction of aggregate types such as tuples, lists and user-defined types (the last two will be introduced in Chapters 3 and 6, respectively).

In most cases, it will be seen that the use of pattern matching reduces the risk of programming errors and enhances program readability.

2.5.1   Alternative patterns

Pattern matching template

The general template for achieving pattern matching in functions is:

$$
\begin{array}{lll}
\textit{function\_name} & \textit{pattern\_1} & = & \textit{function\_body\_1} \\
\textit{function\_name} & \textit{pattern\_2} & = & \textit{function\_body\_2} \\
\end{array}
$$

$$
\begin{array}{lll}
\textit{function\_name} & \textit{pattern\_N} & = & \textit{function\_body\_N}
\end{array}
$$

When the function is applied to an argument, Miranda sequentially scans the definitions, from the topmost definition, until the actual parameter matches one of the patterns. The associated function body is then evaluated. At its simplest, a function will have only one pattern. Since a formal parameter is an instance of a pattern, all the function definitions so far presented are also examples of this form.

The following implementation of the function **not** (the equivalent of the built-in function ~ — which inverts the truth value of its parameter) demonstrates a simple use of pattern matching:

```
not True = False
not False = True
```

Similarly:

```
solomonGrundy "Monday"  = "Born"
solomonGrundy "Sunday"  = "Buried"
solomonGrundy anyday    = "Did something else"
```

In this example, the **anyday** pattern will match any other input and will therefore act as a default case. Notice that this default must be the bottommost definition (see Section 2.5.2.).

Exercise 2.4

Modify both versions of the function **solomonGrundy** so that **Thursday** and **Friday** may be treated with special significance.

2.5.2   Legal patterns

Patterns may consist of constants (for example, integers but not fractional numbers, or the Boolean values **True** and **False**), tuples and formal parameter names.

Patterns containing arithmetic, relational or logical expressions are generally not allowed; the following are both wrong:

```
wrong (x + y) = "silly"
also_wrong ("a" ++ anystring) = "starts with a"
```

However, it is legitimate to have patterns of the form (n + k), where n will evaluate to a non-negative integer value and k is a non-negative integer constant. Hence the following is legitimate, for all actual values of n greater than zero:

```
decrement (n + 1) = n
```

Unfortunately, this facility does *not* extend to the other operators or to values of n and k that are negative or fractional.

Duplicates

Unlike some other languages that have pattern matching, Miranda permits both constant and formal parameters to be replicated:

```
both_equal (x,x) = True
both_equal (x,y) = False

both_zero (0,0) = True
both_zero (x,y) = False
```

The occurrence of duplicated identifiers in a pattern instructs Miranda to perform an equality check. Thus, in the above example, both_equal will only return True if both the first and second components of its two-tuple argument are the same (are equal to each other), and both_zero will only return True if both components are equal to 0.

The equality check is *only* performed if an identifier is duplicated in a single pattern: duplication of identifiers "vertically" across several patterns is commonplace and has no special meaning. Thus, in the following examples, the multiple occurrences of the identifier x do *not* cause an equality check to be performed:

```
step_up (0,x) = x
step_up (1,x) = x+1

plus (0,x) = x
plus (x,0) = x
plus (x,y) = x+y

twenty_four_hour (x,"a.m.") = x
twenty_four_hour (x,"p.m.") = x + 12

equals_ten (x, 10) = True
equals_ten (x, y) = False
```

Note that this cannot be used to compare functions for equality:

```
Miranda both_equal (sqrt, sqrt)
program error: attempt to compare functions
```

Non-exhaustive patterns

In the not function (shown in Section 2.5.1), both possible values for the Boolean type were checked. If the programmer has not considered all the possible input options then Miranda will still permit the script file but may generate a run-time error.

```
not False = True
```

```
Miranda not False
True
```

```
Miranda not True
program error: missing case in definition of not
```

Although programmers may be tempted to ignore patterns that they believe will never arise, it is generally sensible to trap unexpected cases with an appropriate "default" pattern. For example, if all of the days of the week were catered for as patterns in the second version of the solomonGrundy function, it might still be desirable to have a final pattern that dealt with any string which did not represent a day of the week.[5]

---

[5]See Section 2.9 for how this pattern may be dealt with by the Miranda **error** function.

Order of evaluation

It must be stressed that Miranda checks each alternative sequentially from the top pattern to the bottom pattern, ceasing evaluation at the first successful match. If the patterns are mutually exclusive then it does not matter in which order they are defined. However, patterns may overlap and then the order of definition is *vital*, as is now shown in the following script file:

```
wrong_or x = True
wrong_or (False,False) = False
```

On exit from the editor Miranda will report:

```
syntax error: unreachable case in defn of "wrong_or"
error found near line 2 of file "script.m"
compilation abandoned
```

It is strongly advised that patterns should be mutually exclusive wherever possible. However, the guideline for designing functions with overlapping alternative patterns is to arrange the patterns such that the more specific cases appear first. In the above example (False,False) was less general than x and should have been the first pattern to be matched against.

Lazy evaluation of function arguments

Finally, a word of caution regarding the "lazy evaluation" of function arguments, as discussed in Section 2.1. Miranda uses a "call-by-need" style of argument evaluation, so that in the following program a divide-by-zero error is avoided:

```
myfst (x,y) = x

result = myfst (34, (23 / 0))
```

```
Miranda result
34
```

However, if myfst were to use pattern matching with constants, then the divide-by-zero error is *not* avoided:

```
myfst (x,0) = x
myfst (x,y) = x

result = myfst (34, (23 / 0))
```

```
Miranda result
```

```
program error: attempt to divide by zero
```

The error occurs because the pattern matching on the second component of the tuple (to see if it is equal to zero) forces Miranda to evaluate the division, so that it can decide whether to use the first or the second function body.

2.5.3   Guards

This section demonstrates how pattern matching may be made more selective and powerful by using the keywords **if** and **otherwise.**

if

In the example of `toupper` in Section 2.1.1 there was no check to see if the character to be converted was within the expected range. In the following example, use of Miranda's "guard" mechanism demonstrates how patterns may be constrained:

```
safe_toupper c
          = decode ((code c) - (code 'a') + (code 'A')),
            if (c >= 'a') & (c <= 'z')
safe_toupper c = c
```

Here, the first action is only executed when the guard condition (which follows the comma token (,) and the keyword **if**) evaluates to `True`.[6] In general, the guard can be any expression that evaluates to a Boolean result and more than one guard is permitted. For example:

```
whichsign n  = "Positive", if n > 0
             = "Zero", if n = 0
             = "Negative", if n < 0
```

otherwise

The use of the keyword **otherwise** demonstrates another way of trapping the default case. The action associated with it is only taken when the pattern does not satisfy any guard. The function `safe_toupper` could have been written:

---

[6]In fact the **if** can be omitted but it probably makes the code easier to read if it is included. To ensure good documentation, Miranda has an optional `/strictif` directive that actually enforces the use of the **if** keyword. The comma is mandatory in either case.

```
safe_toupper c
        = decode ((code c) - (code 'a') + (code 'A')),
          if (c >= 'a') & (c <= 'z')
        = c, otherwise
```

Note that this keyword can only appear as the default case to the last body for any given pattern.

Alternative and guarded patterns

There is no restriction on the combination of alternative patterns and guarded patterns. For example:

```
check_equiv (0,x)  = "Equivalent", if x="Zero"
                   = "Not equivalent", otherwise
check_equiv (1,x)  = "Equivalent", if x="One"
                   = "Not equivalent", otherwise
check_equiv (n,x)  = "Out of range of this check"
```

2.6 Type information

This section shows how Miranda can be helped to distinguish the type of formal parameters and introduces a mechanism for interaction with the Miranda type system.

2.6.1 Type declarations

For all the functions defined so far, the Miranda system has been able to work out the types of the function parameters from their context. However, this is not always the case. For example, the keyword **show** is overloaded and, on leaving the editor, it is not always possible for Miranda to determine the implicit type of a function that uses **show** in its function body. Thus, Miranda will raise a type error if given a script file containing the following attempted definition:

```
wrong_echo x = (show x) ++ (show x)
```

The solution is to employ the type indicator :: which not only *reports* the type of a function or value identifier when used with the Miranda command interpreter, but can also be used to *declare* the intended type of a function or identifier inside a script file. The general template for its use is:

    function_name :: *parameter_type* -> *target_type*

The actual code can then be given. Hence **wrong_echo** can be corrected as shown in the function **right_echo**:

```
right_echo ::  num -> [char]
right_echo x = (show x) ++ (show x)
```

In addition to resolving any possible type ambiguity, the use of :: is recommended for three other important reasons:

1. As a design aid, since the program designer is forced to consider the nature of the input and output before implementing any algorithm.
2. As a documentation aid; any programmer can immediately see the source and target types of each function.
3. As a debugging aid, since Miranda will indicate differences between inferred types and declared types.

Whilst some of the examples in the rest of this book may not contain explicit type constraints (for pedagogic reasons of simplicity and clarity), the approach is encouraged as being a good programming discipline and all the extended examples will adopt this style.

2.6.2   Polymorphic type constraint

A polytype may also be included as a type constraint. The following functions **third_same** and **third_any** are two versions of the same function which exemplify this property. In the first version, the use of the same polytypes constrains the actual parameters to be of the same type. The second version uses different polytypes to permit actual parameters to be of different types.
Same type version:

```
third_same ::  (*,*,*) -> *
third_same (x,y,z) = z
```

```
Miranda third_same (1,2,3)
3
```

```
Miranda third_same (1,2,'3')
type error in expression
cannot unify (num,num,char) with (num,num,num)
```

Any type version:

```
third_any ::  (*,**,***) -> ***
third_any (x,y,z) = z
```

```
Miranda third_any (1,2,3)
3
```

```
Miranda third_any (1,2,'3')
'3'
```

There is no way to constrain the parameters to have *different* polytypes.

Exercise 2.5

Define a function nummax which takes a number pair and returns the greater of its two components.

2.6.3   Type synonyms

As a further aid to program documentation, Miranda allows a type to be given a name, which may be any legal identifier as described in Chapter 1 (and which must also start with a lower case character). For example the tuple (13, "March", 1066) has the type (num, [char], num). For clarity this type could be given the name date by using the == facility as follows:

```
date == (num, [char], num)
```

Unfortunately, if a value is constrained with the type name date then Miranda will respond with the underlying types rather than the new type name. Thus, though type synonyms are very useful for shortening type expressions in script files, they do not help to make type error messages clearer:

```
mybirthday ::  date
mybirthday = (1, "April", 1900)
```

```
Miranda mybirthday ::
(num, [char], num)
```

For all purposes other than documentation of the script file, the value mybirthday will be treated as a (num, [char], num) aggregate type. Using the == notation *does not introduce a new type*. Values of type date and type (num, [char], num) can be compared and otherwise mixed, *unlike* the strong type discipline imposed, for instance, between nums and chars. Thus, the following is legal:

```
abirthday = (1, "April", 1900)
```

```
Miranda mybirthday = abirthday
True
```

Polymorphic type synonyms

It is also legal to have type synonyms that are entirely or partially comprised of polytypes. If a polytype appears on the right-hand side of a declaration then it must also appear on the left-hand side, between the == token and the new type name. For example, sametype_triple can be declared to be a triple of any type such as numbers or characters by defining it as a polytype:

```
sametype_triple * == (*,*,*)
```

An alternative and more general type synonym would be:

```
triple * ** *** == (***,**,*)
```

This is more general than the first version because it does not require all the elements of the three-tuple to have the same type.

Polymorphic type synonyms can be used to declare the types of functions in much the same way as other type synonyms. The only constraint is that it is necessary to indicate whether the type of the function is intended to be polymorphic or have a specific monomorphic type:

```
revNumTriple ::   (sametype_triple num)
                     -> (sametype_triple num)
revNumTriple (x,y,z) = (z,y,x)
```

or

```
revAnyTriple ::   triple * ** *** -> triple *** ** *
revAnyTriple (x,y,z) = (z,y,x)
```

2.7   Simple recursive functions

Miranda, like other functional programming languages, uses *recursion* as its main iteration control structure; this general mechanism can achieve the same effect as the imperative language features such as "while", "repeat" and "for" loops.[7] A recursive function definition is one where the name of the function being defined appears inside the function body. When the function is applied to an argument, an appearance of the function name in the function body causes a new copy of the function to be generated and then applied to a new argument. If the function name appears as part of an expression then the evaluation of the expression is suspended until the recursive function application returns a value.

Recursion is a very powerful and general mechanism which must be used carefully. At its simplest, it can be used to generate an infinite number of applications of the same function, for example:

---

[7]See also Chapter 4.

```
loop_forever () = loop_forever ()
```

If this function is ever evaluated, it will loop for ever, calling itself again and again and achieving nothing. The function `loop_forever` could also be defined to take a non-empty argument, but is equally useless:

```
loop_forever x = loop_forever x
```

```
Miranda loop_forever 2
BLACK HOLE
```

Evaluating this function by hand shows that whenever `loop_forever` is applied to the message `"BUY US A DRINK"` it immediately invokes another *copy* of the function `loop_forever` and applies it to another *copy* of the message.

```
loop_forever "BUY US A DRINK"
==> loop_forever "BUY US A DRINK"
==> loop_forever "BUY US A DRINK"
==> loop_forever "BUY US A DRINK"
. . . .
```

To create a more useful recursive function definition, it is necessary to ensure that there is some *terminating condition* for the function and also that the recursive calls are successively applied to arguments that *converge* towards the terminating condition.

A number of recursive styles can be identified which achieve the above criteria, the rest of this section shows the most common simple recursive styles: *stack* and *accumulative* recursion.

2.7.1   Stack recursive functions

The following function `printdots` is an example of the recursive style known as *stack* recursion. This function prints the number of dots indicated by its parameter. Firstly, there is a terminating pattern 0. Secondly, each recursive application of `printdots` is to a *different* n. Thirdly, each successive n decreases towards the terminating pattern 0.

```
printdots ::  num -> [char]
printdots 0 = ""
printdots n = "." ++ (printdots (n - 1))
```

A hand evaluation reveals:

```
printdots 3
==> "." ++   (printdots (3 - 1))
==> "." ++   (printdots 2)
==> "." ++   ("." ++ (printdots (2 - 1)))
==> "." ++   ("." ++ ("." ++ (printdots 1)))
==> "." ++   ("." ++ ("." ++ (printdots (1 - 1))))
==> "." ++   ("." ++ ("." ++ (printdots 0)))
==> "." ++   ("." ++ ("." ++ ("")))
==> "." ++   ("." ++ ("." ++ ""))
==> "." ++   ("." ++ "." )
==> "." ++   ("..")
==> "..."
```

This hand evaluation illustrates the appropriateness of the name *stack recursion*; the arguments of all the calculations being *stacked* (rather like a stack of playing cards) until the terminating pattern is met.

Exercise 2.6
   Define a recursive function to add up all the integers from 1 to a given upper limit.

2.7.2   Accumulative recursive functions

An alternative style of recursive function is now shown. The following example plus exploits the fact that two positive numbers can be added, by successively incrementing one of them and decrementing the other until it reaches zero.

```
plus ::   (num,num) -> num
plus (x,0) = x
plus (x,y) = plus (x + 1, y - 1)
```

Hand evaluating the application of plus to the tuple (2,3) gives:

```
plus (2, 3)
==> plus (2 + 1, 3 - 1)
==> plus (2 + 1, 2)
==> plus (2 + 1 + 1, 2 - 1)
==> plus (2 + 1 + 1, 1)
==> plus (2 + 1 + 1 + 1, 1 - 1)
==> plus (2 + 1 + 1 + 1, 0)
==> 2 + 1 + 1 + 1
==> 5
```

This function also meets the fundamental requirements of having a terminating condition and a convergent action. The terminating condition is met in the first pattern, which if matched halts the recursion and gives the result. The convergent action is satisfied by the body of the second pattern which will eventually decrement y towards the first pattern's terminating condition. It can be seen that the name *accumulative* is appropriate in that one of the component arguments is used as an *accumulator* to gather the final result.

Exercise 2.7
   Write `printdots` in an accumulative recursive style. This will require more than one function.
Exercise 2.8
   Write the function `plus` in a stack recursive style.

2.8   Who needs assignment?

Imperative programming languages use a memory-store model with "variables" whose names refer to memory locations. Central to the imperative style is the action of changing the values held in these variables through a process called "assignment". For example, in the C++ language the statement `int x;` gives the variable name `x` to a previously unused memory location which is big enough to store an integer. The value stored at this location might initially be set to 3 using the assignment statement `x = 3;` and subsequently overwritten with a new value 25 using the assignment statement `x = 25;`. Multiple assignment (reassignment) of values to the same memory location is vitally important to the imperative style, yet this mechanism seems absent in the functional style.

   In Miranda there is *no assignment operator*. It is not possible for a programmer to make an explicit change to the value held at a given storage location and it is not possible for a function to change the value of its argument. To those who have some experience of programming in an imperative language, this may come as a shock.

   In order to understand why assignment is not necessary in a functional language, it is worthwhile analysing its rôle in imperative programs:

1. To store input and output values.
   A memory location is set aside to receive incoming data; the program reads in that data and then uses assignment to save the data in the appropriate memory location.
2. To control iteration.
   A memory location is set aside to hold an integer which counts how many

times an iteration construct has looped. Each time around the loop, an assignment statement is used to increment or decrement the value held in the "counter" memory location.

3. To store the results of intermediate calculations.

   Often it is necessary to remember an intermediate value whilst the program does some other calculation; the intermediate result can then be used later. This is usually achieved by assigning the intermediate value to a memory location.

4. To store a history of intermediate results (known as "state" information).

   This is much the same as the previous rôle except that a collection of different memory locations may be required. This involves some additional memory management (using direct addressing of memory) to ensure that each value is stored (using assignment) in the appropriate location, possibly overwriting the existing value at that location. The collection of memory locations is often known as the "state" of the computation.

All of the above imply the need to consider the nature of data storage. In functional languages, it is not necessary to think in terms of data storage locations and so it is correspondingly unnecessary to think in terms of the alteration of the contents of data storage locations. The rôle taken by assignment is either provided transparently by the Miranda system or is a natural consequence of the recursive style of programming:

1. Input to a program appears as the actual parameter to its topmost function and output from the program is the result of the topmost function application. The allocation of storage locations to hold these values is automatically managed by the system and the output of the topmost function application is printed to the screen without the programmer having to specify this action.

2. Iteration control is provided by recursion; the number of iterative steps being controlled by the value of the initial argument.

3. The results of intermediate calculations need not be stored (although a result can be "remembered" as a definition for later use). The automatic storage allocation mechanism of Miranda hides store allocation and deallocation from the programmer, as seen in the following comparison of the imperative and functional treatments of the function swap.

   An ANSI C definition of swap is:

```
void  swap(int *xp, int *yp) {
      int t;

      t = *xp;
      *xp = *yp;
      *yp = t;
}
```

An alternative imperative approach is to pass the two integers as an aggregate type, for example:

```
typedef  struct {
         int x;
         int y;
         } PAIR;

PAIR swap (PAIR arg){
         PAIR result;

         result.x = arg.y;
         result.y = arg.x;
         return result;
         }
```

For both imperative approaches it is necessary to assign to a specific storage variable—either to hold a temporary (intermediate) value or to hold the result. By contrast, the Miranda approach is much simpler:

```
swap (x,y) = (y,x)
```

4. The storage of state information is also dealt with automatically by a functional language implementation. For example, the accumulative recursive style "remembers" the changing state of values from one recursive application to the next by means of the "accumulative" parameter.

Program control

It is worth noting that the three classic program control structures of imperative programming languages are also available to the functional programmer:

1. Iteration: by means of recursion.
2. Selection: by means of pattern matching.
3. Sequencing: by means of the nesting of function applications.

2.9   Error messages

Some functions may not have a sensible result for all of their possible argument values. For example, if the built-in function `div` is applied with a zero denominator then it will terminate with the error message:

```
program error: attempt to divide by zero
```

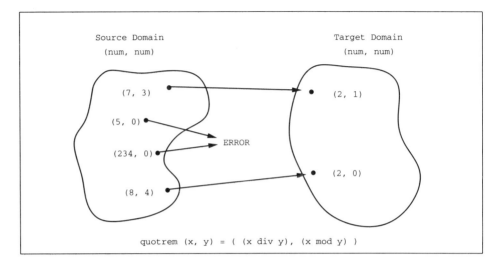

Figure 2.4 Example of a partial function.

A function which has no defined result for one or more of its input values is known as a *partial function*, as illustrated in Figure 2.4. It is often the case that a programmer will need to define a partial function. For example, the function `printdots` (given in Section 2.7.1) should give an error if applied to a value of n which is less than zero. Unfortunately, in the current definition the parameter of recursion, n, will never converge to its terminating condition if it is initially negative. There are three options available to the Miranda programmer to handle this situation:

1. Impose a dummy answer. A negative number of dots is clearly meaningless, but could be dealt with by indicating that negative values generate no dots.
2. Ignore it and let the Miranda system recurse for ever or generate some not very helpful error message, such as:

    `<<not enough heap space -- task abandoned>>`

    Unfortunately this will not necessarily pinpoint which function has failed inside a complex expression or program.
3. Force the Miranda system to give a more meaningful message, by stating which function has failed and why it has failed.

This last option can be achieved using the built-in function **error** as follows:

```
string == [char]

printdots ::  num -> string
printdots 0 = ""
printdots n
    = "." ++ (printdots (n - 1)), if n > 1
    = error "printdots:  negative input", otherwise
```

```
Miranda printdots (-1)
program error: printdots - negative input
```

The function **error** is polymorphic in its return type. It can take any input string and will evaluate to the return type of the function where it appears. As a *side-effect*, its parameter string is printed as a user-provided diagnostic. No further evaluation can occur after **error** is applied.

Exercise 2.9

Write the function **int_divide** using only integer subtraction and addition.

2.10   Programming with functions

This section shows the design of a small program to convert an integer to a string value. This mirrors the function **shownum** for integers, though it must be noted that due to Miranda's strong type system it is not possible for the user to write a **show** program to convert all types. The design of this program is presented in a *top-down* manner. This technique is known as top-down design because each step, except the final step, assumes the existence of functions defined at a later step.[8]

Specification

The program will take an integer as its parameter and will evaluate to a string. The string will be a denary representation of the integer; for a negative integer the string will start with a minus sign character.

---

[8]Chapter 5 shows a way to more closely associate the functions within a program.

Design

Firstly, the sign of the input integer is determined and dealt with. Secondly, a function to process positive integers is developed. This breaks its input into two parts: an integer less than 10 (which can be represented as a single character), together with an integer greater than 10 which requires exactly the same processing.

Implementation

Step 1: Converting any integer to a string

Assuming that a positive number can be represented as a string, then a negative number can also be represented by taking its absolute value (using **abs**) and preceding the string representation by a - character. This description converts directly to the Miranda code for a top-level function int_to_string which will translate an integer value to a string value:

```
string == [char]

int_to_string ::   num -> string
int_to_string n = "-" ++ pos_to_string (abs n), if n < 0
                = pos_to_string n, otherwise
```

Step 2: Converting a positive integer to a string

The next stage of the design is to define pos_to_string to convert a positive integer to a string. Since only integers less than 10 have a single character ASCII representation, the integer to be converted must either be less than 10 (the terminating condition of the function) or requires further processing.

The integer must be split into two parts: the least significant digit (which can be obtained using **mod**), and the integer without its least significant digit (which can be obtained using **div**). At each step, the least significant digit must be converted to a single character string using the function int_to_char. The rest of the integer forms the parameter to another application of pos_to_string. At each successive application, the parameter will reduce and eventually converge to a number less than 10.

Because individual digits are discovered in the reverse order to that which they must appear, it is necessary to concatenate them on the right of any recursive application of pos_to_string.

This description leads directly to the following Miranda code:

```
pos_to_string ::   num -> string

pos_to_string n
              = int_to_char n, if n < 10
              = pos_to_string (n div 10)
                ++ (int_to_char (n mod 10)), otherwise
```

Step 3: Converting an integer less than 10 to a string

The code for this function is based on the same rationale as for the function **toupper** shown in Section 2.1.1 and should be self-explanatory:

```
int_to_char ::   num -> string

int_to_char n = show (decode (n + code '0'))
```

Note that **int_to_char** is presented as a separate function because it is concerned with type *conversion*, whilst **pos_to_string** has an *iterative* purpose.

Putting it all together

In Miranda it does not matter in which sequence the definitions are written. However, it is good style to present the functions in the order of their top-down design.

One function per function

It must be stressed that each function in the above program has a single purpose. This recommended method allows *easier testing* and *easier modification* of individual parts of the program.

2.11 Summary

This chapter has discussed the definition and use of functions. Functions translate a value from a source type to a value in a target type, with *tuples* being used to represent composite domains. An alternative style that does not need tuples is discussed in Chapter 4.

There are many choices available to the designer of functions, including the following:

BIRKBECK
LIBRARY
COLLEGE

1. The types of the function parameters—this includes the choice of which types may be used, whether they are *monomorphic* or *polymorphic* and whether the function is defined for all input values.

   Functions may either be monomorphic, which means that their definition absolutely specifies the required types of the input data, or they may be polymorphic, whereby the actual types of the input data may be different for different applications of the function. Polymorphic function definitions are an important extension to the strong type system introduced in Chapter 1. Functions that are only defined for some values of their input parameter are known as *partial functions*; if they are applied to an argument for which they have no definition, the programmer may signify that the program should terminate immediately with an error message.

2. The use of *recursion* as a general-purpose control structure.

   The mechanism of recursion has been shown to provide the iterative control structures of imperative programming languages (such as "for loops" and "while loops"). Recursive function definition is of fundamental importance to programming in Miranda and in this chapter the two most common forms of recursion (*stack* and *accumulative*) have been introduced. The nature of recursive definitions is further explored in Chapters 3 and 4.

3. The use of the *pattern matching* style of definition.

   The technique of pattern matching may be used when defining functions; this has many advantages, including the introduction of a selection mechanism and providing a way to ensure that a programmer gives consideration to all of the possible inputs to a function.

Chapter 3

Lists

As has been shown in previous chapters, data items of types such as num and bool can only hold one data value at a time. In order to collect more than one value, *tuples* and *strings* can be used; these are known as aggregate data types. However, since they are not recursive by nature, it is not easy to manipulate data items of these types in a recursive manner. The *list* data type is introduced in this chapter as a powerful aggregate data type which is recursively defined and is used to hold many values of a single type. Built-in functions are introduced to construct and deconstruct data items of this new type.

Functions which manipulate lists are naturally recursive. This chapter provides guidelines for the design of such functions using the techniques of case analysis and structural induction; case analysis ensures that the programmer considers all possible inputs to a function, whereas structural induction is a powerful tool for developing recursive algorithms.

Recursive function definition is of such fundamental importance to the manipulation of the list data structure that the general technique is analysed further and five common modes of recursion over lists are discussed. The chapter ends with a detailed example of program design utilizing the above techniques; the program *grep*, a textual search utility, which will be used as an extended example throughout the rest of the book.

3.1   The list aggregate type

Aggregate types

It is often useful to have a single name to refer to items of data that are related in some way. Any data type that allows more than one item of data to be referenced by a single name is called an *aggregate type* or a *data structure*, since the items are represented in a structured and orderly manner.

65

It is clear that objects of the simple types `bool`, `char` or `num` have one value and are not aggregate types. One example of an aggregate type is the tuple, which allows a fixed number of data items to be represented by a single name. This chapter introduces the *list* aggregate type, which is of particular interest to functional language programmers, because it is *recursively defined* and may be easily manipulated by recursive functions.

Lists

The important concept of the list data structure is analogous to a collection of nested boxes. There is a central ("empty") box which may be surrounded by a slightly larger box, which in turn may be surrounded by another box, and so on. The central box contains nothing and cannot be opened, whereas all other boxes contain a data item and another nested-box structure (see Figure 3.1).

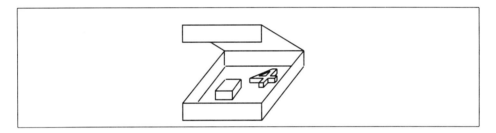

Figure 3.1 Box containing empty box and the data item "4".

To inspect the first item in this data structure, it is necessary to open the outermost box—inside will be the first data item and a smaller box (the rest of the data structure). In order to inspect the second item in the list, it is necessary to do two things—first open the outermost box, then open the box that is found inside. At that point, the second data item in the list is available, together with a smaller box representing the remainder of the data structure (see Figure 3.2).

In order to use such a data structure, the following operations must be provided by the language:

1. A way to construct a new structure (that is, the ability to put things inside a new box).
2. A way to deconstruct an existing structure (that is, the ability to "open a box").
3. A way to recognize the empty box so that there will be no attempt to deconstruct it (which would be an error because it contains nothing).

The following discussion of Miranda lists will first present the notation used and then explain how these three operations may be performed.

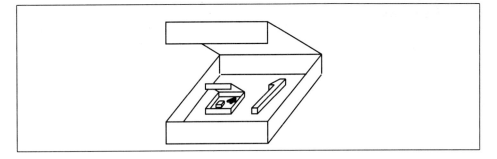

Figure 3.2 Box containing the data item "1" and another box.

3.1.1   List syntax

From the above analogy, it should be clear that the list data structure is naturally recursive in its definition. Informally, a Miranda list may be defined either as being empty or containing one element together with a list (which itself is empty or consists of an element of the same type as the previous element together with a list (which itself is empty or consists of an element of the same type as the previous element together with ... and so on ...)).

From the above, a more formal, recursive definition of a list may now be derived:
   A list is either:
      empty
   or:
      an element of a given type together with
      a list of elements of the same type
There are two notations that Miranda uses to represent lists: an *aggregate* format and a *constructed* format. The aggregate format is introduced below, whereas the constructed format is presented in Section 3.2.

The empty list is represented in both formats by the characters []—this corresponds to the "empty box" which cannot be opened. For lists with one or more elements, the empty box is implicit in the aggregate format and only the data items are given explicitly. For example, a box which contains the number 1 together with the empty box is represented by the aggregate format [1]. Further examples of lists entered at the prompt together with the type indicator now follow:

```
Miranda [1,2] ::
[num]

Miranda ["David Turner's", "Miranda"]  ::
[[char]]
```

```
Miranda [(1,2),(3,1),(6,5)] ::
[(num,num)]

Miranda [[1],[2,2,2]] ::
[[num]]
```

Illegal lists

All the elements of a list *must* have the same type; the Miranda system will detect any attempt to define a list of mixed types. All of the following examples within the script file are therefore illegal:

```
wrong1 = [1, "1" ]
wrong2 = [1, [1] ]
wrong3 = [1, (1, 1) ]
wrong4 = [1, [] ]
```

In each case the first element of the list is a number and so, on exit from the editor, the Miranda type checker expects all the other elements of the list to be numbers as well:

```
type error in definition of wrong4
(line   4 of "script.m") cannot cons num to [[*]]
type error in definition of wrong3
(line   3 of "script.m") cannot cons num to [(num,num)]
type error in definition of wrong2
(line   2 of "script.m") cannot cons num to [[num]]
type error in definition of wrong1
(line   1 of "script.m") cannot cons num to [[char]]
```

The meaning of "cons" will be explained below.

3.1.2 The empty list—[]

The empty list is represented by the characters []. Recursive functions which operate on lists will successively deconstruct each smaller "box" in the list structure and will converge on the empty list []. However, it is important that such a function should not attempt to deconstruct [] since this would give an error.

The value [] is used as the starting point for constructing a list of any type; thus, [] must have the polytype [*]. For example, when [] is used to create a list of numbers it adopts the type [num], but when it is used to create a list of Booleans it adopts the type [bool]. Notice that [] is a data item which can itself appear in lists; both of the following values have type [[*]]:

```
list1 = [ [], [], [] ]

list2 = [[]]
```

3.2   Built-in operations on lists

Miranda provides a number of built-in operations for list manipulation, including those for list construction and deconstruction. An empty list can simply be created by giving a name to the empty list constant []. Other lists can be created by combining an item with an existing list, using the special list constructor : or by combining a list with another list using the built-in operator ++. Two functions are also provided for list deconstruction: hd and tl. The former takes a list and returns its first element; the latter takes a list and returns the list without the first element.

A number of other list manipulating functions (such as extracting the nth item of a list or finding its length) may also be provided as built-in functions. However, they could easily be written by the programmer, as will be seen later in this chapter.

3.2.1   List construction—:

Apart from [], the only list operator that is actually required is the polymorphic operator : (pronounced "cons") which *prepends an item to an existing list of the same type as that item*. To use the nested-box analogy, : takes a data item and a box and puts both into a bigger box; this creates a new list. The type constraint is important—the second argument must either be empty or contain items of the same type as the first argument. A list of one item can be created from a single item and [] because [] is a polytype list and so can be combined with an item of any type. The type of : is:[1]

```
Miranda : ::
*->[*]->[*]
```

In the following example script file, all of the identifiers are of type [[char]]:

```
alist = "a" :   []
blist = "fed" :   "cb" :   alist
clist = "C" :   ["c", "c", "c"]
dlist = "d" :   "dd" :   "d" :   []
```

It is also possible to identify individual list components, using the pattern matching definition style introduced in Section 1.4:

---

[1]This represents a "mapping" or function type; for many purposes it is similar to a (*,[*])->[*] type, but see also the section on currying in Chapter 4.

```
(firstItem :  otherItems) = [3, 2, 1]
```

```
Miranda firstItem
3
Miranda otherItems
[2,1]
Miranda 4 : 2 : 3 : []
[4,2,3]
```

The use of : provides the list in its constructed format though the system responds by giving the list in its aggregate format.

The (firstItem : otherItems) definition is similar to that of tuple matching, shown in Chapter 1. The use of : in this manner is possible because it is not a normal function or operator but a special form of what is known as a *constructor*. It is not concerned with manipulating the values of its arguments but with constructing a new list. *One of the most important properties of constructors is that they provide a unique representation for each value of an aggregate type.* Thus, a new list can be constructed—and so deconstructed—in only one way. In the above example, the only possible value for firstItem is the number 3 and the only possible value for otherItems is the number list [2,1].

The operator : is also different from other operators so far seen in that it associates to the right; that is (1:2:[]) is really (1:(2:[])). If : associated to the left giving ((1:2):[]), then the construction (1:2) would fail because 2 is not a list.

List construction abuse

The following examples demonstrate common mistakes. The first example is wrong, in that the number 1 is *cons*-ed onto a list whose items are strings (whereas Miranda expects the items to be numbers, to be consistent with the first argument to :). In the second example, the first argument to : is a list of type number and therefore Miranda expects the second argument to be a list whose items are themselves lists of numbers. An error occurs because the second argument is in fact a list whose items are numbers. The third example has a similar error, in that the number 1 is expected to be prepended to a list of numbers, whereas the second argument is a number and not a list.

```
wrong_x = 1 :  ["a","bcd"]
wrong_y = [1] :  [2,3]
wrong_z = 1 :  2
```

```
type error in definition of wrong_z
(line   3 of "script.m") cannot cons num to num
type error in definition of wrong_y
```

```
(line    2 of "script.m") cannot cons [num] to [num]
type error in definition of wrong_x
(line    1 of "script.m") cannot cons num to [[char]]
```

Exercise 3.1
  Give two possible correct versions of **wrong_y**.
Exercise 3.2
  Which of the following are legal list constructions?

```
list1 = 1 : []
list2 = 1 : [] : []
list3 = 1 : [1]
list4 = [] : [1]
list5 = [1] : [1] : []
```

Append

Miranda provides another polymorphic list operator ++ (pronounced "append").
This takes two lists of the same type and concatenates them to create a new list
of the same type. The terminating [] value of the first list is discarded. The type
of ++ is:[2]

```
Miranda ++ ::
[*]->[*]->[*]
```

Sample session:

```
Miranda [1] ++ [2,3]
[1,2,3]

Miranda [] ++ [1]
[1]

Miranda [] ++ []
[]

Miranda 1 ++ [2,3]
type error in expression
cannot unify num with [num]
```

---

[2]This type is similar to ([*],[*])->[*], see also Chapter 4 on currying.

Properties of append

Two properties of ++ are worth noting:

1. The operator ++ could associate from the left or from the right and produce the same result. An advantage here is that expressions involving ++ do not require bracketing.
2. The operator ++ is not a constructor because it cannot provide a unique representation for a list. This is demonstrated by the fact that the comparison:

    ```
    ["A","A"] = firstList ++ secondList
    ```

    could be satisfied either by both `firstList` and `secondList` having the values `["A"]` or by one of them having the value `[]` and the other having the value `["A","A"]`.

    Theoretically ++ is unnecessary since it can be defined in terms of : (as shown in Section 3.7.2). Nevertheless, it is provided as a built-in operator because it is such a frequent programming requirement.

3.2.2 List deconstruction

Miranda provides two polymorphic functions to extract items from a list, called **hd** and **tl**.[3]

The function **hd** (pronounced "head") operates on a list to select its first element (that is, it "opens the box" and extracts the data item). The type of **hd** is therefore:

```
[*]->*
```

Examples:

```
Miranda hd [1]
1

Miranda hd [1,2,3,4]
1

Miranda hd ["Schoenfinkel","male","mathematician"]
Schoenfinkel

Miranda hd [[1,2,3],[8,9]]
[1,2,3]

Miranda hd [(1,2),(7,-1),(0,0)]
(1,2)
```

---

[3]Section 3.4 shows how easily they could be defined if they were not already provided.

The function `tl` (pronounced "tail") is complementary to `hd` in that it operates on a list to yield that list with its first element removed (that is, it "opens the box" and extracts the inner box). The type of `tl` is therefore:

```
[*]->[*]
```

Thus, if `tl` is applied to a value of type `[num]` then it will return a value of type `[num]` (even if the resulting list is `[]`).

Examples:

```
Miranda tl [1,2,3,4]
[2,3,4]

Miranda tl ["Schoenfinkel","male","mathematician"]
["male","mathematician"]

Miranda tl [[1,2,3],[8,9]]
[[8,9]]

Miranda tl [(1,2),(7,-1),(0,0)]
[(7,-1),(0,0)]

Miranda (tl [1])
[]

Miranda (tl [1]) ::
[num]
```

The relationship between hd, tl and :

Both `hd` and `tl` give rise to errors when applied to empty lists:

```
Miranda hd []

program error: hd []

Miranda tl []
[
program error: tl []
```

Thus, when programming with lists, it is necessary to use either a guard or pattern matching to avoid such errors. This test often arises as a natural consequence of the fact that the empty list is the terminating condition for functions that are defined recursively over a list (as shown later in this chapter).

Apart from the case of the empty list, hd and tl and : are related in such a way that for any list:

    (hd anylist) : (tl anylist) = anylist

Exercise 3.3

Miranda adopts the view that it is meaningless to attempt to extract something from nothing; generating an error seems a reasonable treatment for such an attempt. What would be the consequences if hd and tl were to evaluate to [] when applied to an empty list?

3.2.3   Other list operators

A number of other operators are provided for list manipulation. Three of these operators are familiar, being congruent to the string manipulation operators introduced in Chapter 1. These are: -- (list subtraction), # (list length) and ! (list indexing). For example:

    Miranda ['c','a','t'] -- ['a']
    ct

    Miranda # [345,2,34]
    3

    Miranda ["chris", "colin", "ellen"] ! 0
    chris

The other list operators are: "dotdot" notation, which is used as an abbreviation for lists representing a series of numbers, presented below; and "list comprehension", discussed in Chapter 5, which provides a tool for intensionally specifying the contents of a list through calculation (rather than extensionally stating each element).

3.2.4   Dotdot notation

The simplest form of "dotdot" notation is to place two numbers in a list (using the aggregate format), separated by two dots as follows:

    Miranda [1..4]
    [1,2,3,4]

The above example shows that Miranda responds by "filling in" the missing numbers between the first and the last. This abbreviated form may only be used for ascending lists—if a descending list is specified, the system returns the empty list. However, negative numbers may be specified:

```
Miranda [4..1]
[]

Miranda [-2..2]
[-2,-1,0,1,2]

Miranda [-2..-4]
[]
```

Lists of numbers which form an arithmetic series are also allowed. If the first number is followed by a comma and a second number (before the two dots) then this will specify the interval between each number in the series:

```
Miranda [1,3..9]
[1,3,5,7,9]

Miranda [-2,0..10]
[-2,0,2,4,6,8,10]

Miranda [1,7..49]
[1,7,13,19,25,31,37,43,49]

Miranda [1.1,1.2..2.4]
[1.1,1.2,1.3,1.4,1.5,1.6,1.7,1.8,1.9,2.0,2.1,2.2,2.3,2.4]
```

If the last number does not belong in the sequence then the list will stop before exceeding the last number:

```
Miranda [1,3..10]
[1,3,5,7,9]
```

With this second form of "dotdot" abbreviation, it is also possible to define descending sequences:

```
Miranda [3,1..-5]
[3,1,-1,-3,-5]

Miranda [3,1..-8]
[3,1,-1,-3,-5,-7]

Miranda  hd (tl (tl (tl [3,1..-5])))
-3
```

3.3   Lists and other aggregate types

This section briefly looks at the relationship between lists and the other Miranda aggregate types: strings and tuples.

Lists and strings

Strings and lists of strings are semantically related, since they both represent a sequence of characters. In fact, the string double-quote notation is just a convenient shorthand for a list of characters, as seen by the type indication for a string:

```
Miranda "sample" ::
[char]
```

This explains why all of the Miranda list operators work on both strings and lists. Notice that the above sample string could equally well have been written:

```
Miranda ('s' : 'a' : 'm' : 'p' : 'l' : 'e' : []) ::
[char]
```

or

```
Miranda ['s','a','m','p','l','e'] ::
[char]
```

Exercise 3.4

At first sight it would appear that **show** can be bypassed by defining a function that quotes its numeric parameter:

```
numbertostring :: num -> [char]
numbertostring n = "n"
```

Explain what the above function *actually* does.

Lists and tuples

It can be seen that lists and tuples are similar in that they are both aggregate data structures (that is, they collect together many data elements). However, they differ in three ways:

1. Their types: all the items in a list must be of the same type,[4] whereas tuple elements may be of differing types. However, lists and tuples can mix; it is legal to have tuples with list components and vice versa. In the latter case, it is necessary to ensure that the tuple elements of the list are of the same length and have the same component types.

```
wrong_list = [(1,2,3), (True,False)]
```

```
type error in definition of wrong_list
cannot cons (num,num,num) to [(bool,bool)]
```

```
good_tuple = ([1,2,3], [True,False])
good_list = [(12,"June",1752), (13,"March",1066)]
```

2. A list is a *recursively defined* type (it is defined in terms of itself), and therefore the type contains no information about the number of elements in the list. By contrast, a tuple is *not* recursively defined and the type of a tuple determines exactly how many elements it will contain. It is for this reason that lists may be constructed incrementally, whilst tuples may not.

3. Equality testing: tuple comparison can only be made against tuples of the same composite type and hence the same number of components, whereas lists of any length may be compared.
   Comparing tuples:

```
Miranda (1,2,3) = (1,2)
type error in expression
cannot unify (num,num) with (num,num,num)
```

Comparing lists:

```
Miranda [1,2,3] = [1,2]
False
```

3.4 Simple functions using lists

Functions over lists may be defined in the same manner as all other functions; they can be recursive, polymorphic and use pattern matching. The nature of recursive, and especially polymorphic recursive, functions is dealt with in later sections; this section overviews the use of pattern matching on lists. There are four things that can appear in function patterns involving lists:

1. Formal parameters—which can be substituted by any actual value.

---

[4]See Chapter 6 for ways of creating a new type of list which may have elements of different underlying types.

2. Constants—including the empty list [].
3. Constructed lists using : notation (the aggregate form is also legal, but is not recommended for general use).

Examples of simple functions using lists:

```
isempty ::   [*] -> bool
isempty [] = True
isempty anylist = False

isnotempty ::   [*] -> bool
isnotempty anylist = ~(isempty anylist)

bothempty ::   ([*],[**]) -> bool
bothempty ([],[]) = True
bothempty anything = False

startswithMira ::   [char] -> bool
startswithMira ('M' : 'i' :  'r' :  'a' :  rest) = True
startswithMira anylist = False
```

In the final example, it is necessary to bracket the ('M' : 'i' : 'r' : 'a' : rest) list construction so that it is treated as a single value, which can then be pattern matched. Further examples of pattern matching using list construction include possible implementations of the built-in functions hd and tl:

```
myhd ::   [*] -> *
myhd [] = error "myhd"
myhd (front :  rest) = front

mytl ::   [*] -> [*]
mytl [] = error "mytl"
mytl (front :  rest) = rest
```

The use of pattern matching in these examples emphasizes that there is no possible way of deconstructing [] to give component values.

3.5   Recursive functions using lists

Many of the functions over lists are recursive because the list itself is a recursive data structure. Whilst recursion involving numbers generally requires the recognition of zero to provide a terminating condition, list processing generally requires the recognition of the empty list. This section shows that the two recursive styles shown in Chapter 2 can also be used to manipulate lists.

Stack recursion over lists

The template for many functions on lists is very similar to that of stack recursive functions shown in Section 2.7.1:

> template []   =   *some final value*
> template (front: rest) =   *do something with front and*
>   *combine the result with a*
>   *recursion on template applied*
>   *to rest*

For example, the following function adds all the items in a number list. It specifies that the sum of an empty list is 0, whilst the sum of any other list is the value of the front item added to the sum of the rest of the list:

```
nlist == [num]

sumlist ::  nlist -> num
sumlist [] = 0
sumlist (front :  rest) = front + sumlist rest
```

Exercise 3.5
   Write a stack recursive function to add all numbers less than 3 which appear in a list of numbers.

Accumulative recursion over lists

The following example reworks sumlist to show its equivalent accumulative recursive implementation:

```
nlist == [num]

sumlist ::  nlist -> num
sumlist any = xsum (any, 0)

xsum ::  (nlist, num) -> num
xsum ([], total) = total
xsum (front :  rest, total) = xsum (rest, front + total)
```

However, if it were desired to consider the sum of an empty list to be meaningless or an error, it would be sensible to validate the input list in sumlist and process it in the auxiliary function xsum. In the following version, if sumlist recognizes an empty list then it treats this as an error and does no further processing. In contrast, when **xsum** recognizes an empty list it treats this as the *terminating condition* for the recursion and returns the desired total:

```
nlist == [num]

sumlist ::  nlist -> num
sumlist []  = error "sumlist - empty list"
sumlist any = xsum (any, 0)

xsum ::  (nlist, num) -> num
xsum ([], total) = total
xsum (front :  rest, total) = xsum (rest, front + total)
```

It is worth noting that validation is only done once in this example and has been separated from the calculation. In contrast, the following version is undesirable in that an extra pattern is needed to detect the terminating condition and also that the validation is confused with the calculation. As discussed in Section 2.10, from a software design perspective it is generally poor practice to make a function do more than one thing.

```
nlist == [num]

muddledsum ::  nlist -> num
muddledsum any = xmuddledsum (any, 0)

xmuddledsum ::  (nlist, num) -> num
xmuddledsum ([], total)
          = error "muddledsum"
xmuddledsum ((item :  []), total)
          = (item + total)
xmuddledsum (front :  rest, total)
          = xmuddledsum (rest, front + total)
```

A template for accumulative recursive functions is:

$$main \; [] \; = some \; terminating \; condition$$
$$or \; error \; condition$$
$$main \; any = aux \; (any, \; (initial \; value \; of \; accumulator))$$

$$aux \; ([], \; accumulator) = accumulator$$
$$aux \; ((front: \; rest), \; accumulator)$$
$$= aux(rest, \; do \; something \; with \; front$$
$$and \; accumulator))$$

Exercise 3.6

The following function `listmax` is accumulative recursive. Rather than using an explicit accumulator, it uses the front of the list to hold the current maximum value.

```
numlist == [num]

listmax :: numlist -> num
listmax [] = error "listmax - empty list"
listmax (front : []) = front
listmax (front : next : rest)
    = listmax (front : rest), if front > next
    = listmax (next : rest), otherwise
```

Rewrite `listmax` so that it uses an auxiliary function and an explicit accumulator to store the current largest item in the list.

3.6 Polymorphic recursive functions on lists

Many list-handling functions are designed to explore or manipulate the list structure itself rather than the list elements. These are called "polymorphic" functions because the elements of the source lists may be of any type; otherwise they are the same as non-polymorphic functions, as has already been shown with the simple functions `isempty` and `bothempty` in Section 3.4. Polymorphic recursive functions on lists are particularly interesting, in that they are the basis for a rich variety of tools of general utility for list processing. This section presents two of these functions over lists: `length`, and `mydrop`. The treatment of `mydrop` will also demonstrate that not all software design principles are set in stone.

length

The following definition of `length` follows the template provided to describe stack recursive functions. It provides the same functionality as the built-in `#` operator. Informally, the length of a list can be seen as one of two possibilities: the length of an empty list (which is 0) or the length of a non-empty list. The latter can be seen to be 1 plus the length of a list containing one less item.

```
length ::    [*] -> num
length [] = 0
length (front :   rest) = 1 + length rest
```

mydrop

The polymorphic function `mydrop` returns part of its second argument (a list of items of any type) by removing the first n items, where n is the first argument. It provides similar functionality to the `drop` function provided in the Miranda Standard Environment:

```
mydrop ::   (num, [*]) -> [*]
mydrop (0, anylist)        = anylist
mydrop (any, [])           = error "mydrop"
mydrop (n, (front :  rest))  = mydrop (n - 1, rest)
```

This function has been presented in the way that most functional programmers would probably write it. However, it goes against the advice given for the function `sumlist`. A better design might be:

```
mydrop ::   (num, [*]) -> [*]
mydrop (n, anylist)
    = error "mydrop:  negative input", if n < 0
    = error "mydrop:  input too big", if n > (# anylist)
    = xdrop (n, anylist), otherwise

xdrop ::   (num, [*]) -> [*]
xdrop (0, anylist)      = anylist
xdrop (n, front :  rest) = xdrop (n - 1, rest)
```

This definition satisfies the principle of a function only doing one kind of activity, because it separates the validation from the rest of the processing. However, it is algorithmically unsatisfying in that the entire length of anylist must be calculated, even though xdrop will work as desired on any list with at least n elements. For example, the length of a million item list may have to be calculated, even though the programmer only wanted to discard its first element!

An alternative solution is to replace # in the **if** guard with a more finely tuned function which only checks that anylist is of the minimum necessary length:

```
mydrop   ::   (num, [*]) -> [*]
mydrop   (n, anylist)
      = error "drop:  negative input", if n < 0
      = error "drop:  input too big",
         if shorterthan (n, anylist)
      = xdrop (n, anylist), otherwise
```

Exercise 3.7

What happens if a negative value of n is supplied to the first version of `mydrop`?

Exercise 3.8

Write the function `shorterthan` used by the final version of `mydrop`.

A further example is the function `mymember` which checks whether an item appears in a list. This function also provides similar functionality to the function `member` provided in the Miranda Standard Environment. The specification is simple:

1. The terminating condition where the list is empty—hence nothing can appear in it, and so `mymember` evaluates to `False`.
2. The terminating condition where the item to be found matches the head of the list—and so `mymember` evaluates to `True`.
3. The item does not match the head of the list—and so it is necessary to see if the item appears in the rest of the list.

Translation to Miranda is as simple as the function specification:

```
mymember ::  ([*],*) -> bool
mymember ([], item) = False
mymember (item :  rest, item) = True
mymember (front :  rest, item) = mymember (rest, item)
```

3.7 Thinking about lists

The list-handling functions introduced so far have been simple, to write because their Miranda code follows directly from their natural language specification. Unfortunately not all functions are so intuitively defined. To make the programmer's task easier, this section discusses two important tools for designing functions, and list-handling functions in particular. The first tool is commonly known as *case analysis*, which stresses the importance of looking at each expected function parameter. The second tool is known as *structural induction* and offers an important technique to aid the design of recursive algorithms.

3.7.1 Case analysis

It is impossible to consider every possible argument value to a list-handling function. In practice, it is only necessary to consider a limited number of cases:

1. The empty list [] which must *always* be considered because it is either a terminating value or an illegal option.
2. The general list (front :   rest) which also must *always* be considered; the function body corresponding to this pattern is where the recursive application is normally found.
3. Specific "n item" lists. For example the single item list (item :   []), since there is a class of functions (for example listmax in Exercise 3.6) that require at least one element in the list for a meaningful result.

List reversal

This section explores the design of the function myreverse, which reverses the order of the items in a list (and therefore has the type [*] -> [*]).[5] The discussion also highlights some important properties of list manipulation using : and ++.

The function definition can be derived by case analysis of possible input values:

1. The empty list.
2. A list of one item.
3. A list of two items, which is the simplest case where the list is transformed.
4. A general list.

List reversal for the first two cases is trivial:

```
myreverse []    = []
myreverse [item] = [item]
```

Considering the third case, the desired result can be seen as simply reversing the two elements of the list. This means that the list must be deconstructed to give a name to each of the two elements and then reconstructed with the elements reversed.

The deconstruction of the list can be done using pattern matching with either the aggregate format or the constructed format for the list:

```
myreverse1 [front, final]  = ???
myreverse2 (front : rest) = ???
```

Remember that final and rest are not the same thing—the former refers to an item, whereas the latter refers to a list (which contains both the final item and the empty list).

Similarly, there are three ways to reconstruct the list—using either the : operator or using the list aggregate format or using the ++ operator. Here are the six possibilities:

---

[5] Note that the Miranda Standard Environment also provides a function called **reverse** which has the same functionality.

```
myreverse11 [front, final] = final : front : []
myreverse12 [front, final] = [final, front]
myreverse13 [front, final] = [final] ++ [front]
myreverse21 (front : rest) = (hd rest) : front : []
myreverse22 (front : rest) = [(hd rest), front]
myreverse23 (front : rest) = rest ++ [front]
```

Notice that both `myreverse21` and `myreverse22` require `rest` to be further broken down by use of the `hd` function, and so in this situation the aggregate pattern seems to be more useful. However, `myreverse13` requires both `front` and `final` to be converted into lists before they can be appended. This conversion is achieved by enclosing each in square brackets, which is equivalent to using `:` and the empty list `[]`.

As a guiding principle, the use of `:` in the pattern is preferred for the general recursive case (as will be seen below), and in the base cases either format may be used. For `myreverse`, the most straightforward of the correct definitions given above is:

```
myreverse [front, final] = [final, front]
```

The reader should be wary of the following two errors:

```
wrong_myreverse1 [front, final] = final : front
wrong_myreverse2 [front, final] = final ++ front
```

Both of the above definitions fail to compile because the operator (either `:` or `++`) does not get arguments of the correct types. The latter definition is actually legal for a list whose items are themselves lists, but it is semantically wrong because the list items are inappropriately compressed:

```
wrong_myreverse2 [[1], [2]]
==> [2] ++ [1]
==> [2,1]
```

Considering the final case, the recursive nature of list processing becomes more obvious. As a first step, reversing, for example, [1,2,3] can be treated as reversing [2,3] appended to [1], that is (`myreverse [2,3]`) `++` [1]. Reversing [2,3] is, of course, covered by the third case and the list [2,3] can easily be extracted from [1,2,3] using pattern matching.

The above discussion leads to the provisional function definition:

```
myreverse ::   [*] -> [*]
myreverse []              = []
myreverse [item]          = [item]
myreverse [front, final] = [final, front]
myreverse (front :  rest) = (myreverse rest) ++ [front]
```

The provisional function evaluates in the following manner:

```
myreverse [1,2,3]
==> (myreverse [2,3]) ++ [1]
==> [3,2] ++ [1]
==> [3,2,1]
```

Rationalization of list reversal

In practice, the above definition may be simplified, in that the final three patterns can all be catered for by the final function body. Applying the final pattern to a single or double item list shows that both the patterns for single and double item lists are redundant. This is because the reverse of the single item list is a special case of the final pattern [item] is just (item :   []). The function myreverse thus simplifies to:

```
myreverse [*] -> [*]
myreverse [] = []
myreverse (front :   rest) = (myreverse rest) ++ [front]
```

A hand evaluation reveals:

```
myreverse [1,2]
==> (myreverse [2]) ++ [1]            || using the final pattern
==> ((myreverse []) ++ [2]) ++ [1] || using the final pattern
==> ([] ++ [2]) ++ [1]               || using the first pattern
==> [2] ++ [1]                        || ([] ++ [item]) == [item]
==> [2,1]
```

3.7.2   Structural induction

Case analysis is a useful method of ensuring that a programmer considers all possible inputs to a function. This gives immediate solutions to all "base" cases which are directly provided for in the function specification and also highlights those cases which require further processing. In the previous example of myreverse an intuitive recursive solution was evolved for the general list (front:rest); however not all problems are as amenable to such intuition. There is, therefore, a need for a more systematic method of analysis. The nature of this analysis will depend on the nature of the parameter of recursion (that is the parameter which converges towards a terminating condition). For lists, a technique known as *structural induction* is recommended because it provides a way to reason about a list's recursive structure.

Structural induction requires two steps:

1. Consider all the base cases as for case analysis.
2. Consider the general case. The design of the function body may be facilitated by the following technique: assume that a function body exists for a list `rest` and then construct a definition for the case (`front:rest`). The assumption is normally known as the *induction hypothesis*.

The use of structural induction to design two functions (**startswith** and **append**) is now presented. The first function **startswith** will be used in the extended example later in this chapter.

Specification of startswith

The function **startswith** takes two lists and returns a Boolean value. If the first list is an initial sublist of the second list then the function evaluates to **True**, otherwise it evaluates to **False** (for example, **startswith** (`[1,2,3],[1,2,3,4,5]`) evaluates to **True**). By definition, an empty list is an initial sublist of all lists.

Design of startswith

The function **startswith** will take a pair of lists whose elements may be compared for equality. It therefore has the type (`[*],[*]`) -> **bool**.

The design will consider the general case and then the base cases. In this example, it helps to consider the general case first, in order to determine the parameter of recursion. However, the program designer may consider the base cases first if appropriate.

The general case is where neither list is empty—there is no direct solution from the specification and so this requires further processing. The general form of the first list is (`front1 :   rest1`) and the general form of the second list is (`front2 :   rest2`). In this general case, the induction hypothesis is that the application **startswith** (`rest1, rest2`) will evaluate to the appropriate truth value. Given this assumption, the creative step is to realize that the general case should evaluate to **True** if **startswith** (`rest1, rest2`) evaluates to **True** and also `front1` is the same as `front2`. This highlights the fact that each list converges and both are parameters of recursion. The design translates directly to the following incomplete Miranda code:

```
startswith (front1 : rest1,  front2 : rest2)
        = (front1 = front2) & startswith (rest1, rest2)
```

The base cases are:

1. An empty first list—by definition this case always returns `True`. This is the terminating case for successful matches:

   ```
   startswith ([], anylist) = True
   ```

2. An empty second list—which always evaluates to `False`. This is the terminating case for unsuccessful matches because there is still some of the first list to be compared. If the first list had also been empty, this would have been matched by the first base case:

   ```
   startswith (anylist, []) = False
   ```

The complete definition is:

```
startswith ::   ([*],[*]) -> bool

startswith ([], anylist) = True
startswith (anylist, []) = False
startswith (front1 :   rest1, front2 :   rest2)
       = (front1 = front2) & startswith (rest1, rest2)
```

List append

The following discussion emphasizes the advantages of using structural induction rather than case analysis, especially when a large number of cases arise, since the philosophy of structural induction is to generalize rather than specialize.

The infix operator `++` may itself be defined as a prefix function, in terms of `:`. The specification of the following function **append** is very similar to that of `++` as stated earlier in this chapter; it takes a pair of lists of the same type and concatenates them to create a new list of that type; that is, it has the tuple type `([*],[*]) -> [*]`, which differs only slightly from `++` which has the curried type `[*]->[*]->[*]` (as will be explained in Chapter 4). The `[]` component of the first list is always discarded; if the first list is empty the function evaluates to the second list.

An attempt at defining **append** using case analysis is to write down the possible combinations of types of lists to be appended:

```
append ([],            [])               =  Body_1
append ([],            item2 : [])       =  Body_2
append ([],            front2 : rest2)   =  Body_3
append (item1 : [],    [])               =  Body_4
append (item1 : [],    item2 : [])       =  Body_5
append (item1 : [],    front2 : rest2)   =  Body_6
append (front1 : rest1, [])              =  Body_7
append (front1 : rest1, item2 : [])      =  Body_8
append (front1 : rest1, front2 : rest2)  =  Body_9
```

It is clear that providing function bodies for each of these possible cases will involve a lot of programmer effort. Much of this effort can be saved if structural induction is employed.

A definition for the general case Body_9 is based on the induction hypothesis that there is already a definition for append (rest1, front2 : rest2). The induction step is to produce a definition for append (front1 : rest1, front2 : rest2) which uses the property that front1 must become the first item of the resultant list:

```
append (front1 : rest1, front2 : rest2)
    = front1 : append (rest1, front2 : rest2)
```

It is clear that the parameter of recursion is the first list—the second list never alters. Hence front2:rest2 could be written more simply as anylist. There is now only one base case to consider: when the first list is empty (Body_3). By definition this evaluates to the second list. The full Miranda code is thus:

```
append  ::   ([*],[*]) -> [*]

append  ([], anylist)
    =  anylist
append  (front1 :  rest1, anylist)
    =  front1 :  append (rest1, anylist)
```

All the other cases can be removed from consideration; in particular, it can be seen that the single item list is not a special case. *In general, single (or n-item) lists should only be treated in a special manner by the function definition if they are treated as special cases by the function specification.*

Exercise 3.9

Use structural induction to design the function mytake, which works similarly to mydrop but takes the first n items in a list and discards the rest.

Exercise 3.10

Write a function fromto which takes two numbers and a list and outputs all the elements in the list starting from the position indicated by the first number up to the position indicated by the second number. For example:

```
Miranda fromto (3, 5, ["a","b","c","d","e","f"])
["d","e","f"]
```

3.7.3   Problem solving using structural induction and top-down design

This section looks at a slightly larger problem, the solution to which illustrates the use of structural induction in conjunction with the top-down design technique (discussed in Section 2.10).

The problem to be considered is that of sorting information in an ascending order. There is a wealth of literature on how this may be best achieved (for example, Standish, 1980); one of the simplest methods, known as *insertion sort*, is now presented.

Sorted list specification

1. An empty list is defined as already sorted.
2. A list of only one element is defined as already sorted.
3. The list (`front:rest`) is sorted in ascending order if `front` is less than all items in `rest` and `rest` is sorted in ascending order.
4. For the purposes of this example, only number lists will be considered.

Top-down design

There are a number of strategies to achieve insertion sort; the approach taken here is to start with an unsorted list and an empty list and then insert the items of the former into the latter one at a time, ensuring that the latter list is always sorted. This approach makes the assumption that it is possible to insert one item into an already sorted list to give a new sorted list. For example, to sort the list [3,1,4,6,2,4], the following changes will occur to the two lists:

	Unsorted list	Sorted list
Initially	[3,1,4,6,2,4]	[ ]
First pass	[1,4,6,2,4]	[3]
Second pass	[4,6,2,4]	[1,3]
Third pass	[6,2,4]	[1,3,4]
Fourth pass	[2,4]	[1,3,4,6]
Fifth pass	[4]	[1,2,3,4,6]
Final pass	[ ]	[1,2,3,4,4,6]

Insertion sort implementation

To meet the above design, the function `isort` must employ an accumulator (which is initialized to be empty) to build the final sorted list. There is also the need for a function to insert each element from the unsorted list into the accumulator. This leads directly to the Miranda code:

```
nlist == [num]

isort anylist = xsort (anylist, [])

xsort ::  (nlist, nlist) -> nlist
xsort ([], sortedlist)
     = sortedlist
xsort (front :  rest, sortedlist)
     = xsort (rest, insert (front, sortedlist))
```

Insert design

The design of the function `insert` is simple; the item to be inserted is compared against each element of the sorted list in turn, until its correct position is found.

Insert implementation

The base case is that of inserting an item into an empty list which just gives a singleton list of that item:

```
nlist == [num]
insert :: (num, nlist) -> nlist
insert (item, []) = [item]
```

The general case is that of inserting an item into a non-empty sorted list:

```
insert (item, (front : rest)) = ???
```

This involves finding the first item in that list which is greater than the item to be inserted and placing the new item before it.

There are two subcases to consider:

1. The front of the list is greater than the new item. The new sorted list is now the new item constructed to the existing sorted list:

```
= item : front : rest, if item <= front
= ???, otherwise
```

2. The front of the list is not greater than the new item, and so it is necessary to place the new item somewhere in the rest of the sorted list. The inductive hypothesis is to assume that `insert` works correctly for the smaller list `rest`. The inductive step is to use this assumption to form the general function body so that `insert` will work correctly for the larger list (`front : rest`). This gives:

```
front : insert (item, rest)
```

Note that if the new item is larger than any existing list member then eventually the rest of the list will converge towards []; this has already been covered in the base case.

Piecing all this together gives:

```
nlist == [num]

insert ::   (num, nlist) -> nlist
insert (item, [])
    = [item]
insert (item, front :   rest)
    = item :   front :   rest, if item <= front
    = front :   insert (item, rest), otherwise
```

Insertion sort limitations

This sorting algorithm is not particularly efficient, nor is it very general (it will only sort numbers in ascending order). Chapter 4 presents a more general purpose version that will sort a list of any type in any order. Chapter 5 presents a more elegant algorithm known as *quicksort*.

3.7.4   Lazy evaluation of lists

When a function is applied to a data structure, it only evaluates that data structure as far as is necessary in order to produce the required result. This is similar to the behaviour of the built-in operators for logical conjunction (&) and logical disjunction (\/). For example, applying the function **hd** to the list [1,2,3] only requires the value of the first item in the list. If the following items were not yet fully evaluated, for example if the list were [1,(1 + 1),(1 + 1 + 1)], then evaluating **hd** [1,(1 + 1),(1 + 1 + 1)] would *not* cause the additions to be done. The following Miranda session illustrates this behaviour:

```
Miranda hd [23, (4 / 0), 39]
23

Miranda [23, (4 / 0), 39] ! 0
23

Miranda [23, (4 / 0), 39] ! 1

program error: attempt to divide by zero

Miranda [23, (4 / 0), 39] ! 2
39
```

Thi lazy behaviour provides the basis for elegant yet efficient solutions as will be shown in Section 5.4.

3.8 Modes of recursion

This section reviews the two familiar styles of recursive functions over lists (stack and accumulative recursion) and introduces three new styles (filter, tail and mutual recursion). The different styles of recursion may often be mixed to form even more expressive control structures. However, the programmer should choose the style which most closely mirrors the natural specification of the problem.

Stack recursive functions

Stack recursion was first introduced in Chapter 2, where the **printdots** function was used as an example. In general, stack recursive functions such as **length** have a growing stage where evaluation is suspended, and a reducing stage wherein the final result is evaluated. The reducing stage can only arise when the parameter of recursion reaches the value that causes the non-recursive option to be taken. At this point, the parameter of recursion is said to have *converged* and the reducing stage is triggered by the fact that the non-recursive option returns a value instead of causing another function application.

A further example of a stack recursive function is **occurs** which counts how many times a particular item appears in a given list. There are three cases to consider:

1. The terminating condition of the empty list which has no occurrences of any item and so evaluates to zero.
2. The item matches the head of the list and so the number of occurrences is one plus the number of occurrences in the rest of the list.

3. The item does not match the head of the list and so the number of occurrences is zero plus the number of occurrences in the rest of the list.

Translating the above specification to a stack recursive implementation gives:

```
occurs ::   ([*],*) -> num
occurs ([], item)             = 0
occurs ((item : rest), item)  = 1 + occurs (rest, item)
occurs ((front : rest), item) = 0 + occurs (rest, item)
```

Two alternative recursive implementations of the above specification are now discussed.

Filter recursive functions

A variation on the stack recursive approach is filter or partial stack recursion, which is demonstrated in the following implementation of occurs. The definition just presented is inelegant, in that the artificial value 0 was invented to denote the non-occurrence of an item in a list. For example, the application occurs ([0,22,3,5,0,1,1,9,101,0],0) recursively expands to (1 + 0 + 0 + 0 + 1 + 0 + 0 + 0 + 0 + 1 + 0), whereas it would be more elegant to have an algorithm that recursively expanded to just (1 + 1 + 1), thereby dropping the superfluous zeros.

The stack recursive algorithm for the function occurs can be modified to adopt a filter recursive approach as follows:

1. If the list is empty, the result is the same as for stack recursion.
2. If the item matches the head of the list, the result is the same as for stack recursion.
3. If the item does not match the head of the list, the number of occurrences is just the number of occurrences in the rest of the list.

As with the stack recursive version, the new version eventually reaches an empty list and evaluates to zero; thus there is no danger of a "dangling" addition:

```
occurs ::   ([*],*) -> num
occurs ([], item)             = 0
occurs ((item : rest), item)  = 1 + occurs (rest, item)
occurs ((front : rest), item) = occurs (rest, item)
```

Applying this version of occurs on the above example almost filters out all of the unwanted zeros—there is still the trivial case of a final addition for the empty list!

Accumulative recursive functions

The recursive style using *accumulators* (introduced in Section 2.7.2) is also applicable to list-handling functions and, as already shown in the definitions of `sumlist` and `xsum` (in Section 3.5), it is often necessary to provide a main and auxiliary function definition. The main function normally provides any necessary preliminary validation and initializes the accumulator. Rewriting the function `occurs` in this style gives:

```
occurs  ::  ([*],*) -> num
occurs  (any, item) = xoccurs (any, item, 0)

xoccurs ::  ([*],*,num) -> num
xoccurs ([], item, total) = total
xoccurs ((front :  rest), item, total)
        = xoccurs (rest, item, total + 1), if front = item
        = xoccurs (rest, item, total), otherwise
```

This version of `occurs` will achieve the same results as the two previous versions, but is more difficult to read and reason about, probably because its definition is more procedural in nature and further away from its natural language specification.

Tail recursive functions

The polymorphic definition of the function `mymember` in Section 3.6.1 is an example of a *tail recursive* function. A tail recursive function is one wherein at no stage is evaluation suspended.[6] Another example is the function `mylast`, which selects the final item in a non-empty list or raises an `error` if the list is empty:

```
mylast [*] -> *
mylast [] = error "mylast:  empty list"
mylast (front :  []) = front
mylast (front :  rest) = mylast rest
```

Note that this function is so commonly required that it is also provided in the Miranda Standard Environment (with the name `last`).

---

[6]This has an important consequence for functional language implementation because many implementations detect tail recursive functions and produce code which uses constant stack storage space (Field and Harrison, 1988; MacLennan, 1990).

The functions `mymember` and `mylast` are "pure" tail recursive functions; they exhibit neither stack nor accumulative recursive style. Accumulative recursive functions are also tail recursive when they do not suspend any evaluation. By contrast, stack recursive functions can never be tail recursive.

3.8.1   Mutual recursion

Sometimes it is tempting to define functions in terms of each other (that is, these functions are mutually recursive). For example, the following (not recommended) program deletes all text within brackets from a given string:

```
string == [char]

nasty_skipbrackets ::  string -> string

nasty_skipbrackets [] = []
nasty_skipbrackets ('(' :  rest)
    = nasty_inbrackets rest
nasty_skipbrackets (front :  rest)
    = front :  nasty_skipbrackets rest

nasty_inbrackets ::  string -> string

nasty_inbrackets []
    = error "text ends inside a bracket pair"
nasty_inbrackets (')' :  rest)
    = nasty_skipbrackets rest
nasty_inbrackets (front :  rest)
    = nasty_inbrackets rest
```

Is mutual recursion desirable?

Mutually recursive solutions are often considered undesirable because it is generally unclear which function is calling the other with any particular values. Furthermore, it is also impossible to test each individual function separately. Fortunately, the mutual dependencies can often be eliminated.

In the following program, the function `skipbrackets` scans the text until it finds the start of brackets. At this point it passes the remainder of the input text to `inbrackets`, which strips the rest of the current bracketed expression and returns the remaining text. The function `skipbrackets` can now use this result to find the next bracketed expression:

```
string == [char]

skipbrackets ::  string -> string

skipbrackets []
     = []
skipbrackets ('(' :  rest)
     = skipbrackets (inbrackets rest)
skipbrackets (front :  rest)
     = front :  skipbrackets rest

inbrackets ::  string -> string

inbrackets []
     = error "text ends inside a bracket pair"
inbrackets (')' :  rest)
     = rest
inbrackets (front :  rest)
     = inbrackets rest
```

Exercise 3.11
  Modify the `skipbrackets` program to cater for nested brackets.

3.9   Extended example—grep

This section introduces the development of the UNIX program *grep* which will
be used as an extended example throughout this book. The rest of this chapter
shows how the Miranda facilities already demonstrated may be used to develop a
real software tool. The program will be developed incrementally as new features
of Miranda are introduced in subsequent chapters to make the design easier to
understand and of more general utility.

Grep specification

Grep is a UNIX program which displays each line from its input that contains
an instance of a given pattern. As such, it is clearly very useful for a number of
different tasks, including the location of keywords and predefined names within a
program or selecting interesting parts of a document.

Table 3.1 Options for the UNIX *grep* facility.

Character	Meaning
c	any non-special character *c* matches itself
c	turn off any special meaning of character *c*
^	beginning of line
$	end of line
.	any single character
[...]	any one of characters in ...; ranges like a-z are legal
[^...]	any one of characters not in ... ; ranges are legal
*r**	zero or more occurrences of a regular expression *r*
r1r2	regular expression *r1* followed by regular expression *r2*
No regular expression matches a newline	

For example, assuming the file called "textbook" contains the lines:

```
Programming in Miranda
by
C.Clack, C.Myers and E.Poon
```

then typing:

```
grep "Miranda" "textbook"
```

will result in the first line of the file being displayed.

In practice *grep* is more than a simple pattern matching tool; it also caters for what are known as *regular expressions*; (Aho *et al.*, 1974; Kernighan and Pike, 1984). In a regular expression certain characters may be *meta-characters*, which have special meanings. In the case of *grep* the meanings of characters, in order of precedence, are given in Table 3.9.[7]

Thus, it is possible to search for a pattern that is anchored at the beginning or end of a line and more importantly to search for patterns that contain "wild cards". For example, ^M.R will match any line starting with M followed by any character, followed by R as the third character.

Similarly, M.*R will match:

```
MIR or M.R or MXR or MAAAAAAR or MABCR or MR
```

anywhere on the searched line.

---

[7]This table was adapted from Section 4.1 of the *Unix Programming Environment* (Kernighan and Pike, 1984). The actual UNIX tool has several more options.

Furthermore,

```
[a-zA-Z] [a-zA-Z_1-9]*
```

will match any line that starts with an alphabetic character, followed by zero or more occurrences of an alphabetic character, digit or underscore, *in any combination*, such as:

```
fun
Miranda
legal_name
aux1
aux2_fun
```

It should be clear from the above why *grep* is sometimes known as a "filter" program; only the part of the input that matches the pattern is output, all other parts are filtered out.

Grep development considerations

The development of *grep* will be presented in a number of stages:

1. A simple program to indicate if a given pattern appears in a line. This is *grep* without any meta-characters. This version of *grep* will deal with just one line of input, and merely return the Boolean value **True** or **False**, depending on whether the given pattern has been matched or not.
2. A program to allow the * meta-character to appear in the pattern. The rationale for considering this as the next case is; if zero or more occurrences of a normal character can be matched then it is likely that zero or more occurrences of a wild card can also be matched.
3. An extended program to cater for many lines of input returning the text of each line that has a successful match. This is presented in Chapter 4.
4. A safer version using enumerated types, is presented in Chapter 6.
5. A version that deals with file handling is presented in Chapter 8.
6. A program to cater for the other regular expression meta-characters, including wild cards. This is presented in Chapter 9.

3.9.1   A simple version of grep

Specification

The *grep* program will return the truth value of whether the first component of its tuple pair argument is a substring of the second component. Therefore it has the type:

```
([char],[char]) -> bool
```

Design

The requirement for a successful *grep* search is that the regular expression (the pattern) either matches from the front of the searched line, or it matches from the front of the rest of the searched line. This is the general case of the structural induction. The terminating cases are:

1. The empty regular expression, which matches any line.
2. The empty searched line, which only matches an empty regular expression.

Implementation

Since it is the intention to deal with regular expressions, it is worthwhile providing a simple front-end to perform this action before any further processing:

```
string == [char]

grep ::  (string, string) -> bool
grep (regexp, line) = sublist (regexp, line)
```

The rest of the design translates directly to the Miranda code:

```
string == [char]

sublist ::  (string, string) -> bool
sublist ([], any) = True
sublist (any, []) = False
sublist (regexp, line)
      = startswith (regexp, line)
         \/ sublist (regexp, tl line)
```

It is important that the two base cases are defined in the above sequence. The cases are not mutually exclusive; if they were swapped then matching an empty regular expression and an empty input line would incorrectly evaluate to **False**.

Design of startswith

This has already been done in Section 3.7.2.

Exercise 3.12

   It would appear that **sublist** no longer needs its first function pattern because this is checked as the first pattern in **startswith**. Explain why this is incorrect, and also whether the second pattern of **sublist** can safely be removed.

Exercise 3.13

An incorrect attempt to optimize the `startswith` program would combine `startswith` and `sublist` in one function:

```
stringpair == ([char], [char])

sublist :: stringpair -> bool
sublist ([], any) = True
sublist (any, []) = False
sublist ((regfront : regrest), (lfront : lrest))
       = ((regfront = lfront) & sublist (regrest, lrest))
         \/ sublist (regfront : regrest, lrest)
```

This follows the general inductive case that the result is true if the front two items of the lists are equal and the result of a sublist search of the rest of the two lists is also true. Alternatively, the entire regular expression matches the rest of the search line. Show why this approach is wrong.

3.9.2 Incorporating the zero or more occurrences

The next stage of the development is to allow for zero or more occurrences of a given character to appear in the searched line. For example:

```
A*BC       appears in              AAABC
                                   ABC
                                   BC
                                   AAABAAABC


A*A        appears in              AAAAAA
                                   AA
                                   A
```

At this point it is also worth recalling that `*` itself can be matched by preceding it with a `\` which turns off its special meaning:

```
A\*B       appears in              A*B

A\*B       does not appear in      AABC
                                   ABC
                                   BC
                                   AAABAAABC
```

The need for lexical analysis

The design of *grep* is now made more complex by the necessity of always checking for the *meta-character following any other character. There are two approaches to handling this. One approach is that the auxiliary function `startswith` could look ahead for the meta-character *. However, this *confuses* the activity of recognizing the meta-characters in the regular expression with the activity of comparing the regular expression with the current search line. This makes the resultant function `startswith` very complicated and will go against the advice in Chapter 2 that a function should only do one thing.

In preference, the regular expression could be preprocessed to attribute every character with a "match-type token" to indicate whether it is to be matched *once only*, as a normal character, or whether it is to be matched *zero or more* times.[8] For this version of *grep*, a new function called `lex` is used to do the preprocessing; this function will initially recognize \ and * but will be extended later to deal with the other meta-characters.[9] The easiest way of representing the two attributes is probably a tuple of the form (`MATCH_TYPE`, `actual_value`). For example (`"ONCE"`, ch) or (`"ZERO_MORE"`, ch), as shown in Figure 3.3.

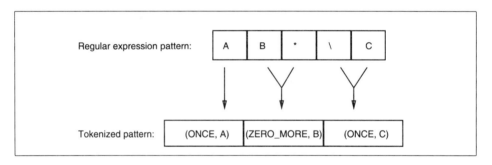

Figure 3.3 Example of a regular expression in tokenized form.

Pattern matching, by case analysis, can now be employed to convert the raw regular expression into a list of regular expression elements:[10]

---

[8]With this approach, `startswith` is also saved the bother of checking for the escape sequence \c, where c is any character.

[9]This technique of transforming the regular expression into a sequence of actual values and their match-type token is known as lexical analysis (Aho *et al.*, 1974; Kernighan and Pike, 1984) hence the name of the function `lex`.

[10]The reader is referred to Chapter 6 for a more elegant approach using *enumerated types*.

```
string  == [char]
mtype   == string
regtype == mtype * string
reglist == [regtype]

lex ::  string -> reglist

lex [] = [] = []

lex ('\\' :  ch :  '*' :  rest)
        = ("ZERO_MORE", ch) :  lex rest
        || note the two char '\\'
        || is treated as the single char '\'
lex ('\\' :  ch :  rest) = ("ONCE", ch) :  lex rest
lex ('\\' :  [])         = [("ONCE", '\\')]
lex (ch :  '*' :  rest)  = ("ZERO_MORE", ch) :  lex rest
lex (ch :  rest)         = ("ONCE", ch) :  lex rest
```

3.9.3 Redesign of startswith

Matching strategy

Incorporating *ZERO_MORE* match-types into the `startswith` function requires the careful consideration of two additional factors:

1. Each element of the regular expression list may be either a *ONCE* match-type or a *ZERO_MORE* match-type. It is necessary to treat them separately because they lead to different inductive hypotheses.

2. There are many possible sub-lines within a line that can match a regular expression, especially one involving a *ZERO_MORE* match-type; for example, *A*A* matches both *A* and *AAAAAAAAA*. In order to continue the design, it is necessary to adopt a strategy to deal with all possibilities in a consistent manner. The most common strategies are:

   (a) Look for the shortest possible match; for example, to match the regular expression *A*A* it is only necessary to inspect the first character in the string *AAAAAAA*. (Notice, however, that matching *A*B* against *AAAAAAAB* still requires the inspection of the entire second string.)

   (b) Look for the longest possible match; for example, to match the regular expression *A*A* it is necessary to inspect all of the characters in the string *AAAAAAA*.

Since **grep** only returns a Boolean value, either strategy is valid; the efficiency of the strategy depends mainly on the nature of the regular expression and the searched line. The program presented in this book will follow the strategy of the shortest possible match.[11]

Design and implementation

The design proceeds by identifying the important cases for analysis:

1. The general case, where both the searched list and the regular expression list are non-empty. This must be split into two subcases to cater for the two different match-types.
2. The base cases, for the empty regular expression list and for the empty searched list. In the latter case, once again there is a need to cater for the two different match-types.

This leads to the following five alternative patterns:

```
startswith ([], any)
    =  Body_1
startswith (("ONCE", ch) : regrest, [])
    =  Body_2
startswith (("ZERO_MORE", ch) : regrest, [])
    =  Body_3
startswith (("ONCE", ch) : regrest, (lfront : lrest))
    =  Body_4
startswith (("ZERO_MORE", ch) : regrest, (lfront : lrest))
    =  Body_5
```

Finally, in accordance with the advice given in Chapter 2, a default pattern is added to help with debugging:

```
startswith anyother = error "startswith: illegal pattern"
```

The definitions of Body_1, Body_2 and Body_4 are essentially the same as those for the previous version of **startswith** (as explained in Section 3.7.2). However, the other definitions need further attention.

---

[11]However, many text editors with a "search and replace" command adopt the longest possible match strategy.

Body_5—ZERO_MORE general case

Given the pattern `(("ZERO_MORE",ch) : regrest, (lfront : lrest))`, there are two successful matching possibilities: either to *zero* occurrences of `ch` or to the *first* of *one or more* occurrences of `ch` (which requires further processing to determine how many more occurrences of `ch` exist). The "shortest possible" match strategy first assumes a match to zero occurrences of `ch` and has the inductive hypothesis that `(startswith (regrest, lfront : lrest))` will operate correctly. If the recursion evaluates to `True` then the entire search evaluates to `True`. Otherwise, the strategy is to "backtrack" to consider the possibility of a single occurrence match. This search will be successful if `ch` matches `lfront` and also if all of the current regular expression matches the rest of the search line.[12]

This leads to the following Miranda code for Body_5:

```
startswith (regrest, (lfront : lrest))
\/
((ch = lfront) & startswith (("ZERO_MORE",ch) : regrest, lrest))
```

It is interesting to observe that if `\/` did not delay the evaluation of its second argument then the function would evaluate all possible matches for the regular expression to the searched list. By contrast, any actual evaluation is limited to a sequential search from the shortest to the longest, stopping when an overall match is found.

Body_5 at work

The following shows the code for `Body_5` at work on two exemplary cases:

1. A successful match of the regular expression `"A*A"` against the input line `"AAB"` which demonstrates the shortest possible match strategy.
2. A successful match of the regular expression `"A*B"` against the input line `"AAB"` which demonstrates the backtracking mechanism.

For clarity, the hand evaluation is shown using the "raw" regular expression and searched-line strings rather than their tokenized list versions.

1. Shortest match strategy

```
grep ("A*A", "AAB")
==> startswith ("A*A", "AAB")  || i.e. Pattern_5
==> startswith ("A", "AAB")    || i.e. Pattern_4
==> True
```

---

[12]Note that if the searched list contains a long sequence of `ch` characters then this could lead to a large number of delayed decisions and indeed backtracking may occur many times before the appropriate match is found.

2. Backtracking mechanism

```
grep ("A*B", "AAB")
==> startswith ("A*B", "AAB")                  || i.e. Pattern_5
==> startswith ("B", "AAB")                    || i.e. Pattern_4
==> False
      \/
     (
     "A" = "A"
         &
      startswith ("A*B", "AB")                 || i.e. Pattern_5
         ==> startswith ("B", "AB")            || i.e. Pattern_4
         ==> False
             \/
            (
            "A" = "A"
                &
             startswith ("A*B", "B")    || i.e. Pattern_5
                ==> startswith ("B", "B")  || i.e. Pattern_4
                ==> True
            )
         ==> True
     )
  ==> True
```

Body_3—ZERO_MORE at end of line

This leaves the case for `Body_3`, which can be considered as a successful zero-occurrence match. One of the parameters of recursion has reached termination (or was [] to start with), but the other still needs further processing to handle regular expressions of the form $A*B*$ (which can successfully match an empty search list). The inductive hypothesis is the same as for `Body_5`: the inductive step is therefore to recurse using the rest of the regular expression—the evaluation will either converge towards an empty regular expression and succeed or a *ONCE* match-type will be found in the regular expression and the overall search will fail. The code is:

```
startswith (("ZERO_MORE", ch) : regrest, [])
      = startswith (regrest, [])
```

Final code for startswith

Piecing this all together gives:

```
string      == [char]
mtype       == string
regtype     == (mtype,string)
reglist     == [regtype]

startswith ::  (reglist, string) -> bool

startswith ([], any) = True
startswith (("ONCE", ch) :  regrest, []) = False
startswith (("ZERO_MORE", ch) :  regrest, [])
    = startswith (regrest, [])
startswith (("ONCE", ch) :  regrest, lfront :  lrest)
    = (ch = lfront) & startswith (regrest, lrest)
startswith (("ZERO_MORE", ch) :  regrest, lfront :  lrest)
    = startswith (regrest, (lfront :  lrest)) \/
      ((ch = lfront) &
      startswith (("ZERO_MORE", ch) :  regrest, lrest))
startswith any = error "startswith"
```

In order to complete the implementation, the `grep` and `sublist` functions need amending to preprocess the raw regular expression:

```
sublist ::  (reglist, string) -> bool

sublist ([], any) = True
sublist (any, []) = False
sublist (regexp, line)
    = startswith (regexp, line) \/
          sublist (regexp, tl line)

grep ::  (string, string) -> bool
grep (regexp, line) = sublist (lex regexp, line)
```

Furthermore, the `sublist` function needs a little extra modification so that a regular expression such as `A*` matches the empty string (as shown in the answer to the final exercise in this chapter).

Exercise 3.14

Explain the presence of the final pattern in the function `startswith`, even though it should never be encountered.

Exercise 3.15

What would happen if the second and third pattern in `startswith` were swapped?

Exercise 3.16

Alter the `sublist` function so that `"A*"` matches the empty string.

3.10   Summary

This chapter has introduced the recursively defined aggregate list data type. A new list may be created from an existing list and a new value by use of the *constructor* :. Chapter 6 will extend this concept to user-defined recursive types with user-defined constructors.

The techniques of *case analysis* and *structural induction* were introduced as an aid to designing list-handling functions. Recursive function definition is of such fundamental importance to the manipulation of the list data structure that the general technique was analysed further and five common modes of recursion over lists were discussed: tail recursion, stack recursion, filter recursion, accumulative recursion and mutual recursion. Chapter 4 shows how higher order functions may be used to encapsulate common recursive forms.

This chapter ended with the design and development of the *grep* program, using the tools and techniques learned so far. Later in the book we will show how more advanced techniques can be applied to the same real-world example to produce a better design.

Chapter 4

Curried and Higher Order Functions

Chapter 2 has shown that functions are values in themselves and can be treated as data items (see Section 2.2). This chapter shows that functions may in fact be passed as parameters to other functions; a function that either takes another function as an argument or produces a function as a result is known as a *higher order function*.

Two further concepts are introduced in this chapter: *currying* and *function composition*. Currying (named in honour of the mathematician Haskell Curry) enables functions to be defined with multiple parameters without the need to use a tuple. A curried function also has the property that it does not have to be applied to all of its parameters at once; it can be *partially applied* to form a new function which may then be passed as a parameter to a higher order function. Function composition is used to chain together functions (which may themselves be partial applications) to form a new function.

Several powerful "families" of higher order functions on lists are shown; these functions can be combined and composed together to create new higher order functions. Higher order functions may be used to avoid the use of explicit recursion, thereby producing programs which are shorter, easier to read and easier to maintain.

4.1 Currying

It is sometimes tedious to use tuple notation to deal with functions that require more than one parameter. An alternative way of writing the function definition and application is to omit the tuple notation as shown in the definition for **get_nth** (which selects the nth item from a list, and is similar to the built-in ! operator):[1]

---

[1] Note that the brackets around (**front** : **any**) are not tuple brackets but part of the list construction and must not be removed.

```
get_nth   any   []                      =   error "get_nth"
get_nth   1     (front :  any)          =   front
get_nth   n     (front :  rest)         =   get_nth (n - 1) rest
```

The type indication is new:

```
Miranda get_nth ::
num->[*]->*
```

This is different from previous responses for function definition, which had a single arrow in the type. In the curried definition shown above, there are two arrows which implies that two functions have been defined. These type arrows always associate to the right,[2] so that an equivalent type response is:

```
num->([*]->*)
```

This illustrates that **get_nth** is a function which has a number source type and generates an intermediate result which is itself a function; this second, but anonymous, function translates a polytype list into a polytype.

The presence of multiple arrows in the type indicates that **get_nth** is a *curried* function. This curried version of **get_nth** may now be applied to two arguments, without using tuple brackets, giving the desired result:

```
Miranda get_nth 2 ["a","bb","ccc"]
bb
```

In practice, any uncurried function could have been defined in a curried manner, regardless of the number of components in its argument. *From now on most functions will be presented in a curried form.*

4.1.1   Partially applied functions

Although currying allows a simpler syntax, its real advantage is that it provides the facility to define functions that can be *partially applied*. This is useful because it enables the creation of new functions as specializations of existing functions. For instance, the function **get_nth** may be used with just one argument to give rise to new functions:

```
get_second   =   get_nth 2
get_fifth    =   get_nth 5
```

```
Miranda get_second ::
[*]->*
```

---

[2]Remember that function *application* associates to the left.

```
Miranda get_fifth ::
[*]->*
```

```
Miranda get_second ["a","bb","ccc"]
bb
```

A hand evaluation of the above application of **get_second** shows:

```
get_second ["a","bb","c"]
==> (get_nth 2) ["a","bb","ccc"]
==> get_nth 2 ["a","bb","ccc"]
==> get_nth 1 ["bb","ccc"]
==> "bb"
```

The partial application of (**get_nth** 2) thus generates an intermediate function, waiting for application to a final argument in order to generate a result. A partial application may also be used as an actual parameter to another function; the expressive power of this feature will become evident later in this chapter during the discussion of *higher order functions*.

4.1.2 Partially applied operators

The Miranda arithmetic and relational operators all have an underlying infix format. This means that they cannot be partially applied. For example, both of the following definitions will fail:

```
wrong_inc = 1 +

wrong_inc = + 1
```

It is, of course, possible to define simple, prefix, curried functions which do the same as their operator equivalents and can then be partially applied:

```
plus ::   num -> num -> num
plus x y = x + y

inc = plus 1
```

As there are not many operators, this approach provides a brief, simple and pragmatic solution. An alternative approach is to use the Miranda *operator section* mechanism. With this approach *any* dyadic operator (that is, an operator taking two arguments) may be used in a prefix, curried manner by surrounding it with brackets.

For example, the following two expressions are equivalent:

```
1 + 2
(+) 1 2
```

The latter demonstrates firstly, that the syntactic form (+) is a prefix function and secondly, that it takes its two distinct arguments and hence is curried.

The following definitions further demonstrate the power of the bracketing notation:

```
inc = (+) 1

twice = (*) 2
```

The unrestricted use of operator sections can sometimes lead to cluttered code, and so it may be preferable to provide names for prefix, curried versions of the operators. Using these names will lead to code that is longer, but more comprehensible. The following definitions provide suggested names which may be used (where appropriate) in subsequent examples throughout the book:

```
plus                = (+)
minus               = (-)
times               = (*)
divide              = (/)

both                = (&)
either              = (\/)

append              = (++)
cons                = (:)

equal               = (=)
notequal            = (~=)

isitgreaterthan     = (<)
greaterthan         = (>)

isitlessthan        = (>)
lessthan            = (<)
```

Notice that number comparison has two variants, for example isitlessthan and lessthan.[3] These two functions are quite different:

1. isitlessthan is normally used in a partially applied manner to provide a predicate, for example:

---

[3] The following discussion applies equally to the functions isitgreaterthan and greaterthan.

```
is_negative ::   num -> bool
is_negative = isitlessthan 0
```

```
Miranda is_negative (-1)
True
```

2. `lessthan` is normally used as a prefix replacement for the infix operator `<`:

```
Miranda lessthan 0 (-1)
False
```

The partial application (`lessthan 0`) is interpreted as "is 0 less than some integer?".

This kind of distinction applies to all *non-commutative* operators.

In general, Miranda allows both *presections* (for example, (`1+`)) and *postsections* (for example, (`+1`)). There is one important exception: it is not possible to define a postsection for the subtraction operator. This is because (`-1`) already has a special meaning—minus one!

4.2   Simple higher order functions

Higher order functions are a powerful extension to the function concept and are as easy to define and use as any other function. The rest of this section shows a number of simple higher order functions whilst the next section extends the principle to higher order functions over lists.

4.2.1   Function composition

The built-in operator `.` (pronounced "compose") is different to previously shown built-in operators in that it takes two functions as its parameters (and hence is also a higher order function). A frequent programming practice is to apply a function to the result of another function application. For instance, using the function `twice` (defined in the previous section):

```
quad x = twice (twice x)

many x = twice (twice (twice (twice x)))
```

In this sort of function definition, the use of bracket pairs is tedious and can lead to errors if a bracket is either misplaced or forgotten. The operator `.` enables most of the brackets to be replaced:

```
quad x = (twice .   twice) x

many x = (twice .   twice .   twice .   twice) x
```

Not only is this notation easier to read but it also emphasizes the way the functions are combined. The outermost brackets are still necessary because . has a lower precedence than function application. The compose operator is specified by $(f . g) x = f (g \ x)$, where the source type of the function f must be the same as the result type of the function g.

Function composition provides a further advantage beyond mere "syntactic sugaring", in that it allows two functions to be combined and treated as a single function. As shown in Chapter 1, the following intuitive attempt at naming **many** fails because **twice** expects a number argument rather than a function translating a number to a number:

```
wrong_many = twice twice twice twice
```

```
type error in definition of wrong_many
cannot unify num->num with num
```

The correct version uses function composition:

```
many ::   num -> num
many = twice .   twice .   twice .   twice
```

```
Miranda many 3
48
```

The use of . is not limited to combining several instances of the same function (which itself must have identical source and target types); it can be used to combine any pair of functions that satisfy the specification given above. For example:

```
sqrt_many = sqrt .   many

sqrt_dbl = sqrt .   (plus 1) .   twice
```

Note that in the final example (plus 1) is a monadic function (it takes just one parameter); the use of **plus** on its own is inappropriate for composition because it is dyadic.

Composing operators

If an operator is to be used in a function composition then it must be used in its sectional form. For example:

```
Miranda ((+ 2) . (* 3) 3
11
```

This rule also applies to ˜ and #, which must be treated as prefix operators rather than functions:

```
Miranda ((˜) . (< 3)) 4
True
```

```
Miranda ((#) . tl) [1,2,3]
2
```

Exercise 4.1

Give the types of the following compositions:

```
tl . (++ [])
abs . fst
code . code
show . tl
```

4.2.2 Combinatorial functions

The following functions are similar to . in that they facilitate the use of higher order functions. These functions are known as *combinators* (Diller, 1988; Field and Harrison, 1988; Revesz, 1988; Turner, 1979) and, traditionally, are given single upper case letter names (which is not possible under Miranda naming rules). This text only introduces versions of the combinators B, C and K, which are of general utility. There are many more possible combinators which have mainly theoretical interest and serve as the basis for many implementations of functional languages. For more information the reader is referred to the Bibliography.

Compose

The B combinator is the prefix equivalent of . and is defined below as the function "compose":

```
compose = (.)   || B combinator
```

The function compose can now be used in a similar way and with the same advantages as its built-in equivalent.

Swap

The C combinator is known as "swap" and serves to exchange the arguments of a (curried) dyadic function:

```
swap ff x y = ff y x    || C combinator
```

Note that the Miranda Standard Environment provides the function `converse`, which has the same functionality.

Cancel

The K combinator is known as "cancel" because it always discards the second of its two arguments and returns its first argument:

```
cancel x y = x    || K combinator
```

Note that the Miranda Standard Environment provides the function `const`, which has the same functionality as `cancel`.

Exercise 4.2

Theoreticians claim that all of the combinators (and consequently all functions) can be written in terms of the combinator K (`cancel`) and the following combinator S (`distribute`):

```
distribute f g x = f x (g x)
```

Define the combinator `identity` (which returns its argument unaltered) using only the functions `distribute` and `cancel` in the function body. Provide a similar definition for a curried version of `snd`.

4.2.3   Converting uncurried functions to curried form

The user-defined functions presented in the first three chapters of this book have been defined in an uncurried format. This is a sensible format when the functions are intended to be used with all of their arguments, but it is not as flexible as the curried format. If curried versions are required then it would be possible to rewrite each function using curried notation; however, this would involve a lot of programmer effort (and consequently would be prone to programmer error). A more pragmatic approach is to write a function that will generate curried versions of uncurried functions—this function could be written once, then used as and when necessary.

This section presents a function, make_curried, which will convert any uncurried, dyadic function (that is, a function which takes a tuple with two components) to curried format. The programmer can then use this function as a template for further conversion functions as required.

The conversion function make_curried is itself in curried form and takes three parameters. The first parameter represents the uncurried function and the next two parameters represent that function's arguments. All that the function body needs to do is apply the input function to these last two parameters collected into a tuple (since an uncurried function only works on a single argument):

```
make_curried ::   ((*,**) -> ***) -> * -> ** -> ***
make_curried ff x y = ff (x,y)
```

Now, given the definition:

```
maxnum ::   (num,num)->num
maxnum (x, y) = x, if x > y
              = y, otherwise
```

then clearly the application maxnum 1 2 will fail, as the function maxnum expects a number pair. Using make_curried gets around this problem:[4]

```
make_curried maxnum 2 3
==> maxnum (2, 3)
==> 3
```

Similarly, new curried versions of existing functions can be created with the minimum of programmer effort:

```
newmaxnum = make_curried maxnum
```

The function make_curried is another example of a higher order function because it expects a function as one of its parameters. In general, any function that takes a function as at least one of its parameters or returns a function, as its result is known as a higher order function.

Exercise 4.3
Explain why make_curried cannot be generalized to work for functions with an arbitrary number of tuple components.

Exercise 4.4
Write the function make_uncurried which will allow a curried, dyadic function to accept a tuple as its argument.

---

[4]This is an excellent example of the fact that function application associates from the left, to give ((make_curried maxnum) 2) 3 rather than make_curried (maxnum (2 3)) which would be an error.

Exercise 4.5

The built-in function `fst` can be written using `make_uncurried` and the `cancel` combinator:

```
myfst = make_uncurried cancel
```

Provide a similar definition for the built-in function `snd`.

4.2.4   Iteration

An important advantage of the functional approach is that the programmer can create a rich set of iterative control structures and hence be more likely to choose one which represents the problem specification. This subsection illustrates this point in the definition of a "repeat" loop construct. This function is *not* similar to the `repeat` function available in the Miranda Standard Environment—it is, however, similar to the `iterate` function.[5]

The following (non-robust) function repeatedly applies its second parameter to its final parameter, which serves as an *accumulator* for the final result. The parameter of recursion is n which converges towards zero:

```
myiterate ::   num -> (* -> *) -> * -> *
myiterate 0 ff state = state
myiterate n ff state = myiterate (n-1) ff (ff state)
```

The function `myiterate` can be used to give a non-recursive definition of any function that bases its recursion on a fixed number of iterations. For example, the function `printdots` (from Chapter 2) may be defined as:

```
printdots n = myiterate n ((++) ".") ""
```

In `printdots` the empty string `""` is the initial value of the `state` parameter (or accumulator), which changes at each recursive step. A hand evaluation of (`printdots 2`) reveals:

```
printdots 2
==> myiterate 2 ((++) ".") ""
==> myiterate 1 ((++) ".") (((++) ".") "")
==> myiterate 1 ((++) ".") ("." ++ "")
==> myiterate 1 ((++) ".") (".")
==> myiterate 0 ((++) ".") (((++) ".") ".")
==> myiterate 0 ((++) ".") ("." ++ ".")
==> myiterate 0 ((++) ".") ("..")
==> ".."
```

---

[5]The function could alternatively be defined as `myiterate n ff state = (iterate ff state) ! n`.

If the function to be repeated also requires the iteration count as a parameter, the following variant `myiterate_c` may be used (assuming the iteration counter counts down towards zero):

```
myiterate_c ::  num -> (* -> num -> *) -> * -> *
myiterate_c 0 ff state = state
myiterate_c n ff state
           = myiterate_c (n - 1) ff (ff state n)
```

Exercise 4.6

Explain why `myiterate` is non-robust and provide a robust version.

Exercise 4.7

Imperative programming languages generally have a general-purpose iterative control structure known as a "while" loop. This construct will repeatedly apply a function to a variable whilst the variable satisfies some predefined condition. Define an equivalent function in Miranda.

4.3   Higher order functions on lists

Many of the list-handling functions presented in Chapter 3 exhibit similar forms of recursion but use different operations to achieve their results. Miranda provides the facility to generalize these functions and removes the need to program with explicit recursion.

This section shows three families of curried, polymorphic, higher order functions on lists:

1. The "map" family, which retains the list structure but transforms the list items.
2. The "fold" family, which distributes an operator over a list, typically to produce a single value result.
3. The "select" family, which retains the list structure but may delete items from the list, according to a given predicate.

4.3.1   The map family

It is often useful to apply a function to each item in a list, returning a list of the consequences. For example, `map_inc` will apply `inc` to each item in a given number list and `map_twice` will apply `twice` to each item in a given number list:

```
inc = (+ 1)
twice = (* 2)

map_inc []                      = []
map_inc (front :   rest)    = (inc front) :   (map_inc rest)

map_twice []                    = []
map_twice (front :   rest) = (twice front) :   (map_twice rest)
```

A template for any function of this form is:

    map_ff [] = []

    map_ff (front : rest) = (ff front) : (map_ff rest)

It can be seen from this template that the only important difference between `map_inc` and `map_twice` is the name of the function that is applied to the **front** item (represented by *ff* in the template). Rather than having to define functions of this form using explicit recursion, it is possible to define them using the built-in higher order function `map`. This function has *ff* as its first argument and the list to be transformed as its second argument:

```
Miranda map inc [1,3,2,6]
[2,4,3,7]
```

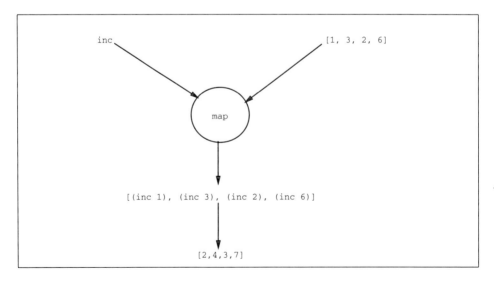

Figure 4.1 The behaviour of the function **map**.

The behaviour of the function **map** is further illustrated in Figure 4.1 and the following examples:

```
Miranda map (+ 1) [1,2,3]
[2,3,4]
```

```
Miranda map (twice . inc) [1,2,3]
[4,6,8]
```

```
Miranda map (plus 2) [1,2,3]
[3,4,5]
```

```
list_inc = map inc
```

```
Miranda list_inc ::
[num] -> [num]
```

```
Miranda list_inc [1,2,3]
[2,3,4]
```

It is important to note that (map inc) is a partially applied function (where inc is a function argument to map) and is *not* a function composition:

```
Miranda (map inc) ::
[num] ->[num]
```

```
Miranda (map . inc) ::
cannot unify num->num with num->*->**
```

Furthermore, as in all other situations, the arguments to and the results produced by map are evaluated lazily:

```
Miranda map (+ 1) [1,2,3]
[2,3,4]
```

```
Miranda map (/ 0) [1,2,3]
[
program error: attempt to divide by zero
```

```
Miranda fst (3, map (/ 0) [1,2,3])
3
```

```
Miranda (hd.tl) (map (3 /) [1,0,3])
program error: attempt to divide by zero
```

```
Miranda hd (map (3 /) [1,0,3])
3.0
```

Designing map

In fact, map is very easy to write. All that is necessary is to generalize from the
map_ff template by passing ff as an additional argument:

```
map ff []              = []
map ff (front :  rest) = (ff front) :  (map ff rest)
```

The function map is polymorphic, as can be seen from its type:

```
Miranda map ::
(*->**)->[*]->[**]
```

The function can transform a list of any type provided that the source type of ff
matches the type of the items in the list.

Mapping over two lists

The principle of list transformation using map can be extended to cater for more
than one list. For example, the following function takes two lists and recursively
applies a dyadic function to the corresponding front items:

```
map_two ::   (*->*->**)->[*]->[*]->[**]
map_two ff [] [] = []
map_two ff (front1 :  rest1) (front2 :  rest2)
    = (ff front1 front2) :  (map_two ff rest1 rest2)
map_two ff any1 any2
    = error "map_two:  lists of unequal length"
```

```
Miranda map_two (make_curried max) [1,2,3] [3,2,1]
[3,2,3]
```

Exercise 4.8
In the definition of map_two, source lists of unequal length have been treated as an error.
It is an equally valid design decision to truncate the longer list; amend the definition to
meet this revised specification.

Exercise 4.9
    Write a function applylist which takes a list of functions (each of type *->**) and
an item (of type *) and returns a list of the results of applying each function to the item.
For example: applylist [(+ 10),(* 3)] 2 will evaluate to [12,6].

Exercise 4.10

Explain why the following definitions are equivalent:

```
f1 x alist = map (plus x) alist
f2 x = map (plus x)
f3 = (map . plus)
```

4.3.2 List folding—reduce and accumulate

This subsection discusses how a dyadic function can be distributed so that it works over a list, typically evaluating to a single value, for example to give the sum of all the numbers in a list. As with the discussion of map, it will be shown how explicit recursion can be removed by means of a single higher order function. Two strategies are used:

1. Stack recursion, to define a function called **reduce** (known in the Miranda Standard Environment as foldr).
2. Accumulative recursion, to define a function called **accumulate** (known in the Miranda Standard Environment as foldl).

The higher order function reduce

On inspecting the structure of the following definitions of sumlist, divall and anytrue, it can be seen that they share a common structure:

```
sumlist []                  = 0
sumlist (front :  rest)  = front +  (sumlist rest)


divall []                   = 1.0
divall (front :  rest)   = front /  (divall rest)


anytrue []                  = False
anytrue (front :  rest)  = front \/  (anytrue rest)
```

Functions of this form place the dyadic operator between each of the list items and substitute a terminating value for the empty list. For example, the sum of the list [1,2,5,2] may be thought of as the result of $1 + 2 + 5 + 2 + 0$. Generalizing gives the template:

$$
\begin{aligned}
reduce\_ff \quad &[] &= \quad &default \\
reduce\_ff \quad &(front : rest) &= \quad &(ff\ front) \oplus (reduce\_ff\ rest)
\end{aligned}
$$

This template is appropriate for all dyadic infix functions $\oplus$. In the above examples, the default value has been chosen such that the following specification holds:

$$any \oplus default = any$$

When the default value has this property, it is formally known as the *Identity* element of the dyadic function:

Table 4.1 Identity elements of common dyadic functions.

any	$\oplus$	*Identity*	=	any
any_int	+	0	=	any_num
any_bool	\/	False	=	any_bool
any_string	++	" "	=	any_string
any_list	I+	[]	=	any_list

Notice it is not always necessary to choose the identity as the default. For example:

```
product_times_ten [] = 10
product_times_ten (front :   rest)
      = front * (product_times_ten rest)
```

Furthermore, many dyadic functions do not have an identity and so great care must be taken in the choice of a sensible default value. For example, it is not obvious what would be a sensible default value for the operator mod.

Miranda provides a built-in higher order function called foldr to generalize *reduce_ff*. However, a user-defined version (here called reduce) can also be written, using a similar approach to that taken with the design of map.

Designing reduce

The above examples considered the distribution of built-in infix operators over lists. However, reduce will be designed to accept prefix functions, mainly because user-defined functions are normally defined in prefix form. The design proceeds by replacing $\oplus$ with a prefix version ff in the template:

$$reduce\_ff \ \ [] \qquad\qquad = \quad default$$
$$reduce\_ff \ \ (front : rest) \quad = \quad (ff \ front) \ (reduce\_ff \ rest)$$

All that is now necessary is to make ff and *default* become explicit arguments:

```
reduce   ::   (* -> ** -> **) -> ** -> [*] -> **

reduce   ff default [] = default
reduce   ff default (front :   rest)
      =  ff front (reduce ff default rest)
```

Examples of partial applications which use `reduce` are now presented (employing the curried functions defined in Section 4.1.2):

```
anytrue            = reduce either False
sumlist            = reduce plus 0
divall             = reduce divide 1.0
product_times_ten  = reduce times 10
```

```
Miranda reduce plus 0 [1,2,3]
6
```

```
Miranda sumlist [1,3,5]
9
```

A hand evaluation of the last application shows:

```
sumlist [1,3,5]
==> reduce (+) 0 [1,3,5]
==> (+) 1 (reduce (+) 0 [3,5])
==> (+) 1 ((+) 3 (reduce (+) 0 [5]))
==> (+) 1 ((+) 3 ((+) 5 (reduce (+) 0 [])))
==> (+) 1 ((+) 3 ((+) 5 0))
==> (+) 1 ((+) 3 5)
==> (+) 1 8
==> 9
```

The function `reduce` is stack recursive, in that it stacks a growing unevaluated expression until the empty list is encountered. At this point it unstacks from the innermost right to the outermost left, combining them pairwise by means of application of the function parameter `ff`. In the unstacking phase, this can be seen as "folding" the list from the right, usually into a single value; hence the alternative name, `foldr`, which is used by the equivalent Miranda Standard Environment function.

The function `reduce` is not restricted to a single value result; it can also return an aggregate type, as illustrated in the following example:

```
do_nothing ::    [*] -> [*]
do_nothing = reduce (:)   []
```

```
Miranda do_nothing [1,5,8]
[1,5,8]
```

A hand evaluation shows how this works:

```
do_nothing [1,5,8]
==> reduce (:) [] [1,5,8]
==> (:) 1 (reduce (:) [] [5,8])
==> (:) 1 ((:) 5 (reduce (:) [] [8]))
==> (:) 1 ((:) 5 ((:) 8 (reduce (:) [] [])))
==> (:) 1 ((:) 5 ((:) 8 [] ))
==> (:) 1 ((:) 5 [8])
==> (:) 1 [5,8]
==> [1,5,8]
```

The overall result is an aggregate type because the dyadic function being distributed (in this case (:)) returns an aggregate type. Notice that the target type of the function being distributed must be the same as the source type of its second argument (that is, it must have type * -> ** -> **). Also notice that (:) has no identity—however, [] was chosen as the sensible default value because it produces a list as required.

It is also possible to use **reduce** to distribute partial applications and function compositions across lists, as demonstrated below:

```
addup_greaterthan ::   num -> num -> num -> num
addup_greaterthan x y z  = y + z, if x < y
                         = z, otherwise
```

```
Miranda reduce (addup_greaterthan 3) 0 [1,7,3,9,8,4,1]
28
```

```
Miranda reduce ((:) . inc) [] [1,2,3]
[2,3,4] : int list
```

The final example above is particularly interesting as it has the same action as **map inc [1,2,3]**. A hand evaluation shows how it works:

```
reduce ((:) . inc) [] [1,2,3]
==> ((:) . inc) 1 (reduce ((:) . inc) [] [2,3])
==> (:) (inc 1) (reduce ((:) . inc) [] [2,3])
==> (:) 2 (reduce ((:) . inc) [] [2,3])
==> (:) 2 (((:) . inc) 2 (reduce ((:) . inc) [] [3]))
==> (:) 2 ((:) (inc 2) (reduce ((:) . inc) [] [3]))
==> (:) 2 ((:) 3 (reduce ((:) . inc) [] [3]))
==> (:) 2 ((:) 3 (((:) . inc) 3 (reduce ((:) . inc) [] [])))
==> (:) 2 ((:) 3 ((:) (inc 3) (reduce ((:) . inc) [] [])))
==> (:) 2 ((:) 3 ((:) 4 (reduce ((:) . inc) [] [])))
==> (:) 2 ((:) 3 ((:) 4 []))
==> (:) 2 ((:) 3 [4])
==> (:) 2 [3,4]
==> [2,3,4]
```

Exercise 4.11
  Rewrite the function map in terms of reduce.

The higher order function accumulate

It is possible to define a very similar function to reduce that makes use of the accumulative style of recursion. Miranda provides the built-in higher order function foldl, which starts evaluating immediately by recursing on the tail of the list with the default value being used as the accumulator. A user-defined version called accumulate is given below:

```
accumulate   ::   (*->**->*) -> * -> [**] -> *

accumulate  ff default [] = default
accumulate  ff default (front :   rest)
          =   accumulate ff (ff default front) rest
```

Equivalence of reduce and accumulate

On many occasions reduce can be substituted with accumulate, as shown in the next three examples which rework the previous reduce examples. However, this is not always the case, as will be demonstrated in the subsequent treatment for reverse.

```
anytrue            = accumulate either  False
sumlist            = accumulate plus    0
product_times_ten  = accumulate times   10
```

A hand evaluation of sumlist [1,3,5] reveals that the same answer is obtained as for the reduce version, but in a very different manner:

```
sumlist [1,3,5]
==> accumulate (+) 0 [1,3,5]
==> accumulate (+) ((+) 0 1) [3,5]
==> accumulate (+) 1 [3,5]
==> accumulate (+) ((+) 1 3) [5]
==> accumulate (+) 4 [5]
==> accumulate (+) ((+) 4 5) []
==> accumulate (+) 9 []
==> 9
```

By contrast, it is not possible to substitute `accumulate` for `reduce` in the `divall` example, nor `reduce` for `accumulate` in the following definition of `myreverse`:

```
myreverse = accumulate (swap (:))  []
```

Note that the above user-defined version is directly equivalent to the definition of the built-in function `reverse`, as presented in Section 28 of the Miranda on-line manual:

```
reverse = foldl (converse (:)) []
```

Comparing reduce and accumulate

The reason why `reduce` cannot be substituted for `accumulate` in the above defini tion of `reverse` is best illustrated through a diagrammatic comparison of the two functions. The following example compares the distribution of the infix + operator across the list `[1,2,3]`, with a default value of 0. If the `reduce` function is used then this may be considered diagrammatically as placing the default value at the right-hand end of the list and bracketing the expression from the right (hence the alternative name `foldr`):

$$
\begin{array}{ccccccc}
1 & : & 2 & : & 3 & : & [\,] \\
\downarrow & & \downarrow & & \downarrow & & \\
1 & + & (2 & + & (3 & + & 0))
\end{array}
$$

By contrast, if the `accumulate` function is used then this may be considered dia grammatically to place the default value at the left-hand end and bracketing the expression from the left (hence the alternative name `foldl`):

$$
\begin{array}{ccccccc}
& 1 & : & 2 & : & 3 & : & [\,] \\
& \downarrow & & \downarrow & & \downarrow & \\
((0 + & 1) & + & 2) & + & 3
\end{array}
$$

Of course, `reduce` and `accumulate` are defined to take curried, prefix functions rather than infix operators and so the actual diagrams would be slightly more complex. For example, `(reduce (+) 0 [1,2,3])` would produce `((+) 1 ((+) 2 ((+) 3 0)))` and `(accumulate (+) 0 [1,2,3])` would produce `((+) ((+) ((+) 0 1) 2) 3)`. However, the above two diagrams provide a better visual mnemonic.

In general, it is only safe to substitute one of the *fold* functions with the other if the function parameter `ff` is associative and also commutative (at least with its identity). As explained in Chapter 1, an infix operator $\oplus$ is associative if the following holds for all possible values of x, y and z:

$$
x \oplus (y \oplus z) = (x \oplus y) \oplus z
$$

Similarly, a prefix function *ff* is associative if the following holds for all possible values of x, y and z:

$$ff \; x \; (ff \; y \; z) = ff \; (ff \; x \; y) \; z$$

A prefix function is commutative with its identity value if the following holds for all possible values of x:

$$ff \; Identity \; x = ff \; x \; Identity$$

It can now be seen that substituting `reduce` for `accumulate` in the definition of `reverse` will fail because both of the two conditions given above are violated. The function (swap (:)) is neither associative nor does it have an identity value.

The relevance of these two criteria can also be illustrated diagrammatically. By using the two rules of *associativity* and *commutativity with the identity*, and by reference to the diagrams used above, it is possible to transform the diagram for `reduce (+) 0 [1,2,3]` into the diagram for `accumulate (+) 0 [1,2,3]` (once again infix form is used in the diagram for clarity):

$$
\begin{array}{lll}
 & & 1 + (2 + (3 \; + 0)) \\
by \; rule \; 1 = & & (1 + 2) + (3 \; + 0) \\
by \; rule \; 1 = & & ((1 + 2) + 3) \; + 0 \\
by \; rule \; 2 = & 0 + & ((1 + 2) + 3) \\
by \; rule \; 1 = & (0 + & (1 + 2)) + 3 \\
by \; rule \; 1 = & ((0 + & 1) + 2) + 3
\end{array}
$$

Exercise 4.12

Some functions cannot be generalized over lists, as they have no obvious default value for the empty list; for example, it does not make sense to take the maximum value of an empty list. Write the function `reduce1` to cater for functions that require at least one list item.

Exercise 4.13

Write two curried versions of `mymember` (as specified in Chapter 3.6), using `reduce` and `accumulate`, respectively, and discuss their types and differences.

4.3.3   List selection

There are a large number of possible list selection functions, which remove items from a list if they do not satisfy a given predicate (that is, a function that translates its argument to a Boolean value). This subsection presents two functions which are typical of this family of functions.

List truncation

The following function takes a list and a predicate as arguments and returns the initial sublist of the list whose members all satisfy the predicate:

```
mytakewhile  ::   (* -> bool) -> [*] -> [*]

mytakewhile  pred [] = []
mytakewhile  pred (front :   rest)
             = front :  (mytakewhile pred rest), if pred front
             = [], otherwise
```

Example:

```
Miranda mytakewhile (notequal ' ') "how_long is a string"
how_long
```

This function behaves in the same manner as the Miranda Standard Environment `takewhile` function.

List filter

The next example is the function `myfilter` which uses a predicate that is based on the item's value. This function may be specified in terms of filter recursion, as shown in Section 3.8:

```
myfilter  ::   (* -> bool) -> [*] -> [*]
myfilter  pred [] = []
myfilter  pred (front :   rest)
          = front :  (myfilter pred rest), if pred front
          = myfilter pred rest, otherwise
```

Examples:

```
Miranda myfilter (isitlessthan 3) [1,7,2,9,67,3]
[1,2]
```

```
rm_dups ::   [*] -> [*]
rm_dups [] = []
rm_dups (front :   rest)
   = front :  (rm_dups (myfilter (notequal front) rest))
```

This function behaves in the same manner as the Miranda Standard Environment `filter` function.

Grep revisited

Using `filter`, the *grep* program shown in Section 3.9 can now be extended to mirror the UNIX *grep* behaviour, so that only those lines which match the regular expression are printed from an input stream. It should be noted that the code is presented in curried and partially applied form and assumes that `sublist` is also curried:

```
string == [char]

grep ::  string -> [string] -> [string]
grep regexp = filter (xgrep regexp)

xgrep ::  string -> string -> bool
xgrep regexp line = sublist (lex regexp) line
```

Exercise 4.14

Define the function `mydropwhile` which takes a list and a predicate as arguments and returns the list without the initial sublist of members which satisfy the predicate.

Exercise 4.15

The *set* data structure may be considered as an unordered list of unique items. Using the built-in functions `filter` and `member`, the following function will yield a list of all the items common to two sets:

```
intersection ::   [*] -> [*] -> [*]
intersection aset bset = filter (member aset) bset
```

Write a function `union` to create a set of all the items in two sets.

4.4   Program design with higher order functions

This section shows how programming with higher order functions leads to more general purpose programs. Higher order functions eliminate explicit recursion and so lead to programs that are more concise and often nearer to the natural specification of a problem.

4.4.1   Making functions more flexible

Many functions can be made more general by substituting explicit predicate functions with a parameter; the decision as to which predicate is actually employed is thereby deferred until the function is applied. In the following example, *insertion sort* (presented in Section 3.7.3) is generalized so that it will sort a list of any type in either ascending or descending order. The only alteration that is required to the original specification is to substitute a comparison function in place of the infix < operator for `insert` and `isort`. The following code reworks the example presented in Section 3.7.3 in curried form:

```
ordertype * == * -> * -> bool
isort ::  ordertype * -> [*] -> [*]
isort order anylist
     =  xsort order anylist []

xsort ::  ordertype * -> [*] -> [*] -> [*]
xsort order [] sortedlist
     =  sortedlist
xsort order (front :  rest) sortedlist
     =  xsort order rest (insert order front sortedlist)

insert  ::  ordertype * -> * -> [*] -> [*]
insert  order item []
     =  [item]
insert  order item (front :  rest)
     =  item :  front :  rest, if order item front
     =  front :  (insert order item rest), otherwise
```

The extra parameter `order` provides the comparison function, whilst also dictating the type of the list. In this manner, the functionality of `isort` has been increased significantly since a different `order` can be slotted in place by a simple partial application:

```
desc_sort ::  [*] -> [*]
desc_sort = isort greaterthan

stringsort ::  [char] -> [char]
stringsort = isort lessthan
```

Notice that the type declaration allows the overloaded relational operators to be truly polymorphic (as with **desc_sort**) or forces them to be monomorphic (as with **stringsort**).

As a bonus, it is possible to remove some of the explicit recursion from these function definitions by replacing the explicitly defined `isort` with **reduce** as follows:

```
isort order = reduce (insert order) []
```

Exercise 4.16

An equivalent version of `stringsort` using `accumulate` would require that the arguments to (`insert lessthan`) be reversed. Why is this the case?

4.4.2   Combining higher order functions

This subsection briefly looks at some of the many ways of combining higher order functions.

Example—combining accumulate and map

The following is a simple example using `map` and `accumulate` to convert a string to an integer:

```
string_to_int ::   [char] -> num
string_to_int astring
   = accumulate (plus .  (times 10)) 0 (map ctoi astring)

ctoi ::  char -> num
ctoi x = (code x) - (code '0')
```

This may be rewritten, using further function composition, as follows:

```
string_to_int ::   [char] -> num
string_to_int astring
   = ((accumulate (plus .  (times 10)) 0) .  (map ctoi))
                                            astring

ctoi ::  char -> num
ctoi x = (code x) - (code '0')
```

Notice that for any definition *f x = expression x*, where *expression* contains no reference to *x*, then *f* and *expression* must be exactly equivalent (they both operate on *x* to produce a result and the two results are equal by definition). Thus, the given definition can be shortened to one which simply states that *f* and *expression* are equivalent: *f = expression*. This does not alter the type of *f*; it is still a function of one argument. This optimization may be applied to the above definition of `string_to_int` as follows:

```
string_to_int ::  [char] -> num
string_to_int
  = (accumulate (plus . (times 10)) 0) . (map ctoi)


ctoi ::  char -> num
ctoi x = (code x) - (code '0')
```

This example reinforces the observation that function composition is the equivalent of sequencing in an imperative style of programming, though here the program sequence should be read from the rightmost composition towards the leftmost.

Example—combining map and filter

The functions `filter` and `map` may be combined to give a function which takes a list of items, each of type (student, grade), and outputs the names of all students with a grade less than 50%:

```
student == [char]
grade   == num
results == [(student, grade)]
mapping == results -> [student]


weak_students ::  mapping
weak_students
      = (map fst) . filter ((isitlessthan 50) . snd)
```

Different approaches to combining functions

There are a number of approaches to combining functions and higher order functions; to illustrate this point, two of the many possible versions of the function `length` are now shown.

The first version has an underlying design that considers the length of a list as the sum of a list which has had all of its items transformed into the number 1. Hence the implementation must *first* transform each of its argument's list elements into a 1 and *second* perform the summation. This can be written using **accumulate**, **map** and the combinator **cancel** as follows:

```
length = (accumulate (+) 0) . (map (cancel 1))
```

An alternative design is to think in terms of function composition and consider the length of a list as the *ongoing* summation of each list element transformed into the number 1:

```
length = reduce ((+) . (cancel 1)) 0
```

There are no rigid rules concerning which style to use. The best advice is to choose the definition which most closely mirrors the natural specification; however this will differ from problem to problem and from program designer to program designer. Probably the biggest danger is to be tempted to go too far with the facilities shown in this chapter:

```
guesswhat  =  (foldr (+) 0).(foldr ((:).((#).(:[]))) [])
```

Exercise 4.17

A function `foldiftrue` which `reduces` only those elements of a list which satisfy a given predicate could be defined as:

```
foldiftrue :: (* -> bool) -> (* -> ** -> **) -> ** -> [*] -> **
foldiftrue pred ff default []
    = default
foldiftrue pred ff default (front : rest)
    = ff front (foldiftrue pred ff default rest), if pred front
    = foldiftrue pred ff default rest, otherwise
```

Write this function in terms of a composition of `reduce` and `filter`.

Exercise 4.18

What is the purpose of the function `guesswhat`?

4.5   Summary

Much of the power of Miranda derives from its ability to treat functions themselves as objects to be manipulated as easily as single values and data structures; a function that either takes a function as an argument or returns a function as its result is known as a *higher order function*.

All the functions introduced in this chapter are higher order functions. They make extensive use of a functional programming language feature known as *currying*; this technique allows the programmer to express the *partial application* of a function to less than all of its arguments. Since a partial application is itself a function, this provides a simple and uniform mechanism for treating functions as values; they may be passed as arguments to other functions and they may be returned as the result of a function.

In order to emphasize the treatment of functions as values, a number of *combinators* have been introduced. These combinators are higher order functions that manipulate other functions. They may often help to simplify code by providing simple, general-purpose manipulation of functions and their arguments. In particular, *functional composition* encapsulates the common practice of using the result of one function application as the input parameter to a second function. The composition operator facilitates the repeated use of this technique, producing a "pipeline" style of programming.

Higher order functions provide an elegant mechanism to remove the need for explicit recursion. To demonstrate this facility for lists, three families of curried, polymorphic higher order functions on lists have been introduced:

1. The `map` family, which retains the list structure but transforms the list items.
2. The `fold` family, which distributes an operator over a list, generally to produce a single value result.
3. The `select` family, which may select items from a list, according to a given predicate.

Chapter 5

Environments and Evaluation

For the solution of large-scale programming problems, it is essential that the programmer takes a *modular* approach; first the problem must be subdivided into manageable sub-problems, then each sub-problem is solved and the results combined to provide the overall solution to the problem. This itself may be a recursive process requiring several subdivisions and recombinations.

Hughes (Hughes, 1984) argues that the ways in which one can divide up the original problem depend directly on the ways in which one can combine the solutions of the sub-problems in order to arrive at the overall solution. Hughes provides an attractive analogy with carpentry: a carpenter knows how to make joints to enable pieces of wood to be combined to make a single object (a chair, perhaps)—without the various kinds of joint, the carpenter would have to carve a chair out of a solid block of wood (a much harder task!). The diversity of joints available to the carpenter determines the diversity of objects which can be built with ease (that is, without resort to solid carving). Similarly, the diversity of the methods of combination available to a programmer determines the diversity of problems which may be solved with ease.

This chapter discusses two methods of combination that have an important impact on the structure and design of programs:

1. The organization and control of environments.
2. The use of lazy evaluation.

Organizing environments (by means of Miranda's **where** mechanism and by *list comprehensions*) gives the programmer a means of grouping dependent functions and identifiers into a coherent programming block. The programmer may control the "visibility" of function names, thereby controlling the parts of the program where they can and cannot be used; this is a form of *encapsulation*, which makes the resultant code safer, easier to understand, easier to maintain and more reusable. The exploitation of lazy evaluation and infinite lists builds on the discussion in Section 3.2.4 to give programmers a new way of thinking about problems. Functions and environments may be combined in new ways; thus, laziness augments the available methods of combination in the language and provides new and elegant mechanisms for structuring programs.

5.1   Environments

When a Miranda script file is compiled, the system builds what is known as an *environment*, which comprises all the script file definitions and all the definitions from the Standard Environment (as given in Section 28 of the on-line manual). Each definition is said to *bind* a name to a value; this is often referred to as a *binding*. When an object is defined it has access to all other bindings in the environment. Any subsequent re-edit repeats this process; it removes the old definitions and constructs a new environment by adding the new definitions to those given in the Standard Environment.

When a function is defined, its body has a *new* environment consisting of the environment defined above (often referred to as the "inherited environment") together with the names of the function's formal parameters (which are only bound to actual values when the function is applied). This new environment is specific to the function body and does not affect subsequent function definitions.

Free and bound names

In order to determine the value of a name that appears in a function's body, one of two rules is applied:

1. Any appearance of a formal parameter name takes its value from the actual parameter to which the function is applied. In other words, the local environment ignores any previous binding for that name in the inherited environment. Formally, the name is said to be *bound* in that function. This rule also holds for the name of the function itself.
2. Any other name that appears in the function body takes its value from the inherited environment; formally, it is said to be *free* in that function. Any function that does not have any free values is said to be closed or to exhibit *closure*.

Scope

The region of program text in which a binding is effective is known as its *scope*. Thus, the two rules presented above are often known as the *rules of scope*.

Outside the scope of a particular binding, the name for that binding has no value and any reference to the name will result in an error (as will be demonstrated below). The only exception to this rule is where a name is reused in a function-body environment—in this case, if the name is used inside the function body it has one value, and if it is used outside the function body may have a different value. It should be clear that the redefinition of names in this way is not advisable because of the confusion that can arise.

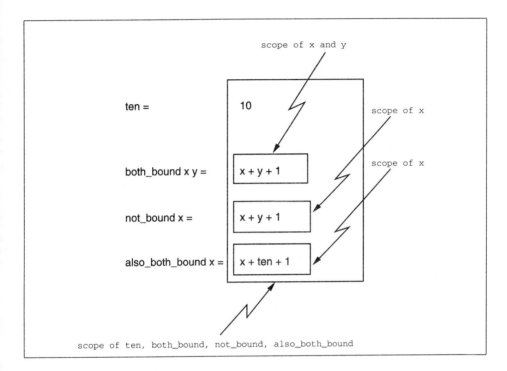

Figure 5.1 The scope of bindings.

Notice that the environment of an expression (that is, the set of names that are accessible to the expression) depends only on the *textual position* of the expression in the program.

The terms "bound" and "in scope" are often interchangeable, as are the terms "unbound" and "out of scope". For example, if a name that is free in a function does not appear in the inherited environment then Miranda will report that it is undefined, as shown in Figure 5.1. On exit from the editor, Miranda will report the error message and *all* bindings from the faulty script will be discarded, for example:

```
compiling script.m
checking types in script.m
(line   5 of "script.m") undefined name "y"
```

The error message displayed above means that Miranda cannot find a meaning for y in the environment of the function not_bound, although Miranda may have a meaning for y in the local environment of another function. In the above case, there was a value associated with the name y, but this was bound in the function both_bound.

What can be bound?

Reserved names[1] *cannot* be re-bound, whilst it is recommended that function names and type names *should not* be re-bound. Thus, the following example, which rebinds predefined names, is legitimate but deplorable, in that it is not immediately obvious what the function does:

```
nasty  [] char = False
nasty  (hd :  tl) char
    =  True, if hd = char
    =  nasty tl char, otherwise
```

Even though char is a basic type and hd and tl are functions that are normally provided by Miranda, their original meanings are suspended throughout the scope of the function nasty. The function happens to work because the names char, hd and tl are bound as formal parameters in the local environment for the function nasty. However, it must again be stressed that this style is dangerous and definitely *not* recommended.

5.1.1   The need for encapsulation

The next part of this chapter shows the need to restrict the scope of identifiers and functions:

1. To avoid name clashes.
2. To link together closely-related functions.

Restricting the scope of an identifier or a function implies that it can only be used in a small part of the program. This provides the ability to structure the program as several smaller sub-programs. The process of building a sub-program which contains identifiers and functions which cannot be used by the rest of the program is often known as *encapsulation*.

---

[1]See Appendix A.

Name clashes

For small programs, any potential name clashes can easily be avoided. The development of small programs is normally only undertaken by one person who can keep track of the limited number of names. For larger programs, it is much harder to guarantee the uniqueness of names because of their increased number and the fact that more than one programmer will normally be involved in the software development process. In this context, it is certainly unreasonable to expect a programmer to invent new names for every new object in the system. Similarly, programmers should not be expected to know the names of objects that they are not directly interested in.

The next part of this chapter shows that unique names are not really a problem because names can be limited to a particular scope; that is, programmers can control their own program environment.

Linking related functions

A function's formal parameters are only in scope within the function body; this adds a little to the environment but this does not give much control. What is really needed is a means of defining a function or value to have a limited scope; that is, to have expressions that are not generally free in the script file, but are in scope only for a particular function body.

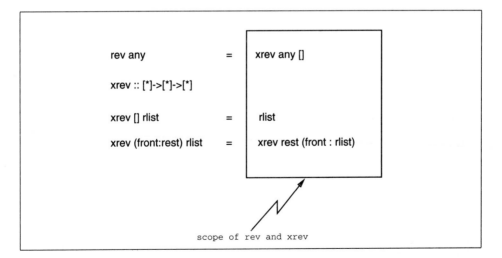

Figure 5.2 A subsidiary function with global scope.

The simple example of **rev**, shown in Figure 5.2, makes use of an auxiliary

accumulative function **xrev**. The latter is not robust (as it does not validate its parameter), nor is it reasonable to expect someone to know that it requires its second parameter to be instantiated to []. The next section will discuss how to restrict the scope of (or *encapsulate*) **xrev** so that it can only be used by **rev**.

5.2   Block structure: where expressions

The requirement for encapsulation can be met by binding **xrev** in the local environment for the function body of **rev**, such that the existence of **xrev** is concealed from any other function. In Miranda this may be achieved by using the keyword **where** as shown in Figure 5.3.

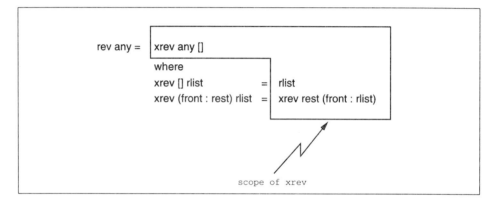

Figure 5.3 A subsidiary function with restricted scope.

The fact that **xrev** is bound in the function **rev** is emphasized by the fact that any attempt to use it on its own will give rise to an error:

```
Miranda xrev [1,2,3] []
UNDEFINED NAME - xrev
```

Use of the keyword **where** follows the "offside rule" introduced in Chapter 2. It may appear after the function body for any particular pattern and is in scope for that entire function body, including guards, but is not in scope for the function bodies of other patterns for the same function definition. These rules are illustrated in the rest of this section.

Shortening expressions

The following example shows one of the simplest uses of **where**, which is to make code more readable by replacing long expressions with shorter ones. In Figure 5.4, the single names `low` and `high` replace the unwieldy expressions `(fst (split pred rest))` and `(snd (split pred rest))`. Once again, the new binding is not available outside the restricted scope.

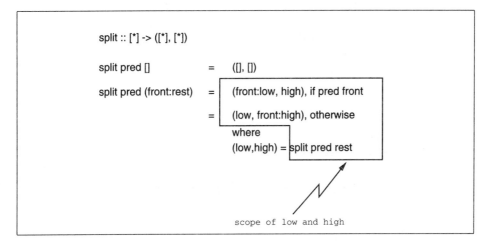

Figure 5.4 The scope of names in a **where** block.

Notice that the local `(low, high)` definition is available to both guards for the pattern `(front :  rest)`, but is *not* available to the function body for the first pattern `[]`.

Multiple definitions within a where clause

There is no restriction on the number of definitions that can appear within a **where** expression and, as expected, if more than one definition appears then the **where** sub-environment is built in exactly the same way as the top-level environment. This is demonstrated in the following program (part of a text justifier) which throws away all leading "white space" characters in a string and which compresses all other occurrences of multiple white space characters into a single space:

```
string == [char]
compress ::  string -> string
compress astring
    = (squeeze .  drop) astring
      where
      space = ' '
      tab = '\t'
      newline = '\n'

      isspace c
        = (c = space) \/ (c = tab) \/ (c = newline)

      || this is not the Standard Environment drop
      drop [] = []
      drop (front :  rest)
          = drop rest, if isspace front
          = (front :  rest), otherwise

      squeeze [] = []
      squeeze (front :  rest)
          = space :  squeeze (drop rest), if isspace front
          = front :  squeeze rest, otherwise
```

Nested where clauses

Local **where** clauses may be nested; perhaps the major use is to reflect the top-down design of a program, whilst restricting the scope of all of the auxiliary functions. The offside rule applies to the nested **where** block in the same way that it applies to the first **where** block. The following reworks the int_to_string conversion program of Chapter 2:

```
string   == [char]
int_to_string ::  num -> string
int_to_string n
      = "-" ++ pos_to_string (abs n), if n < 0
      = pos_to_string n, otherwise
        where
        pos_to_string n
            = int_to_char n, if n < 10
            = pos_to_string (n div 10)
              ++ (int_to_char (n mod 10)), otherwise
              where
              int_to_char n = decode (n + code '0')
```

Another example of the use of nested **where** clauses is given in the implementation of *quicksort* as shown in Figure 5.5. Quicksort is a recursive sorting algorithm which works by choosing one of the values in the list as a pivot; the list is then split into a sublist of all values less than the pivot, the pivot itself and a sublist of all values greater than the pivot; the quicksort algorithm is then applied to each of the two sublists just generated (choosing a new pivot for each sublist). Empty sublists are ignored and eventually every value will have been considered as a pivot—all the pivots are now in order and can be collected together to form the sorted list, as required.[2]

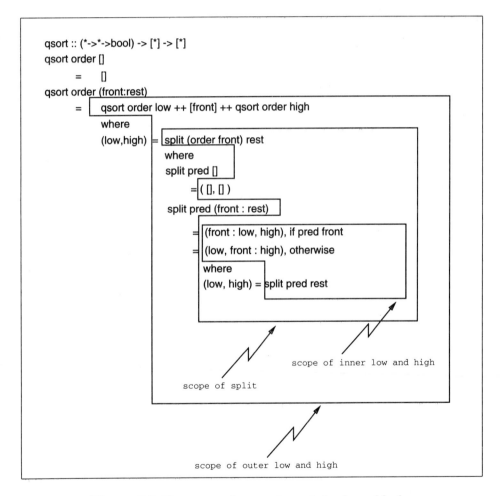

Figure 5.5 The scope of names in nested **where** blocks.

---

[2]For more details see (Standish, 1980).

The implementation uses the `split` function to decompose the unsorted list, to yield a tuple pair of those values that satisfy the ordering function and those that do not.[3] The example demonstrates how **where** expressions may be nested, with the effect that the names `low` and `high` can be used in two different contexts. In general, this is considered to be bad style because of the potential confusion over names. However, the example serves to illustrate that it is possible, and indeed this poor naming policy is unfortunately not uncommon amongst programmers.

Exercise 5.1

Write a function, using **where** definitions, to return the string that appears before a given sublist in a string. For example, `beforestring "and" "Miranda"` will return the string `"Mir"`.

Exercise 5.2

The Standard Environment function `lines` translates a list of characters containing newlines into a list of character lists, by splitting the original at the newline characters, which are deleted from the result. For example, `lines` applied to:

    "Programming with Miranda\nby\nClack\nMyers\nand Poon"

evaluates to:

    ["Programming with Miranda","by","Clack","Myers","and Poon"]

Write this function using a **where** definition.

Sharing common subexpressions

Using **where** can also produce more flexible code when a subexpression appears more than once in another expression. For instance, the function `oklength` checks to see if a given string is of at least a specified size `lowerbound` and not larger than `upperbound`:

```
oklength  ::  [*] -> num -> num -> [*]
oklength  s lowerbound upperbound
      =  (# s) >= lowerbound & (# s) <= upperbound
```

However, (`# s`) appears twice and might have to be altered twice if the function specification changed. If a **where** definition is used then the alteration can be done in one place only, thereby making the programmer's task easier and the code safer.

---

[3]To sort integers in ascending order, the ordering function should be `isitlessthan` since it is used in a partially applied manner within `split`.

```
oklength  ::   [*] -> num -> num -> [*]
oklength  s lowerbound upperbound
      =   slen >= lowerbound & slen <= upperbound
          where slen = # s
```

The new version is not only easier to read, but will execute more efficiently, since the common subexpression will only be evaluated once.[4] The advantage of this modular approach becomes increasingly more apparent as the subexpression occurs more often in the main expression.

Eliminating unnecessary parameters

The following curried version of the sublist function from the *grep* program (shown in Chapter 3) uses an auxiliary function xsublist, whose binding is confined to sublist but does not carry around the regexp parameter on each of its recursive applications. Although regexp is free in xsublist, it is in scope and hence accessible to xsublist:

```
string == [char]

mtype == string
regtype == (mtype, string)
reglist == [regtype]

sublist ::   reglist -> string -> bool
sublist   regexp line
      =   (startswith regexp line) \/ xsublist line
          where
          xsublist  []
                =   False
          xsublist  (any :  lrest)
                =   (startswith regexp lrest)
                    \/ (xsublist lrest)
```

This is quite a popular functional programming style because it is generally easier to read functions with less parameters. Unfortunately, this style can be abused. The following definition of unclearmap also saves on passing a parameter (ff), but may be considered less clear because it is not obvious from where xmap expects its list parameter:

---

[4]This beneficial feature is known as *sharing* and is a form of lazy evaluation, as will be shown in Section 5.4.

```
unclearmap ::   (* -> **) -> [*] -> [**]
unclearmap ff
=  xmap
    where  xmap [] = []
           xmap (front :   rest) = (ff front) :   xmap rest
```

A clearer version would include the list parameter:[5]

```
clearmap ::   (* -> **) -> [*] -> [**]
clearmap ff anylist
=  xmap   anylist
    where  xmap [] = []
           xmap (front :   rest) = (ff front) :   xmap rest
```

5.2.1   A larger example of where blocks

The following program (adapted from (Park and Miller, 1988)) generates a list of random numbers and illustrates the use of **where** to provide a local (restricted) environment.

```
>||Literate script (Page 1 of 2 pages)


Program to generate a list of random real numbers
for systems with 46-bit mantissas, with a function
to constrain the result to integer limits


generate N random numbers
and a new seed from an initial seed

>randomize ::   num->num->(num,([num],num))
>randomize n firstseed
>       = error "randomize:  negative number", if n < 0
>       = genlist n firstseed [], otherwise
>         where
>         c1 = 16807.0
>         upperbound = 2147483647.0
>         nextseed seed
>             = (c1 * seed) - ( upperbound
>                  * (entier ((c1 * seed)/upperbound)) )
>         genlist 0 seed ranlist
>             = (seed, (ranlist,upperbound))
>         genlist n seed ranlist
>             = genlist (n-1) (nextseed seed) (seed:ranlist)
```

---

[5]Notice that the types of `unclearmap` and `clearmap` are identical.

```
>||Literate script continued (Page 2)

constrain real number to an acceptable integer range

>constrain ::  num->([num],num)->[num]
>constrain k (rlist,u)
>          = map (xconstruct k u) rlist
>            where
>              xconstruct k u r = 1 + entier ((r / u) * k)

the function could be used in the following manner:
(constrain 3) (snd (randomize 50 1.1))
This creates a list of 50 random numbers,
in the range 0 to 3, with an initial seed of 1.1
```

Type expressions

Note that type expressions may *not* appear inside **where** blocks. Thus, in the above example, it is unfortunately not possible to specify the type of the function genlist.

5.3   List comprehensions

This section presents another method of restricting the scope of identifiers; the "list comprehension" facility which is a way to specify the elements of a list through calculation (*intensionally*), rather than by explicitly stating each element (*extensionally*).[6]

Simple list comprehension definition and usage

The template for a simple list comprehension consists of an *expression* which is used to calculate the components of the resultant list, together with an *iterative construct* which defines successive values for a local *identifier* by providing these values as a list. The local identifier is only in scope in the *expression* (it is *encapsulated*); for each successive value of the local identifier, the expression is recalculated to provide a new component of the resultant list:

[*expression* | *identifier* <- *value_list*]

---

[6]In this respect, it is similar to the "dotdot" notation shown in Chapter 3.

It helps to pronounce the vertical bar as "such that" and the arrow as "is drawn from". Any expression may occur to the left of the vertical bar. For example:

```
squares3 = [ x * x | x <- [1,2,3]]
```

This reads as:

> "*the list of all values* $x * x$
> *such that* x *is drawn from the list* [1,2,3] ".

The values for the local identifier are drawn from the *value_list* in order, from left to right. In this case, initially x gets the value 1 and the first value of the resultant list is calculated as $(1 * 1 = 1)$, then x gets the value 2 and the next element of the result list is calculated as $(2 * 2 = 4)$ and finally x gets the value 3 and the final element is calculated as $(3 * 3 = 9)$. Hence entering squares3 at the Miranda prompt gives the list [1,4,9].

The list comprehension is thus a shorthand for an anonymous function over a list. The above could have been rewritten with a named local function:

```
squares3 =   xsquares3 [1,2,3]
             where
             xsquares [] = []
             xsquares (front :   rest)
                    = (front * front) :   xsquares rest
```

The above example can be generalized to give a list of squares for any given number:

```
squaresN n = [ x * x | x <- [1..n]]
```

Inside this list comprehension x is a local identifier and n is free but in scope (because it is bound to the actual parameter for squaresN).

The next example is interesting in that the local identifier is only needed as a dummy to control the iteration; the number of dots is determined by the number of times the expression '.' is recalculated, which is controlled by the number of different values for the local identifier j, which is controlled by the function parameter n.

```
printdots n = ['.'  | j <- [1..n]]
```

The elegance of simple list comprehensions is further demonstrated in the following definition for the higher order function map:

```
map f itemlist = [f item | item <- itemlist]
```

The function map and the simple list comprehension often provide equally concise definitions of the same function and may be used interchangeably, for example:

```
squares3 = [ x ^ 2 | x <- [1,2,3]]

squares3 = map (^ 2) [1,2,3]
```

General list comprehensions

The template for a general list comprehension is:

[expression | qualifiers]

A general list comprehension produces the list of all elements given by *expression* such that the *qualifiers* hold. There may be many *qualifiers*; if there are more than one, they must be separated by a semicolon (pronounced "and"). There are two forms of qualifier:

1. A generator, which provides successive values for a local identifier (as illustrated in the previous section). Each local identifier is in scope in *expression*, in the qualifier wherein the identifier is defined, and in all qualifiers to the *right* of that defining qualifier.
2. A filter, which is a Boolean expression to restrict the range of the values given to a local identifier defined in a generator to the *left* of the filter.

The following examples (the first taken from the Miranda On-line Manual)) demonstrate further aspects of list comprehension as a mechanism to create a local environment:

1. Multiple qualifiers.
2. Multiple local identifiers.
3. Recursive list comprehensions.

The function `factors` shows the use of a qualifier in conjunction with a filter:

```
factors n = [ r | r <- [1..(n div 2)]; n mod r = 0]
```

This can be read as:

> *The list of all elements r*
> *Such that*
> > *r is drawn from the list of integers*
> > *starting at 1 and ending with (n div 2)*
> *And*
> > *(n mod r) is equal to 0*

If n in the above example is 9 then r will be drawn from the list [1,2,3,4], but only those values for which (9 mod r) = 0 will be allowed. Thus, r will take the successive values 1 and 3 and the result will be the list [1,3].

Note that the rules of scope for the local identifier r mean that the qualifiers could not have been written in reverse order. The following examples compare two versions with n set to the value 17:

```
Miranda [r |  r <- [1..(17 div 2)]; 17 mod r = 0]
[1]
```

```
Miranda [r | 17 mod r = 0; r <- [1..(17 div 2)]]
[
UNDEFINED NAME - r
```

Multiple generators represent nested loops, with the leftmost generator being the outermost loop:

```
cartesianA n m = [ (x,y) | x <- [1..n]; y <- [1..m] ]
```

This is read as:

> *The list of all two-tuples (x, y)*
> *Such that*
>   *x is drawn from the list [1..n]*
> *And*
>   *y is drawn from the list [1..m]*

In the above example, the leftmost generator for x performs the outermost loop and so the resultant list for `cartesianA 2 3` is `[ (1,1), (1,2), (1,3), (2,1), (2,2), (2,3) ]`. By contrast, with the definition:

```
cartesianB n m = [ (x,y) | y <- [1..m]; x <- [1..n] ]
```

the resultant list for `cartesianB 2 3` is `[(1,1), (2,1), (1,2), (2,2), (1,3), (2,3)]`.

If two local identifiers are drawn from the same list then a shorthand notation is available; the single generator `x,y <- [1..3]` is equivalent to the two generators `x <- [1..3]; y <- [1..3]`. Hence:

```
squarecoords n = [ (x,y) | x,y <- [1..n] ]
```

This can be read as:

> *The list of all two-tuples (x, y)*
> *Such that*
>   *x is drawn from [1..n]*
> *And*
>   *y is drawn from [1..n]*

Hence `squarecoords 2` evaluates to: `[(1,1),(1,2),(2,1),(2,2)]`.

The final example (also from the Miranda On-line Manual) generates all the possible permutations for a given list, demonstrates a list comprehension with more than one local identifier, more than one local calculation and also involves a recursive application of **permutations**. Notice that the local identifiers in a list comprehension come into scope from left to right, so that a generator can make use of identifiers already defined to its left, but not vice versa.

```
permutations  [] = [[]]
permutations  anylist
           =  [ front :   rest | front <- anylist;
                 rest <- permutations(anylist--[front]) ]
```

The list comprehension in this example can be read as:

> *The list of all lists (front : rest)*
> *Such that*
>   *front is drawn from the list anylist*
> *And*
>   *rest is drawn from the result of the recursive call to permutations,*
>   *when applied to the argument anylist -- [front])*

Exercise 5.3
   Define a list comprehension which has the same behaviour as the built-in function
`filter`.
Exercise 5.4
   Rewrite *quicksort* using list comprehensions.

5.4   Lazy evaluation

This section explores a style of programming that is not generally available in other
languages: programming by means of infinite lists of data, together with the use
of *generator* functions and *selector* functions.

5.4.1   Lazy evaluation of lists

As has been shown in previous chapters, Miranda is a *lazy* functional language;
this means that parameters to functions are evaluated only when necessary and
that shared subexpressions are never evaluated more than once. Furthermore, the
items in a list are only evaluated if their values are necessary to produce a result.
In other words, Miranda will not always fully evaluate a function's environment.
For example, in the following Miranda session:

```
Miranda const 3 (4 / 0)
   3
```

the (4 / 0) is not needed and so is not evaluated.

Similarly:

```
Miranda hd [3, (4/0)]
3
```

Evaluation of a list has two distinct stages: a function such as **hd** may cause the first item of a list to be evaluated, but does not need to evaluate the rest of the list; by contrast, a function such as **length** may need to know the number of items in a list without needing to evaluate the items in the list. Thus:

```
Miranda length [3, (4/0), 5]
3
```

Lazy evaluation implies that both evaluation stages of a list are only undertaken as necessary. Since the tail of a list may never be evaluated, it is possible to exploit this fact to define *potentially infinite lists* (perhaps using a recursive function) and then only use that part of the list that is required. For example:

```
natsfrom n = n :   natsfrom (n + 1)
```

This will generate the list (n :   (n + 1) :   (n + 2) :   ...). If an expression such as **natsfrom 1** were typed at the Miranda prompt then Miranda would attempt to print out the entire list and will continue to do so until the user forcibly interrupts the process or Miranda suffers some internal error.[7]

Clearly **natsfrom** on its own is useless, but when combined with other functions it becomes very powerful. This is shown in the following higher order function **make_index_pairs** which takes a list of items and produces a list of pairs, where each item has been paired with an index number. The function **natsfrom** is used to generate an infinite list of indices (because **make_index_pairs** must work on input lists of any length) and **zip2** ensures that just enough of the infinite list is selected in order to give an index to each item:

```
make_index_pairs ::   [*]->[(num,*)]
make_index_pairs names = zip2 (natsfrom 1) names

|| where zip2 is defined in the Standard Environment
|| and is similar to map_two defined in Chapter 4
```

```
Miranda make_index_pairs ["chris","colin","ellen"]
[(1,"chris"),(2,"colin"),(3,"ellen")]
```

It is worthwhile comparing this definition to a recursive version where a subsidiary function **makepairs** must explicitly control the index number generation:

---

[7]Remember that Miranda has infinite-precision integers, which means that it will generate integers until the system memory is no longer big enough to represent the integer.

```
make_index_pairs ::   [*]->[(num,*)]
make_index_pairs names
        = makepairs 1 names
          where
          makepairs n [] []
          makepairs n (front2 :   rest2)
                = (n, front2) :  (makepairs (n + 1) rest2)
```

Note that the two versions exhibit exactly the same behaviour and have exactly
the same type.

5.4.2   Infinite "dotdot" lists

Miranda recognizes the utility of infinite lists by providing a special form of the
"dotdot" notation (introduced in Section 3.2.4) whereby potentially infinite lists
are specified by omitting the final number from the "dotdot" expression. Thus
[1..] represents the potentially infinite list of ascending integers starting at 1,
and [2,4..] represents the potentially infinite list of ascending even numbers
starting at 2.

The function make_index_pairs can now be defined using this notation:

```
make_index_pairs names = zip2 [1..]   names
```

This can be compared favourably with the previous higher order definition, which
required an additional definition for natsfrom. It is also less cluttered than the
following definition using finite "dotdot" notation, which requires identification of
the names parameter and then explicit calculation of its length:

```
make_index_pairs names = zip2 [1..#names] names
```

Finally, the infinite dotdot version could be made more elegant by defining the
name make_index_pairs to be an alias for the partial application of zip2:

```
make_index_pairs = zip2 [1..]
```

Infinite list comprehensions

Not surprisingly, infinite "dotdot" lists are often used in conjunction with list
comprehensions, for example:

```
oddsquares = [ x * x | x <- [1,3..]]
```

which returns a list of all the squares of odd numbers.

The first n items could be selected using `take`:

```
Miranda take 3 oddsquares
[1,9,27]
```

An equivalent recursive program is:

```
oddsquares =   xodds 1
               where
               xodds n = (n * n) :  xodds (n + 2)
```

which would be applied in exactly the same manner.

The next example introduces a variation on the basic mechanism, where a generator may be expressed in terms of itself (this is sometimes called a *recurrence relation*). A recursive generator uses the syntax *n <- exp1, exp2 ..* and is similar to the dotdot expression *[exp1,exp2 ..]*; except that there are no square brackets, and *exp2* is defined recursively in terms of *n*:

```
powers_of_two = [n | n <- 1, 2 * n ..]
```

The above list comprehension can be read as:

> *The list of all items n*
> *Such that*
> 　*n is drawn from the list of values*
> 　*starting with 1 and calculating each new value*
> 　*by multiplying the current value of n by 2.*

Exercise 5.5

Use a list comprehension to write a function that generates a list of the squares of all the even numbers from a given lower limit to upper limit. Change this function to generate an infinite list of even numbers and their squares.

5.4.3　Generators and selectors

In general, lazy evaluation makes it possible to modularize a program as a *generator* function, which constructs a large number of possible answers (perhaps as a potentially infinite list), and a *selector* function, which chooses the appropriate answer. The selector function is applied to the output of the generator function; this is often achieved using function composition. This section takes a further look at this programming style, in conjunction with list comprehensions, infinite lists and also finite but very large lists. As with higher order functions (Section 4.2), there are no rigid rules which style or approach to use. Once again the best advice is to choose the definition which most closely mirrors the natural specification and then optimize if necessary.

Grep as a generator

In Section 4.3.3, the **grep** function was extended so that it would inspect a list of lists of characters (representing maný lines of text) and return those lines which contain a given pattern. Here, the code for **grep** is repeated:

```
string == [char]

grep ::   string -> [string] -> [string]
grep regexp = filter (xgrep regexp)

xgrep ::   string -> string -> bool
xgrep regexp line = sublist (lex regexp) line
```

Assume that the identifier **manual** is bound to a list of lists of characters; the **grep** function can now be utilized to provide a list of all lines in **manual** in which the word **"evaluation"** appears. For example:[8]

```
Miranda grep "evaluation" manual
["Lazy evaluation is elegant.",
 "evaluation of arguments is also an",
 "It also optimizes evaluation."]
```

The above application of **grep** can be viewed as a generator of data; it inspects all of the text in **manual** and returns the appropriate data. Parts of that data can now be selected by a separate function. For example, to select the *first* line in **manual** which mentions **"evaluation"**:

```
Miranda hd (grep "evaluation" manual)
"Lazy evaluation is elegant."
```

Here, the function **grep** generated data and the function **hd** selected a part of that data. Lazy evaluation ensures that **grep** only inspects the text in **manual** as far as necessary to generate *one* line of output data (which is all that **hd** needs).

Interestingly, the same function can be used as both a generator and a selector. For example, to select all lines in **manual** which mention both the word **"evaluation"** *and* the word **"also"**:

---

[8]Miranda would actually print the output all on one line, but it is split across several lines here to make it clearer.

```
Miranda grep "also" (grep "evaluation" manual)
["evaluation of arguments is also an",
 "It also optimizes evaluation."]
```

However, in this case, because **grep** in its role as a selector must inspect all of its argument, then so must **grep** in its role as a generator.

Pipelining generators and selectors

Generator functions and selector functions are often combined using function composition to produce a "pipeline". There may be more than one selector function in the pipeline, as illustrated by the following session which calculates the length of the first line in **manual** which mentions both of the words "evaluation" and "also":

```
Miranda (# . hd . (grep "also")) (grep "evaluation" manual)
34
```

In this case it is also possible to include the generator in the function composition:

```
Miranda (# . hd . (grep "also") . (grep "evaluation")) manual
34
```

In these examples, **hd** only requires the first part of the data from (**grep "also"**), which therefore only needs sufficient data from (**grep "evaluation"**) in order to determine the first line which contains the word "also". Thus, lazy evaluation ensures that only a small part of the text in **manual** is inspected.

The lazy evaluation of generators also applies where the generator is a list comprehension. In the following example, only the first square is calculated by the list comprehension because that is all that the selector **takewhile (< 20)** requires:

```
Miranda takewhile (< 20) [ x * x | x <- [2,4..2000] ]
[4,16]
```

The above expression can be rewritten with the selector inside the list comprehension:

```
Miranda [ x * x | x <- [2,4..2000] ; x * x < 20]
[4,16]
```

However, in the above expression all of the squares from 4 to 4,000,000 are calculated! This is because *selectors inside a list comprehension cannot affect the evaluation of generators inside the same list comprehension.*

5.4.4 Pitfalls for the unwary user of laziness

The ability to specify potentially infinite computation and potentially infinite lists is an extremely powerful tool which must be used with care. There are three major potential pitfalls when employing a selector approach to restricting a lazily generated list:

1. Looking beyond the solution.
2. Never reaching the solution.
3. Losing laziness, and thereby doing too much computation.

Looking beyond the solution

A potential mistake with list comprehensions is to write a function which produces a list containing the required items but continues to look for more items and never terminates because no more exist! An example of this kind of error is now considered:

```
neverending_cubes_lessthan_fifty
        = [x ^ 3 | x <- [1..]; x ^ 3 < 50]
```

Whilst it is quite clear that there are only three cubes which are less than fifty, the function has been defined to consider *all* possible cubes and test *every* one of them to see if it is over fifty. Unfortunately, the function will produce the result [1,8,27 and will then "hang" whilst it continually loops and tests all the other generated cubes.

As explained in the previous section, this error occurs because a filter inside a list comprehension cannot be used to modify the number of times a generator (in the same list comprehension) loops—it can only determine which of the values produced by the generator will be valid for the local identifier.

However, the error of looking beyond the solution is not restricted to the use of list comprehensions. Here is an example which abuses function composition:

```
also_neverending_cubes_lessthan_fifty
        = ((filter (<50)) .  (map (^ 3))) [1..]
```

This function attempts to generate the infinite list of numbers and then to cube all of these numbers and finally to test each cube to check if it is less than fifty; in other words, it loops forever.

In order to correct this error, it is necessary to make use of the fact that each successive cube will be larger than the previous one, and so as soon as one cube fails the test then all subsequent cubes will also fail the test:

```
cubes_lessthan_fifty
        = ((takewhile (< 50)) .  (map (^ 3))) [1..]
```

The function `takewhile` terminates as soon as it finds an element that is less than fifty. The values of the remaining cubes are never needed; they will never be generated and so there will be no infinite computation.

Never reaching the solution

The above discussion showed the dangers of finding the result and going beyond it; however, sometimes the result may never be reached. This mainly arises with list comprehensions that have more than one generator ranging over an infinite list. For example, the function `wrong_triangles` is meant to produce the infinite list of three-tuples (triples) which represent the lengths of the sides of right-angled triangles. However, it fails to produce a single element of that list!

```
wrong_triangles
    = [(a,b,c) | a,b,c <- [1..]; a ^ 2 + b ^ 2 = c ^ 2]
```

To understand the behaviour of the above function, recall the following:

1. The construction `a,b,c <- [1..]` is an abbreviation for the three terms `a <- [1..]; b <- [1..]; c <- [1..]`.
2. Multiple generators represent nested loops, with the leftmost generator controlling the outermost loop. Thus, in the above example, the values generated for `(a,b,c)` will be, in order: `(1,1,1)`, `(1,1,2)`, `(1,1,3)`, `(1,1,4)` and so on until all of the (infinite) values of `c` have been considered.
3. Because the innermost loop for `c` is infinite, the values for `(a,b,c)` where `a` or `b` are greater than 1 *are never considered*.
4. There is no solution to the problem for `a = 1` and `b = 1`, so the function will loop forever.

In recognition of the above problem, Miranda provides a "diagonalizing" list comprehension which combines multiple generators in a different order. If there are two generators `a,b <- [1..]`, the diagonalizing list comprehension tries values in the following sequence: (1,1), (1,2), (2,1), (1,3), (2,2), (3,1), (1,4), (2,3), (3,2), (4,1), (1,5), (2,4), (3,3), and so on. A diagonalizing list comprehension uses the same syntax as a normal list comprehension, *except* that the vertical bar is replaced by two forward-slashes:

```
triangles = [(a,b,c) // a,b,c <- [1..];
                       a^ 2 + b^ 2 = c^ 2]
```

The above definition of `triangles` will still loop forever, but it will test combinations of a, b and c in a "reasonable" order so that solutions are actually generated:

```
Miranda triangles
[(4,3,5),(3,4,5),(8,6,10),(6,8,10),(12,5,13) ...
```

The result is still an infinite list, but one that can generate results that can be used by a selector function.

Losing laziness

It is sometimes tempting to assume that, no matter how a program is written, somehow the Miranda system will always work out the most lazy (that is, least computationally expensive) solution. This is not the case! Unfortunately, it is quite easy to write a selector in such a way (perhaps using pattern matching) that it forces evaluation; hence it does unnecessary computation and so takes an unreasonably long time to execute.

For example, consider the following program which illustrates the use of a generator and several selectors in order to produce the thirteenth prime number:

```
primes12 =  selectors generator
            where
            generator = [2..1000]
            selectors = ((!12) .  (foldr sieve []))
            sieve x [] = [x]
            sieve x any
                 = x :  (filter ((0 =).(mod x)) any)
```

In the above example, the dotdot expression is the generator; it generates a list of numbers between 2 and 1,000. The **primes12** function applies the selectors to the result of this generator. The first selector is **foldr sieve []**, which distributes the function **sieve** across the list, and so performs a standard "sieve of Eratosthenes" to produce a list of prime numbers (assuming that the thirteenth prime is less than 2000). The final selector is (**!12**), which is a prefix sectional form of the list indexing operator (recall that (**!0**) selects the first item in a list). The function works as follows:

```
Miranda primes12
41
```

Initially, it appears that if **generator** is replaced by an infinite dotdot list then **selectors** can be generalized so that it can pick an arbitrary *nth* prime number:

```
nth_prime n =  selectors generator
               where
               generator = [2..]
               selectors = ((!n) .  (foldr sieve []))
               sieve x [] = [x]
               sieve x any
                    = x :  (filter ((0 =).(mod x)) any)
```

Lazy evaluation should ensure that the generator will only do as much work as is required by the last (the leftmost) selector (which is (**!n**)). Now, **nth_prime 12** should produce the same result as the previous version because **generator** will only generate the numbers from 2 to 41. However, this is evidently not the case as the following test reveals:

```
Miranda nth_prime 12
<<not enough heap space -- task abandoned>>
```

The above behaviour happens because one of the selectors *requires all of its input data to be evaluated before it will return a result.*

The offending selector is actually (foldr sieve []). This is somewhat surprising since the following behaves correctly:

```
Miranda ((!12) . foldr (:) [])  [1..]
13
```

Thus, it is not foldr which requires the entire input to be evaluated. The culprit is actually the function sieve—this is because sieve has been defined with pattern matching on its second argument. The consequence of this is that the second argument must be evaluated as far as is necessary to determine whether it is an empty list. However this second argument is the recursive application of foldr, which entails another application of sieve and therefore triggers an evaluation of the next part of the list, and so on. This behaviour is illustrated in the hand evaluation given below:

```
(!0) (foldr sieve [] [2,3,4])
==> (!0) (sieve 2 (foldr sieve [] [3,4]))
==> (!0) (sieve 2 (sieve 3 (foldr sieve [] [4])))
==> (!0) (sieve 2 (sieve 3 (sieve 4 (foldr sieve [] []))))
==> (!0) (sieve 2 (sieve 3 (sieve 4 [])))
==> (!0) (sieve 2 (sieve 3 ([4])))
==> (!0) (sieve 2 ([3,4]))
==> (!0) ([2,3])
==> 2
```

Compare this to the following:

```
(!0) (foldr (:) [] [1,2,3])
==> (!0) ((:) 1 (foldr (:) [] [2,3]))
==> (!0) (1 : (foldr (:) [] [2,3]))
==> 1
```

In the first hand evaluation, foldr sieve [] [2,3,4] cannot produce the initial list item until the entire input list has been scanned. By contrast, the expression foldr (:) [] [1,2,3] can produce the initial item almost immediately because (:) does not require pattern matching; lazy evaluation ensures that the calculation for the rest of the list is never done.

The generalized program can be made lazy if the function sieve does not use pattern matching (which in this case was entirely unnecessary):

```
nth_prime n
        = selectors generator
        where
        generator = [2..]
        selectors = ((!n)  .  (foldr sieve []))
        sieve x any = x :  (filter ((0 =).(mod x)) any)
```

```
Miranda nth_prime 12 [2..]
41
```

5.5   Summary

One of the very first features of Miranda to be covered in this book was the ability to allocate names to expressions. These names are useful because the values of their expressions may be recalled by using the names in subsequent expressions. There are strict rules which govern the binding of names to values and which dictate how these names are made accessible to subsequent expressions. Firstly, every expression has access to those names that exist in its *environment*; secondly, the environment of an expression depends on the textual position of the expression in the program; thirdly, the various environments in the program may be explicitly augmented using **where** definitions and *list comprehensions*.

The main advantage of using these two techniques is that closely related functions and definitions may be self-contained and so not rely on values bound outside the expression (that is, they exhibit closure). They are consequently safer and easier to reuse.

Infinite lists are available to the Miranda programmer as a direct result of the *lazy evaluation* mechanism; the presence of infinite lists, list comprehensions, function composition and higher order functions leads to a style of programming which combines data generators with data selectors. This style is powerful and expressive, but care must be taken to avoid infinite computations and to avoid evaluating too much data.

In particular, it is possible to express the solution to a problem as a combination of a generator of data and a selector which operates on that data (and possibly several subsequent selectors). This encourages an approach to software design whereby a specific problem is solved as the result of a specialization of a general problem, and where the solution is divided into separate components, which are coupled via potentially infinite lists of data, which are evaluated lazily. This approach has the considerable advantage that a selector component can be replaced with a different component in order to solve a different problem. If several selectors are combined using functional composition, this leads to a "pipeline" style of programming, which leads to greater reuse of code and faster code production.

Chapter 6

User-defined Types

Chapter 1 introduced the idea of categorizing program data into various types and the importance of a strong type system has been emphasized throughout this book. However, the available built-in types are somewhat limited, in that they do not always directly model the complex relationships inherent in "real-world" data. This chapter presents a mechanism by which a programmer can create new types. This allows the creation of data structures which are better able to model "real-world" relationships and it encourages the use of the type system to provide *built-in validation* of data.

6.1 The need for new types

A type may be defined with precision by listing the collection of values which belong to the type (that is, the values which exist in the type domain). For example, the type `bool` is precisely defined by listing the two values in its domain: `True` and `False`.[1] This section discusses the need for new types through several abstract examples, concentrating on the collection of values which define a type. This approach is utilized in Section 6.2, where Miranda's actual mechanism for creating new types will be presented.

New types

Miranda provides a small number of useful built-in types. However, the choice of built-in types is a matter for the language designer and it is likely that some other useful types have not been provided. For example, other programming languages do not have a built-in Boolean type. If the type `bool` did not already exist in Miranda,

---

[1] As explained in Chapter 1, we shall ignore the undefined, or error, value in the type domain.

it could be created by specifying the permitted values as { *True or False* }.

If the type num did not already exist, an attempt could be made to create it in a similar way: { *1 or 2 or 3 or 4 or 5 or ...* }. However, this type presents some difficulty because of the very large number of alternative values (in practice limited by the computer architecture). The solution to the problem of a large number of values is to describe the values recursively, as will be seen later in this chapter (Section 6.4).

Special versions of types

Although the type bool is a built-in type for Miranda, it is possible that a programmer might wish to create several special versions of the type and make use of the fact that the type system will ensure that they are used consistently in the program and will not be mixed. For example, { *Windows_true or Windows_false* } could be used to indicate whether the program is connected to a display which supports a windowing environment, whilst { *Multi_user_true or Multi_user_false* } could be used to indicate whether the program is available to a single user or to many users.

This facility for specialization is not limited to Boolean values. For instance, dice-playing games require special meaning to be given to the numbers from one to six, so { *Dice_one or Dice_two or Dice_three or Dice_four or Dice_five or Dice_six* } could be used to indicate the full range of values for a new type called *dice*.

By using these new types, not only can a program be made more readable but there is the considerable advantage that the type system can be used to provide built-in validation (so that *Windows_true* and True can never be confused).

Structured types and constructors

In the pursuit of well-structured data, it is desirable to be able to specify new types in terms of previously defined types. In particular, it should be possible to build upon existing types (including previously specified user-defined types) in order to produce a new type which is able to represent the structured data which occurs in many applications.

A convenient mechanism to achieve this aim is to allow each value of a user-defined type possibly to be followed by a type name to indicate a further sub-level of values. This leads to a hierarchical specification of the values which are valid for a given type. For example, it is possible to define a single type which contains information about whether multiple simultaneous users are allowed, with each of the two values having a further underlying value to indicate whether a windowing system is being used: { *Multi_user bool or Single_user bool* }. In this example, the domain for the new type is fully defined by the values *Multi_user False*, *Multi_user True*, *Single_user False* and *Single_user True*. However, the underlying types need not have finite domains, as shown by the following example: { *Discrete num or Continuous [num]* }.

In the above example, the constant values *Discrete* and *Continuous* provide a unique way to determine the structure of a particular value in the domain of this type; for this reason they are often referred to as *constructors*. Notice that there need not be any underlying type to be "constructed"; `True` and `False` are both simple data values and are also known as constructors. Furthermore, the different constructors for a type can have mixed structure—some may have a complex underlying type, whereas others may have no underlying type at all.

Mixed types

A programmer might wish to create a new type, whose values could be drawn from any one of a mixture of built-in types. For example, a company might describe a customer using a string (that is, type `[char]`) if the customer is an individual, by a `num` or `[num]` if the customer is an internal department or group of departments, or by a (`[char]`,`num`) or (`[char]`,`[num]`) pair if the customer is a department or group of departments of an external company. In this example, the programmer may wish to encapsulate these options into a new type with the alternatives: { *Individual [char] or Department num or Group [num] or Ext_dept ([char],[num]) or Ext_group ([char], [num])* }. Examples of values of this new type are *Individual* "Winston", *Department 45* and *Group [1,3,67]*; thus the domain for this new type contains all the values of the `[char]` domain *together with* all the values of the `num` domain *together with* all the values of the `[num]` domain and so on.

Towards type abstraction

A programmer might wish to specify which values of an existing type are legal for a particular task; for example a twenty-four hour *clock* type should only allow numbers in the range 0 to 23. If the number of alternative values is small then a new type can be generated such as { *Clock_zero or Clock_one or Clock_two or Clock_three or ... or Clock_twenty_three* }.

An alternative would be to create a new type which uses all the values of an underlying type (such as `num`). However, in this case it would be necessary to define a set of operations for the new type, so that values outside of the range 0 to 24 are considered illegal and so that inappropriate operations (such as multiplying together values which represent the hours of the day) are not allowed. Chapter 7 will present the *abstract type* mechanism which allows a programmer to package a new type, together with the operations which are appropriate for that type.

The next section will present the full Miranda syntax for creating new types, which is based on a general mechanism for describing and creating types by means of *defining the permitted values of the type*.

6.2   Algebraic types

In Miranda, a user-defined type is known as an *algebraic type* and is created by
a general-purpose mechanism based on the idea of *constructors*, which were first
discussed in Section 3.2.1. The fundamental principle is that each permitted value
of an algebraic type is distinguished from permitted values of other types by means
of a special tag, known as a constructor. This gives a *unique and unambiguous*
representation for every value of an algebraic type, in exactly the same way that
the built-in constructors : and [] give a unique and unambiguous representation of
any list. A general template for an algebraic type definition is:

> *new_type_name ::=*   *Value1*
> | *Value2*
>   ...
> | *ValueN*

A new type must have at least one value; alternatives[2] are denoted by the vertical
bar | and each value may either be *nullary* or may be constructed from an under-
lying type. A nullary value is a constant value, such as `True` or `False`, and is also
known as a *nullary constructor* (sometimes known as a "constant constructor" for
self-evident reasons). A value therefore has one of two formats:

> *Nullary_constructor_name*

or

> *Constructor_name underlying_type*

The *underlying_type* may be simple or aggregate, built-in or another algebraic type
previously defined in the program.
  Algebraic types are characterized by two important features:

1. They are *not* type synonyms. A type synonym is merely a shorthand denota-
   tion for an already existing type, whereas an algebraic type is a totally new
   type; a type synonym may be mixed with its actual type, whereas algebraic
   types may not be mixed with other types. Thus, in the definition:

   > `positive ::= Positive num`

   the new type name is `positive` and the constructor name is `Positive`. The
   value (`Positive 3`) may *not* be substituted for the value 3 because they are
   of different types.
2. The existing properties of any underlying types are *not* inherited; equality
   and inequality are the only operations which may be legal upon two instances
   of an algebraic type. For example, although the operator `&` is defined for the
   built-in type `bool`, it is not defined for the type `windows ::= Windows bool`

---

[2]Note that alignment of alternatives follows the offside rule detailed in Chapter 2.

and therefore the expression (Windows False) & (Windows True) is meaningless.

Equality and relational tests provide an arbitrary but reproducible ordering.
Because the order is not defined, this behaviour should not be relied upon
in programs. However, Miranda defines equality to be True if both the
constructor names are equal (and any existing underlying values are also
equal). Hence, the expression Constructor1 < Constructor2 will return
True if Constructor1 comes before Constructor2 in the original definition
of the algebraic type, or if they are the same constructor and their underlying
values return True when tested by (<).

Further examples:

```
switch ::= On | Off

colour ::= Rgb (num,num,num)   || Red, Green, Blue
           | Hsl (num,num,num) || Hue, Saturation, Luminance

radius   ::= Radius num

sphere   ::= Sphere radius colour

customer ::= Individual [char]
             | Department num
             | Group [num]
             | Company ([char],num)
```

The rest of this section discusses the various kinds of algebraic types that can be
defined, including algebraic types with just one constructor and one underlying
type, algebraic types with many constructors with different underlying types, and
algebraic types which do not have an underlying type.

6.2.1   Simple algebraic type definition and usage

Algebraic type definition

A simple example of algebraic type definition is:

```
coords ::= Coords (num,num,num)
```

This definition serves two related purposes:

1. To create new algebraic type named coords.
2. To create a new prefix *constructor* Coords

This new constructor takes a number triple and converts it to the new algebraic type; as such, a constructor might be considered as a special form of function without a function body, as can be seen from Miranda's responses:

```
Miranda Coords
<function>

Miranda Coords ::
(num,num,num) -> coords
```

However, there are certain differences between constructors and functions. The differences between functions and constructors are explored in more depth in Section 6.3.

Algebraic type naming

Algebraic type names must be legal identifiers and conform to the rules for Miranda identifiers described in Chapter 1. Constructors must also be legal Miranda identifiers: *except their initial character must be an Upper case character.* There are no further restrictions and constructor names may look just like any other identifier.

For example, legal Miranda identifiers cannot start with a digit. Thus, in particular, it is not possible to model the integers with the definition:

```
wrong_dice ::= 1 | 2 | 3 | 4 | 5 | 6
```

It is equally wrong to use characters or strings as constructors, since a character or string is not a legal Miranda identifier:

```
wrong_dice ::= "One" | "Two" | "Three"
               | "Four" | "Five" | "Six"
```

A legal definition would be:

```
legal_dice ::= One | Two | Three
               | Four | Five | Six
```

As with value identifiers and function identifiers, it is not possible to reuse a constructor name within a program.

Algebraic type instantiation

New instances of coords may be created by supplying the Coords constructor with its expected argument:

```
point_origin = Coords (0.0, 0.0, 0.0)
point_max = Coords (1000.0, 1000.0, 1000.0)
```

The Coords constructor is used in the same manner as the built-in list constructor :.
This is illustrated by comparing its use with that of the prefix version of the latter:

```
Miranda (:) 1 [2,3]
[1,2,3]
```

```
Miranda Coords (3.0, 4.0, 5.0)
Coords (3.0,4.0,5.0)
```

Algebraic type usage

Using algebraic types in functions is just as easy as using existing types and constructors. If there is a requirement to write a function to find the midpoint of two
coords then they may be deconstructed to their underlying type using pattern
matching:

```
midpoint ::  coords -> coords -> coords
midpoint (Coords (x1,y1,z1)) (Coords (x2,y2,z2))
        = Coords ((x1 + x2)/2, (y1 + y2)/2, (z1 + z2)/2)
```

In the application of the function midpoint to the two parameters point_origin
and point_max:

```
Miranda midpoint point_origin point_max
Coords (500.0,500.0,500.0)
```

the formal parameters Coords (x1,y1,z1) and Coords (x2,y2,z2) will be substituted with the actual values: Coords (0.0, 0.0, 0.0) and Coords (1000.0,
1000.0, 1000.0), respectively, and so will be successfully matched.

It can be seen that constructors are used in function patterns in order to *deconstruct* an algebraic type and that they are used in function bodies to *construct* a
value of an algebraic type. Thus, for deconstruction purposes there is no practical
difference between the extraction of the head of a list front from the constructed
list (front : rest) and the extraction of the numbers x1, y1 and z1 from the
constructed Coords (x1,y1,z1). Similarly, for construction purposes there is no
practical difference between the creation of a new list (front : rest) from the
item front and the list rest and the creation of a new coords instance by means
of the application Coords (x1,y1,z1).

Note that, just as with patterns involving the list constructor :, it is necessary
to bracket the Coords constructor with its argument otherwise a syntax error
will occur. This is because a constructor pattern must always be complete (see
Section 6.3.1).

Exercise 6.1
  Write a function to calculate the distance between a pair of **coords**.

Algebraic types are strongly typed

It must be emphasized that using the keyword ::= creates a *new* type which
conforms to the Miranda strong typing philosophy. This has the considerable
advantage that the system will perform data validation and automatically catch
any accidental attempts to use an algebraic type in an illegal manner. In the above
example, it is assumed that the programmer wishes to express the relationship
between three numbers as a new type and does *not* wish to mix a number triple
with a value drawn from this type. Hence, a value that has been defined as a
number triple cannot be legally tested against an instance of a **coords** for equality:

```
Miranda point_origin = (0.0, 0.0, 0.0)
```

```
type error in expression
cannot unify coords with (num,num,num)
```

In a similar manner, any function defined over a tuple of type (num,num,num)
(even if given a name using the == type synonym mechanism) cannot be applied
to **coords** arguments.

6.2.2   Algebraic types with multiple constructors

An algebraic type may also have more than one constructor. This is shown in the
following two examples, the first of which shows an algebraic type with more than
one constructor over the same underlying type; the second shows the benefit of
having constructors with different underlying types.

Multiple constructors over the same type

A new type **fluid** is now defined to express the fact that fluid measurements are different in different countries. The subsequent definition of the function **addFluids** is
designed to eliminate the possibility of a programmer attempting to mix operations
on fluid measures of differing kinds:

```
fluid ::= USgallons num
          | UKgallons num
          | Litres num

addFluids ::  fluid -> fluid -> fluid

addFluids (USgallons x) (USgallons y)
   = USgallons (x + y)
addFluids (UKgallons x) (UKgallons y)
   = UKgallons (x + y)
addFluids (Litres x) (Litres y)
   = Litres (x + y)
addFluids x y
   = error "addFluids:  illegal constructor"
```

It is now guaranteed that inappropriate operations such as adding amounts of different measurements or attempting to multiply two fluid measurements are not performed accidentally. Thus, the following applications will fail:

```
Miranda addFluids (USgallons 3.0) (Litres 54.0)
program error: addFluids: illegal constructor

Miranda (USgallons 3.0) * (USgallons 54.0)
type error in expression
cannot unify fluid with num

Miranda (USgallons 3.0) * (Litres 54.0)
type error in expression
cannot unify fluid with num
```

The last two applications fail because the standard arithmetic and relational operators are not overloaded for algebraic types. Once again, programmers are obliged to think carefully about their intentions and are helped to avoid mistakes by the type checker.

Multiple constructors over different types

It is also possible to have an algebraic type with different underlying types, as is now demonstrated with the following declaration, where an identification code can be either a number or a string:

```
idcode ::= Ncode num | Scode [char]
```

It is now necessary to define a new function to allow comparison between the two types of idcodes:

```
idless ::  idcode -> idcode -> bool

idless (Ncode x) (Ncode y) = x < y
idless (Scode x) (Scode y) = x < y
idless (Ncode x) (Scode y)
    = (int_to_string x) < y
idless (Scode x) (Ncode y)
    = x < (int_to_string y)
    || where int_to_string is as defined in Section 2.10
```

This new comparison function can now be used as any other function, for instance to construct a new sorting function, shown in Section 4.4.1:

```
idsort ::  [idcode] -> [idcode]
idsort = foldr (insert idless) []
```

Of course, it is still necessary to state explicitly the intended constructor for each new `idcode` and Miranda will always respond by echoing the constructor as well as the actual values:

```
Miranda idsort [Ncode 30, Scode "12", Ncode 1, Scode "10"]
[Ncode 1, Scode "10", Scode "12", Ncode 30]
```

6.2.3   Underlying types for algebraic types

There is no restriction on the underlying types for constructors; they can be simple types, aggregate types, polymorphic types, functions or previously user-defined types. This section shows some of these possibilities.

Polymorphic algebraic types

The algebraic type facility parallels the `==` facility in that it is also legal (and often very useful) to have polymorphic algebraic types. For example:

```
samepair * ::= SamePair (*,*)

pair_to_list ::  samepair * -> [*]
pair_to_list (SamePair (a,b)) = [a,b]
```

As with type synonyms, it is necessary to follow the algebraic type name with a declaration of the names of the polytypes involved in the right-hand side of the definition. If there are many different polymorphic types then the algebraic type name must be followed by all of the relevant polytypes:

```
mixedpair * ** ::= MixedPair (*,**)

mixedfst ::  mixedpair * ** -> *
mixedfst (MixedPair (a,b)) = a
```

New algebraic types from old

So far, all the examples of constructors have had built-in underlying types; however, it is often useful to build upon user-defined algebraic types to create more complex types that better represent the real-world data. The following example uses the algebraic type coords to create a new, curried, algebraic type line which represents a straight line in three-dimensional space:

```
line ::= Line (coords) (coords)
```

The following example using line shows both:

1. A name definition using the constructor coords inside the constructor Line.
2. A function definition line_midpoint, where the function pattern only needs to deconstruct the outer layer and therefore only uses the constructor Line:

```
line ::= Line coords coords

aline = Line (Coords(0,0,0)) (Coords (10.0,10.0,10.0))

midpoint ::  coords -> coords -> coords
midpoint (Coords (x1,y1,z1)) (Coords (x2,y2,z2))
      = Coords ((x1 + x2)/2, (y1 + y2)/2, (z1 + z2)/2)

line_midpoint ::  line -> coords
line_midpoint (Line x y) = midpoint x y
```

Functional algebraic types

Just as functions have been considered as values that may appear as the components of lists or tuples, it is possible for them to provide the underlying type for algebraic types, which is often useful when trying to model a dynamic relationship between objects. This is demonstrated in the following example, where a new type is created to hold both a list of components, together with a function which operates on their price to cater for accounting details such as calculating profit margins:

```
component == (num, [char], num)
complist == [component]
|| the type synonym component represents a list of
|| key, description and price

|| sample component list
net_stock_list
        = [(1,"yoghurt",0.84), (2,"peas",1.3),
            (3,"icecream", 2.5)]

stock ::= Stock complist (complist -> complist)
|| a stock item represents a component list
|| together with a function to change the value
|| of each item in the list
```

New instances of stock can be created as follows:

```
gross_stock_list = Stock net_stock_list addTAX
```

where addTAX is defined, for example, in terms of the general-purpose function adjust:

```
adjust ::  num -> complist -> complist
adjust factor cl = [(key,description,newprice)
                    | (key,description,price) <- cl
                    ; newprice <- [price * factor]]

addTAX = adjust 1.175
```

The following function will now generate the information details of a particular stock instance:

```
stockdetails ::  stock -> complist
stockdetails (Stock slist acc_fn) = acc_fn slist
```

The advantage of this approach is that each instance of a stock can have a different accounting function, as long as it is of the correct type. Thus, it is possible to associate different taxation ratings or retail prices to a particular list of components. For example:

```
taxrate = stockdetails gross_stock_list
```

6.2.4 Enumerated algebraic types

The keyword ::= can also be used to create *enumerated* (or *extensional*) types, which provide a set of names representing the full range of values for the type.[3] This

---

[3]This is very similar to enumeration in imperative programming languages.

facility has already been seen with the built in names **True** and **False** which are the only values for the **bool** type. In fact, they are instances of *nullary constructors*; that is, constructors which have no parameters. By contrast, constructors which take a single or tuple argument are known as *unary constructors*. Similarly, Miranda allows constructors to have a higher *arity* with two or more curried arguments.

Enumerated algebraic type definition

The following example introduces an algebraic type representing the possible states of a set of traffic lights. In the UK a set of traffic lights has three colours (red, amber and green) and cycles between four states; the two primary states *green* (go) and *red* (stop), plus two intermediate states *amber* and *(red + amber)*.[4] The sequence of states is *green, amber, red, (red + amber)*.

```
traffic_light ::= Green | Amber
                | Red | Red_amber
```

Green, **Amber**, **Red** and **Red_amber** are actually constructors for **traffic_light**; though in this new sort of construction the constructors construct nothing but themselves!

Enumerated algebraic type usage

The following session shows that enumerated algebraic types may be used in the same manner as any other type:

```
next_state ::  traffic_light -> traffic_light
next_state Green = Amber
next_state Amber = Red
next_state Red = Red_amber
next_state Red_amber = Green
```

   Miranda map next_state [Green, Amber, Red, Red_amber]
   [Amber,Red,Red_amber,Green]

It must also be noted that pattern matching on enumerated algebraic types follows the same rules as for all other types, in that every possible enumeration should be matched. For example, the following definition of **traffic_light** does not match the constructor **Red**:

---

[4]The combination of two colours for one of the intermediate states makes it possible to predict the next state in the sequence without the expense of adding a fourth coloured light. Although four states could be represented by only two coloured lights, there would be an ambiguity between one of the states and a power failure!

```
prior_state ::   traffic_light -> traffic_light
prior_state Green = Red_amber
prior_state Amber = Green
prior_state Red_amber = Red
```

This will compile successfully but generate a run-time error if applied to **Red**:

```
program error: missing case in definition of prior_state
```

Exercise 6.2

Given the algebraic type

```
action ::= Stop | No_change | Start
           | Slow_down | Prepare_to_start
```

write a function to take the appropriate action at each possible change in state for **traffic_light**.

Exercise 6.3

A Bochvar three-state logic has constants to indicate whether an expression is true, false or meaningless. Provide an algebraic type definition for this logic together with functions to perform the equivalent three-state versions of **&**, **\/** and logical *implication*. Note that if any part of an expression is meaningless then the entire expression should be considered meaningless.

Grep revisited

Enumeration can be used to improve the *grep* program by representing the **"ONCE"** and **"ZERO_MORE"** *match types* as follows:

```
mtype ::= ZERO_MORE | ONCE
```

This is a more elegant solution than using strings to represent the match types. It is also safer and guarantees consistency across functions because Miranda will only allow pattern matching with the two constructors. Otherwise, using the approach shown in Chapter 3, it would be possible accidentally to enter a meaningless string, such as **"ZERO_MORE"** (where the digit 0 is mistakenly used instead of the character O) in one of the function patterns for **startswith**. This is a legal string—but it will never be matched. Enumeration ensures that only legal options are considered.

6.3   Constructors and functions

This section summarizes how constructors differ from functions in their use in function patterns and how they are similar for other purposes. Finally, there is a discussion of the consequences of having too many constructors in an algebraic type.

6.3.1   Pattern matching with constructors

There are three kinds of object that can appear in a valid pattern:

1. Constants, such as numbers and strings.
2. Constructors, either nullary or of any arity. However, a constructor pattern *must be complete*; that is, a non-nullary constructor pattern must contain a valid pattern for its parameter(s).
3. Formal parameter names, which cannot be constants or constructors

It must be emphasized that although the application of a constructor to its argument may appear as a pattern, the application of a function *is not* a legal pattern.

The above constraints mean that the following two definitions are incorrect; the first because Measure1 is not defined as a constructor; the second because Litres does not have its parameter:

```
wrong_litre_convert (Measure1 x)
        = Litres (x * 3.7852), if Measure1 = USgallons
          ...., otherwise

wrong_general_convert (USgallons x, Litres)
        = Litres (x * 3.78532)
          ....
```

6.3.2   Constructors as functions

Constructors are similar to functions in that:

1. They translate values from one type to another.
2. Equality is only defined upon an algebraic type value. This means that two nullary constructors can be compared because they each represent a legal value of the type, but two non-nullary constructors cannot be compared because they do not represent any value until they are given the value of their underlying type. Thus True = Meaningless is a legal comparison, but USgallons = UKgallons is illegal. Comparisons of the form USgallons x = UKgallons y are legitimate, but will only return True if both constructors are the same and both underlying values are the same.

3. The constructor name can be composed or passed as a parameter to other functions, for instance:

```
Miranda map Litres [1.0,2.0,3.0]
[Litres 1.0, Litres 2.0, Litres 3.0]
```

If a constructor takes two or more underlying parameters then it may be partially applied in just the same way as a curried function may be partially applied. A partially applied constructor has function type, emphasizing the role of the constructor in converting from one type to another (just as a function translates values of one type to values of another type):

```
Miranda map Sphere [Radius 1, Radius 2, Radius 3]
[<function>,<function>,<function>]

Miranda hd (map Sphere [Radius 1, Radius 2]) (Rgb (3,2,3))
Sphere (Radius 1) (Rgb (3,2,3))
```

Constructors differ from functions in that they have a sense of order. Though intrinsically meaningless, it is possible to evaluate expressions such as:

```
Green < Red
```

The ordering is left to right from the point of definition. However, because it is not sensible to treat constructor names as representing some underlying ordinal type, it is *not* recommended to rely on this language feature.

6.3.3   The dangers of too many constructors

There is sometimes a temptation when programming with algebraic types to define a new type which represents too many things; that is, it has too many constructors. Consider the problem of providing a mechanism for the **fluid** algebraic types to enable values of any one of the three constructors to be converted to values of any one of the other constructors. The sledgehammer approach is to define a function for each conversion, giving rise to six functions: UStoUK, UStoLitre, UKtoUS, etc. The more elegant approach is to provide one general-purpose function; now the problem is how best to parameterize the conversion function to indicate the target constructor. One tempting approach has already been discounted—that of **wrong_general_convert**, shown in Section 6.3.1:

```
wrong_general_convert (USgallons x, Litres)
       = Litres (x * 3.78532)
             ...
```

BIRKBECK
LIBRARY
COLLEGE

The approach was correct in attempting to represent the target as a constructor name, but was syntactically illegal because constructor patterns must be complete. A variation on this approach is to represent the target constructor as an enumeration, as is now shown:

```
fluid     ::=  USgallons num
               | UKgallons num
               | Litres num
               | Fluid_USGALLONS
               | Fluid_UKGALLONS
               | Fluid_LITRES


convert  ::   fluid -> fluid -> fluid
convert       (USgallons x) Fluid_UKGALLONS
         =    UKgallons (x * 0.8327)
convert       (USgallons x) Fluid_LITRES
         =    Litres (x * 3.78532)
              ...
```

This solves the problem, but is rather unwieldy. What has happened is that the pattern matching requirements having been extended from three constructors to six for every function. Yet for this function not every permutation is necessary, and for many other functions the enumerations are not at all necessary. In brief, `fluid` has been "semantically overloaded".[5]

In the above example, it is probably more natural to have types that are less tightly linked, with some appropriate comment:

```
fluid       ::=  Fluid (fluid_name, num)
                 || requires the definition of fluid_name


fluid_name  ::=  Fluid_USGALLONS
                 | Fluid_UKGALLONS
                 | Fluid_LITRES
```

6.4   Recursive algebraic types

This section extends the principle of creating algebraic types that are closer models of the real world, to show how recursive algebraic types may be defined. Recursive types provide a mechanism to define new types with very many (potentially infinitely many) values. The first example shows how the built-in aggregate **list** type could be implemented; the second example shows the **tree** type, which is a more complex data structure.

---

[5]Having too many constructors often interacts badly with an inductive style of program development, because of the cumbersome number of base cases to consider.

6.4.1 Simple recursive algebraic types

The built-in list type has already been semi-formally specified in Section 3.1 as:

1. *empty*
2. *or an element of a given type together with a list of that given type.*

This type is defined recursively and there is no restriction on the number of items in a list (other than the amount of memory available in the computer). The specification meets the structural induction requirements of having a terminating case (the empty list) and a general case (the non-empty list). The built-in constructor for the empty list is [] and the built-in constructor for the non-empty list is : which, considered as a prefix operator, takes an item and a list, and constructs a new list from it.

This built-in recursive type may be denoted using the general mechanism described for algebraic type definition; all that is required is to use the name of the new type being defined as the underlying type for one of the constructors. Thus, in order to provide a user-defined type called list which mimics the built-in polymorphic [*] type, all that is necessary is to translate the above specification directly into the following Miranda definition:

```
list * ::= Nil | Cons * (list *)
```

Instances of lists constructed in this manner are displayed,[6] with their construction made explicit:

```
alist = Nil
blist = Cons 1 alist
clist = Cons 2 blist
```

```
Miranda blist ::
list num

Miranda clist
Cons 2 (Cons 1 Nil)
```

6.4.2 Tree recursive algebraic types

A more general data structure that is not a Miranda built-in type is the *tree*. Of the numerous variations on the tree concept, the following informal specification introduces one of the definitions of a *binary tree* (Standish, 1980).

---

[6]Note that it is not possible to simulate Miranda's alternative square bracket notation. However, for all other purposes Miranda lists and user-defined lists are exactly the same.

A binary tree is either:

1. *empty*
2. *or a node which contains a value, together with a left and a right binary subtree.*

This definition differs from the list, which is essentially a linear structure where each element may follow the next in only one way. With a binary tree, there are two branches at each node and therefore a choice has to be made at each node which branch to follow. The consequence is that tree creation, traversal and manipulation are more complex than their equivalent list operations.

The main advantage of the binary tree structure is for searching; the average number of inspections to extract a given element from a linear list is half the length of the list. However, the average number of inspections to find a member of a averagely balanced sorted binary tree is significantly less,[7] as can be seen from Figure 6.1. The worst case involves four comparisons (that is, half the number of items in the tree) and the average number of comparisons is three.

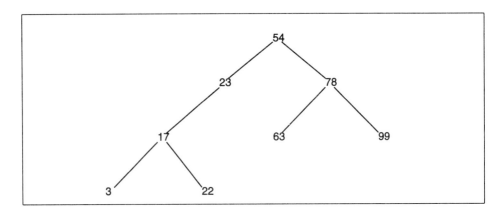

Figure 6.1 A sample tree.

Tree definition

The following translates the informal specification of a tree directly into a Miranda definition of a polymorphic tree, the ordering of which has not yet been determined:

```
tree * ::= Tnil | Tree (tree *, *, tree *)
```

---

[7]For a fully balanced tree (that is, where the items are equally divided between subtrees of the same length) it is actually $\log_2 N$ where N is the number of items in the tree.

There are a number of possibilities as to how this kind of tree can be organized; the most common organization is a sorted tree. The tree presented in Figure 6.1 meets the recursive specification that all the elements of a node's left subtree have a value that is less than the node value itself. Similarly all the elements of a node's right subtree must have a value that is not less than the node's value. The base case of such a tree is the empty tree Tnil which is defined to be sorted.

Growing a tree

The process of making a new (sorted) tree is very similar to making a sorted list using *insertion sort*, first described in Section 3.7.3. There, starting from an empty (sorted) list, elements are inserted one at a time to create an increasingly larger sorted list. Hence, to create a sorted tree, it is first necessary to create an empty (sorted) tree and then provide a function that takes any already sorted tree together with a new item, and returns a new sorted tree.[8]

The only real difference between tree insertion sort and list insertion sort is that the structure of a tree does not require that the existing tree is reordered when a new element is added. All that is necessary is to traverse the tree (according to its ordering specification) until an appropriate empty subtree is encountered and then add the new element. Naturally, for a polymorphic tree, it is also necessary to provide an ordering function as a parameter (as with isort, in Section 4.4.1).

The following two definitions show how an empty tree may be defined and how an item may be inserted into an already sorted tree. Note that the insertleaf function is drawn directly from the definition of the tree. It has the terminating condition of an empty tree and the choice at each non-empty tree as to whether to inspect the left or right subtree. To make this choice requires that tree be deconstructed to obtain the node value. Afterwards a new tree must be reconstructed using the item, the node and the rest of the tree.

```
ordering * == (* -> * -> bool)

insertleaf ::  ordering * -> tree * -> * -> tree *

insertleaf order Tnil item
    = Tree (Tnil, item, Tnil)
insertleaf order (Tree (ltree, node, rtree)) item
    = Tree (put ltree item, node, rtree),
         if order item node
    = Tree (ltree, node, put rtree item), otherwise
      where put = insertleaf order
```

---

[8]It should, of course, be stressed that *tree insertion* is a figurative term; the original tree is not actually altered, but a fresh copy is generated for each additional element.

From list to tree

Just as with the function `isort` in Chapter 4, it is possible to make use of a higher order function to grow a tree from a list without explicit recursion:

```
list_to_tree ::  ordering * -> [*] -> tree *
list_to_tree order itemlist
        = foldl (insertleaf order) Tnil itemlist
```

Or, more concisely:

```
list_to_tree ::  ordering * -> [*] -> tree *
list_to_tree order
        = foldl (insertleaf order) Tnil
```

From tree to list

The complementary function `tree_to_list` also follows directly from the **tree** definition. In effect, the constructor **Tree** has been replaced by the function `tree_to_list` and the tuple notation has been replaced by the append operator **++**:

```
tree_to_list ::  tree * -> [*]

tree_to_list Tnil = []
tree_to_list (Tree (ltree, node, rtree))
    = tree_to_list ltree ++ [node] ++ tree_to_list rtree
```

Because the tree's branching nature has been eliminated, this function is often known as `flatten`.

Exercise 6.4

Explain why it is not sensible to attempt to mirror the tree data structure using nested lists.

Exercise 6.5

A number of useful tree manipulation functions follow naturally from the specification of a binary tree. Write functions to parallel the list manipulation functions **map** and **#** (in terms of the number of nodes in the tree).

Exercise 6.6

What would have been the consequence of writing the function `list_to_tree` as:

```
list_to_tree order
    = reduce (insertleaf order) Tnil
```

Exercise 6.7

Write a function to remove an element from a sorted tree and return a tree that is still sorted.

6.5 Placeholder types

This section introduces *placeholder types*, which are used to allow programmers to defer decisions concerning the type a function or set of functions should have. This may be useful, in that, at different stages in program development, the programmer deals with different problems or different levels of abstraction. Thus, at one stage, the programmer may be concerned with process design rather than data structure design.

For example, early in the design process, it may be decided that a function needs to process data of a given type, perhaps returning a count of the number of items in a aggregate type. At this level of abstraction it is more important that the type is aggregate than its actual representation, which could be a string, a user-defined set, ordered tree or whatever. The choice of aggregate type can better be made after more detailed consideration of the rest of the program.

As a temporary measure, the designer *could* select any arbitrary type that does not give an error, but then they will have to *remember to change* the type if the detailed specification requires it. Alternatively, the designer could choose a polymorphic representation, but this may also prove to be inappropriate or to be too general for the eventual specification. In this case, it is better to defer the decision by *declaring* a new type, using a *placeholder* and to *define* the type later (either by reusing an existing type or using constructors to create an entirely new type). Placeholder types are similar to type synonyms, except that :

1. The symbol `::` is used rather than `==`.
2. The actual type representation has not yet been decided and instead the word **type** is used.

The above situation can now be represented using placeholders:

```
items ::   type

number_of_items ::   items -> num

main_function::   items -> num
main_function x = (number_of_items x) + 5
```

This code can now be processed by Miranda to check for type consistency. If all is well, Miranda will report that functions such as **number_of_items** are SPECIFIED BUT NOT DEFINED but there will be no actual type errors.

Notice that, unlike a type synonym, Miranda treats **items** as a new type:

```
Miranda number_of_items ::
items->num
```

At a later stage in the program development, the actual type will be determined and the code completed:

```
items == [char]

number_of_items ::   items -> num
number_of_items x = # x

main_function ::   items -> num
main_function x = (number_of_items x) + 5
```

Miranda has now been given a type synonym; hence the actual type of the function which accesses the data becomes clear:

```
Miranda number_of_items ::
[char]->num
```

Placeholder types are not particularly useful for small programs, but can be useful to check the type consistency within larger programs—without the need to make a full implementation decision.

6.6   Summary

The strong type system, as presented in Chapter 1, provides a means for enforcing correct usage of Miranda's base, aggregate and function types. The strengths of such a type system are that it promotes good programming style and detects many errors early in the software design cycle. The weakness of such a simple type system is that it imposes strict limitations on what may be expressed.

The first important step towards providing more expressive power was the ability to define functions with polymorphic types, discussed in Chapter 2. In this chapter, the type system was further expanded, using algebraic types, so that the programmer is no longer restricted to the basic Miranda types, but may build new types from the old ones and may expect the type system to apply the same rigour to the new types as to the old.

Finally, this chapter introduced placeholder types, which let the programmer defer the choice of a function's type whilst the program is still in the design stage.

Chapter 7

Abstract Types

This chapter concludes the presentation of Miranda's type system by introducing the *abstract type* mechanism, which allows the definition of a new type, together with the type expressions of a set of "interface" or "primitive" operations which permit access to a data item of the type. The definitions of these primitives are hidden, providing an abstract view of both code and data; this leads to a better appreciation of a program's overall meaning and structure.

The use of type expressions as a design tool and documentary aid has already been encouraged in previous chapters. The **abstype** construct (also known as an "abstract data type" or "ADT"[1]) defines the type expressions for a set of interface functions without specifying the function definitions; the benefits include the separation of specifications from implementation decisions and the ability to provide programmers with the same view of different code implementations. In summary, Miranda's **abstype** mechanism provides the following two new programming benefits:

1. Encapsulation.
2. Abstraction.

Encapsulation

There are considerable benefits if each programmer or programming team can be confident that their coding efforts are not going to interfere inadvertently with other programmers and that other programmers are not going to inadvertently affect their implementation details. This can be achieved by packaging a new type together with the functions which may manipulate values of that type.

---

[1]However, there is a subtle difference between Miranda's **abstype** mechanism and traditional ADTs—see Section 7.1.2.

Furthermore if all the code required to manipulate the new type is collected in one place it is easier to test, modify or maintain and to make accessible to other programmers.

Abstraction

The set of type expressions in an **abstype** is called the *signature* of the **abstype**. The purpose of the interface signature in an **abstype** is to provide a high-level specification of the types of functions which operate on a new type. By using an interface signature, it is possible to "abstract" away from the decision of what underlying type the actual implementation will use. This has the bonus of allowing the implementor considerable freedom to alter the underlying representation at a later time without needing to change a single line of code in the rest of the program (as long as the type and the purpose of each interface function remain the same and the program is recompiled).[2]

For example, if one programmer develops a number of functions that manipulate a data item (perhaps the functions `validate_date` and `days_between_dates` which manipulate `dates`) then it is wasteful for other programmers to develop the same functions. Furthermore, as long as they know the type signatures of the functions and what actions the functions perform then *it is unnecessary for other programmers to understand how the functions are implemented.*

If these operations are linked with the creation of a new type then the advantages of built-in type validation are also available.

Syntax

The syntax for using an **abstype** is given by the following general template:

> **abstype**   *type_declaration*
> **with**   *function_type_signature1*
>   . . .
>   *function_type_signatureN*
>
> *type_declaration_instantiation*
>
> *function_definition1*
>   . . .
> *function_definitionN*

---

[2]This can be particularly useful if the implementation proves too slow or the input data profile changes.

The functions declared within the **abstype** body provide the public interface to the new type; that is, values of this type can only be manipulated via the public interface functions.

Note that the **abstype** itself merely specifies the *name* of a new type and the *types* of the interface functions—the definitions of the type and the interface functions are given immediately afterwards, just as they would be if they were not encapsulated as an **abstype**. This enforces the intention that type information (in the signature) should be separated from implementation information (in the subsequent function definitions).

7.1   Simple abstract type definition and usage

The following example shows how the natural numbers (that is, the non-negative integers) can be considered as an **abstype** package, consisting of a numeric type together with frequently required associated functions. This package would typically be used to manipulate anything for which a negative representation would be meaningless, "prices" and "quantities" being two frequent cases.

It should be noted that the number of functions in the package is limited to mimic those provided by the built-in arithmetic and relational operators; as with the built-in types, there is no need to provide functions for every possible user-specified operation involving natural numbers.[3] The functions that are provided are often known as *primitives* because they can be considered the raw building blocks for the type.

Abstract type definition

```
|| abstype nat specification

abstype nat
with
      makeNat     ::   num -> nat
      natEqual    ::   nat -> nat -> bool
      natLess     ::   nat -> nat -> bool
      || similarly for the other comparison operators

      natMinus    ::   nat -> nat -> nat
      natPlus     ::   nat -> nat -> nat
      || similarly for the other arithmetic operators

      natDisplay ::   nat -> num
```

---

[3]See Section 7.4 for guidelines on which functions should be packaged.

```
|| abstype nat implementation details

nat == num

makeNat x
    = error "makeNat:  non-negative integer expected",
        if (x < 0) \/ (~(integer x))
    = x, otherwise

natDisplay x = x

natEqual = (=)

natLess = (<)

natMinus x y
    = error "natMinus:  negative result", if (x - y) < 0
    = x - y, otherwise

natPlus = (+)

|| and similarly for the other operators
```

The above code illustrates the following points:

1. The abstype is useless on its own—the programmer must also provide under-lying definitions for the type and the interface functions.
2. Every function name declared within a signature must have a corresponding definition. If a definition is missing, an error arises:

```
abstype stack *
with
   emptystack::stack *
   pop ::   stack * -> *
   push ::   stack * -> * -> stack *

stack * == [*]

emptystack = []

pop [] = error "empty stack"
pop (x :   xs) = x
```

```
compiling script.m
checking types in script.m
SPECIFIED BUT NOT DEFINED: push;
```

This rule has the clear advantage that it prevents a programmer from specifying something and then forgetting to code it!

3. Any function definition whose name matches a name which appears within an **abstype** signature must be of the type declared in the signature.

```
abstype stack *
with
  emptystack::stack *
  pop ::   stack * -> *
  push ::   stack * -> * -> stack *

stack * == [*]

emptystack = []

pop [] = error "empty stack"
pop (x :   xs) = x

push xs x = (x, xs)
```

```
compiling script.m
checking types in script.m
abstype implementation error
"push" is bound to value of type: *->**->(**,*)
type expected: [*]->*->[*]
(line  14 of "script.m")
```

This rule reinforces the principle that programmers should first consider the nature of the input and output types of their programs before worrying about the coding details.

4. The interface function definitions could appear anywhere in the program, but it is sensible programming practice to put them next to their declarations.

Abstract type usage

The following session shows how the `makeNat` function can be used to create new instances of **nats**. The function `natPlus` is then used to add these two instances:

```
quantity1 = makeNat 3
quantity2 = makeNat 3
```

```
Miranda quantity1
<abstract ob>

Miranda natPlus quantity1 quantity2
<abstract ob>
```

In all of the above cases, the system response is new, indicating that the representation is hidden. The programmer cannot be tempted to bypass these primitives and attempt direct manipulation of the underlying type. This has the considerable benefit that the underlying types and implementation details may be changed with no need to change any application programs that use the abstract type primitives—this is often termed *abstraction.*

This point is reinforced by the fact that the only type information available is the name of the **abstype:**

```
Miranda quantity1 ::
nat
```

Notice that lazy evaluation has the effect that computation is not actually carried out if there is no value which can be viewed by the user. Thus, in the following example, the **error** function for (makeNat (-3)) is not invoked because the expression is not evaluated:

```
Miranda natPlus (makeNat (-3)) (makeNat 3.1)
<abstract ob>
```

Hiding the implementation means that the only way to access actual values is by one of the **nat** primitives. In the final example below, the attempt to display the value of a **nat** has caused some evaluation and consequently the **error** function has reported that it is not possible to turn a negative number into a **nat:**

```
Miranda natdisplay (natLess quantity1 quantity2)
False

Miranda natdisplay (natPlus quantity1 quantity2)
6

Miranda natDisplay (natPlus (makeNat (-3)) (makeNat 3.1))
program error: makeNat : negative input
```

Exercise 7.1

Provide function definitions for the **nat** primitives if a recursive underlying data representation is used as follows: **algnat ::= Zero | Succ algnat.**

Exercise 7.2

A *date* consists of a day, month and year. Legitimate operations on a date include: creating a date, checking whether a date is earlier or later than another date, adding a day to a date to give a new date, subtracting two dates to give a number of days, and checking if the date is within a leap year. Provide an abstract type declaration for a date.

7.1.1 Polymorphic abstypes

An **abstype** may also be used to declare a new polymorphic type; in this case, the name of the new type must be followed by the polytypes which will be used in the underlying definition. This is demonstrated in the following example of a *sequence*.

A double-ended list (sometimes known as a *sequence*), can be defined such that all the operations normally occurring at the front of a list (:, hd, tl) have mirror operations occurring at the end of the list. The basic set of operations provided are **seqNil** (which returns an empty sequence), followed by **seqConsL**, **seqConsR**, **seqHdL**, **seqHdR**, **seqTlL** and **seqTlR** (which provide the normal list operations at both ends of the sequence); two further functions **seqAppend** and **seqDisplay** are also provided for convenience. This type could be defined recursively or, as shown below, by extending operations on the built-in list type:

```
abstype sequence *
with
    seqNil     ::   sequence *
    seqConsL   ::   * -> (sequence *) -> (sequence *)
    seqConsR   ::   (sequence *) -> * -> (sequence *)
    seqHdL     ::   (sequence *) -> *
    seqHdR     ::   (sequence *) -> *
    seqTlL     ::   (sequence *) -> (sequence *)
    seqTlR     ::   (sequence *) -> (sequence *)
    seqAppend  ::   (sequence *) -> (sequence *)
                    -> (sequence *)
    seqDisplay ::   (sequence *) -> [*]

sequence * == [*]

seqNil = []
seqConsL = (:)
seqConsR anyseq item = anyseq ++ [item]

|| etc

seqDisplay s = s
```

Exercise 7.3

Complete the implementation for the **sequence** abstract type.

7.1.2   Properties of abstract types

Constraints

Five important constraints are imposed on the use of abstract types:

1. The arithmetic operators do *not* work for values of an **abstype**, regardless of the underlying type:

```
Miranda quantity1 + quantity2
type error in expression
cannot unify nat with num
```

2. Because the underlying abstract type representation is hidden, it is not possible to pattern match on an abstract type instance:

```
wrong_equal_numbers  ::  nat -> num -> bool
wrong_equal_numbers  0 0
               =  True
wrong_equal_numbers  quantity1 x
               =  natEqual quantity1 (makeNat x)
```

```
incorrect declaration
specified wrong_equal_numbers :: nat -> num -> bool
inferred wrong_equal_numbers :: num -> num -> bool
```

The above error has occurred because the constant pattern 0 has appeared as the first argument for the function. The use of 0 as a value of type **nat** is restricted to the interface functions; if 0 occurs elsewhere then it is seen to be a value of type **num**.

3. The type name for an **abstype** must be linked to an existing type name through the use of a type synonym. This defines the underlying type for the **abstype**. It is *not* possible to define the underlying type in any other way— a potential mistake is to attempt to define the underlying type directly as an algebraic type. The first example below shows this error, and the second example demonstrates a correct definition:

```
abstype wrong_lights
with
  start_light ::  wrong_lights
  next_light ::  wrong_lights -> wrong_traffic_lights


wrong_lights ::= Green | Red | Amber | RedAmber


start_light = Green


next_light Green = Amber
next_light Amber = Red
next_light Red = RedAmber
next_light RedAmber = Green
```

```
compiling script.m
syntax error: nameclash, "wrong_lights" already defined
error found near line 6 of file "script.m"
compilation abandoned
```

```
abstype traffic_lights
with
  start_light::traffic_lights
  next_light ::traffic_lights -> traffic_lights


lights ::= Green | Red | Amber | RedAmber


traffic_lights == lights


start_light = Green


next_light Green = Amber
next_light Amber = Red
next_light Red = RedAmber
next_light RedAmber = Green
```

4. Only the declared interface functions may access the specified **abstype**. In the last example, any other function can be defined to operate upon values of type `lights`; what is new is that only the declared interface functions can operate upon values of type `traffic_lights`. The fact that the underlying type for `traffic_lights` is `lights` is not relevant to the rest of the program because values of the two types cannot be mixed—they are treated as entirely different types.[4]

---

[4]Note that Miranda does *not* provide data-hiding as part of its **abstype** facility, unlike some other languages, where the underlying type would also be concealed.

5. An **abstype** can only be defined at the top-level of a Miranda session; for example, it is not legal to define an **abstype** within a **where** block or function body.

Ordering abstract type values

Values of an abstract type inherit the ordering characteristics of the underlying type. Thus, if equality and relational ordering are defined on the underlying type then they will be defined for the **abstype** values:

```
Miranda quantity1 <= quantity2
True
```

However, reliance on the use of the built-in equality and relational operators *severely limits* the degree of abstraction achieved by the **abstype**; if the underlying representation of the abstract type is changed then the use of the built-in operators such as = and < cannot be relied upon. It is therefore recommended that if ordering primitives are required then they should be provided explicitly as interface functions.

7.1.3   Converting between abstract types

Sometimes there will be a requirement to convert from one abstract type to another. Initially this may seem difficult, because only the interface functions may use an abstract type's data. For example, if a program contains a **tree** abstract type (see Section 6.4.2) and a **sequence** abstract type (see Section 7.1.1), where should the function **tree_to_sequence** be defined? It cannot be defined inside the **tree** abstract type because it will not have access to the **sequence** underlying representation; similarly, it cannot be defined inside **sequence** because it will not have access to the **tree** underlying representation.

This apparent limitation is solved pragmatically in one of two ways: firstly by converting to a common intermediate data type; alternatively by coalescing the two abstract types.

1. If the two abstract types are not closely linked semantically then it is likely that the conversion mentioned above will not occur often and in this case it is sufficient to provide a "display" function and a "make" function for each; these two functions will use an intermediate form based on built-in types in order to provide the conversion. For example, given the abstract type **tree** and the abstract type **sequence** then the **sequence_to_tree** function can thereafter be defined externally to both abstract types, as is shown in the following program extract:

```
|| Define the tree abstract type:
abstype tree *
with

|| etc

tree * == mytree *
mytree * ::= Tnil | Tree (mytree *) * (mytree *)

displayTree Tnil = []
displayTree (Tree ltree node rtree)
    = displayTree ltree ++ [node]
      ++ displayTree rtree

makeTree order alist
    = accumulate (insertleaf order) Tnil alist
        . . .

|| Define the sequence abstract type:
abstype sequence *
with

|| etc

sequence * == mysequence *
mysequence * ::= Seq [*]

displaySequence (Seq s) = s

|| etc

|| Define a conversion function:

sequence_to_tree order
    = (makeTree order) .  displaySequence
```

2. By contrast, if conversion between two abstract types is a very frequent requirement then this implies that they are in fact very closely linked semantically and should therefore be defined in tandem. The **sequence_to_tree** function can then be defined inside the combined abstract type body and will have access to all the necessary data:

```
abstype seqtree *
  with
     sequence_to_tree::   seqtree * -> seqtree *
     tree_to_sequence::   seqtree * -> seqtree *

                   || etc

seqtree * == myseqtree *

mytree * ::= Tnil | Tree (mytree *) * (mytree *)

myseqtree * ::= Seqtree (mytree *) | Seq [*]


sequence_to_tree (Seq []) = Seqtree Tnil
sequence_to_tree (Seq (front :  rest)) =
                   || etc

tree_to_sequence (Seqtree Tnil) = Seq []
tree_to_sequence (Seqtree (Tree ltree node rtree)) =
                   || etc
```

7.2   Showing abstract types

Most objects in a Miranda program may be printed by using the built-in function
show. However, there is no built-in method for converting objects with an abstract
type to a printable form. Thus, if show is applied to an object of abstract type, it
will normally print as:

This behaviour for the function show may be modified by providing a special
"show" function for a given **abstype**. The rule for doing this is to include in
the definition of the abstract type a function with the name showfoo (where "foo"
is the name of the abstract type involved). Thereafter, if the built-in function show
is applied to an object of type foo then the function showfoo will automatically
be called.

   For example, consider the type traffic_lights where it is required to represent
three lights by characters displayed one above the other (red, amber and green from
top to bottom):

    Miranda red_light::
    traffic_lights

```
Miranda show red_light
*
0
0

Miranda show green_light
0
0
*

Miranda show redamber_light
*
*
0
```

In order for **show** to work in the above manner, it is necessary to define an extra interface function called **showtraffic_lights**:

```
abstype traffic_lights
with
start_light          ::   traffic_lights
next_light           ::   traffic_lights -> traffic_lights
showtraffic_lights   ::   traffic_lights -> [char]

lights ::= Green | Red | Amber | RedAmber

traffic_lights == lights

start_light = Green

next_light Green    = Amber
next_light Amber    = Red
next_light Red      = RedAmber
next_light RedAmber = Green

showtraffic_lights Green    = "0\n 0\n*\n"
showtraffic_lights Red      = "*\n 0\n0 \n"
showtraffic_lights Amber    = "0\n *\n0 \n"
showtraffic_lights RedAmber = "*\n *\n0 \n"
```

In the above example, the special-purpose "show" interface function takes one argument (of type **traffic_lights**) and returns a value of type **[char]**.

Showing polymorphic abstypes

If the **abstype** involved is polymorphic then the new "show" function must take an extra argument, which is a function: that is, a function which knows how to "show" an object of the polymorphic type. In practice, the programmer never has to provide this additional function when **show** is applied because it is automatically provided by Miranda; however, the definition of the new "show" function must assume that the function is passed as the first argument and must use that function appropriately. For example, consider an **abstype** which mirrors the built-in list type:

```
abstype list *
with
   empty        :: list *
   add_to_list ::    * -> list * -> list *
   showlist    ::    (* -> [char]) -> list * -> [char]


alglist * ::= Nil_list | List * (alglist *)


list * == alglist *


empty = Nil_list


add_to_list x y = List x y


showlist f Nil_list    = "[]"
showlist f (List x y) = "( " ++ (f x) ++ " :   "
                                ++ (showlist y) ++ " )"
```

The general rule is as follows. Let "foo" be an abstract type name. To make objects of type "foo" printable, it is necessary to define a "showfoo" such that:

> if foo is a simple type (not polymorphic)
> showfoo :: foo $->$ [char]

> if foo is polymorphic in one type variable (foo *)
> showfoo :: (*$->$[char]) $->$ foo * $->$ [char]

> if foo is polymorphic in two type variables (foo * **)
> showfoo :: (*$->$[char]) $->$ (* * $->$[char]) -> foo * * *$->$ [char]

...and so on. Note that the *show* function must be declared in the signature of the abstract type, and that the name of the function is significant—if it were to be called *banana* rather than *showfoo* then it would not have any effect on the behaviour of **show**. Similarly if it is not of the correct type then again it will not effect **show**, though in this case the compiler will print a warning message.

Exercise 7.4

Provide a *show* function for the **sequence** abstract type.

Exercise 7.5

Assuming that the underlying type for an abstract **date** type is a three number tuple (day, month, year), provide functions to display the day and month in US format (month, day), UK format (day, month) and to display the month as a string, such as "Jan" or "Feb".

7.3   Further examples of abstract types

This section now presents two more examples of the use of abstract types. The first example collects together the functions over a binary tree and presents an elegant method for providing a generic package for trees. The second, larger, example shows how an *array* data structure might be implemented in more than one way without affecting the way it is used in existing programs.

7.3.1   Trees as abstract types—generic packaging

The major disadvantage of defining a polymorphic search tree is that the ordering function must always be passed as an explicit parameter to the interface functions for tree modification and manipulation. This difficulty can be overcome by incorporating the ordering function into the data structure definition; thus, it is only necessary to specify the ordering function when a tree is first created and thereafter all other interface functions can find the ordering function by inspecting the data structure. The advantage of using an **abstype** in this situation is that, once the tree has been established, the user of the interface functions need not be aware of the embedded ordering function.

```
ordering * == (* -> * -> bool)
tree *   ::= Tnil
           | Tree (tree *) * (tree *)
orderedTree * ::= OrderedTree (ordering *) (tree *)

abstype absTree *
  with
        newtree    ::  ordering * -> absTree *
        insertleaf ::  absTree * -> * -> absTree *
        flatten    ::  absTree * -> [*]

absTree * == orderedTree *

newtree order = OrderedTree order Tnil

insertleaf (OrderedTree order anytree) item
    = OrderedTree order (insert anytree)
      where
      insert Tnil = Tree Tnil item Tnil
      insert (Tree ltree node rtree)
          = Tree (insert ltree) node rtree,
            if (order item node)
          = Tree ltree node (insert rtree),
            otherwise

flatten (OrderedTree order anytree)
    = inorder anytree
      where
      inorder Tnil = []
      inorder (Tree ltree node rtree)
          = inorder ltree ++ [node] ++ inorder rtree
```

Instances of this **absTree** can be created by passing the appropriate sorting function, for example:

```
lessthan ::  num -> num -> bool
lessthan = (<)

num_absTree ::  absTree num
num_absTree = newtree lessthan
```

Thus, an **absTree** in increasing numeric order might be as shown in Figure 7.1.

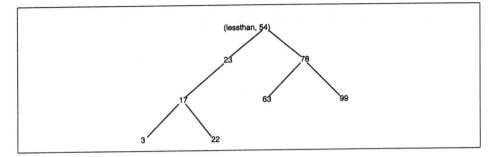

Figure 7.1 Sample Atree.

Exercise 7.6
An alternative representation of the `Atree` would be:

```
abstype other_tree *
with
      || declarations

ordering * == * -> * -> bool
other_tree * ::= Anil (ordering *)
                | ATree (ordering *) (other_tree *) * (other_tree *)
```

What would be the consequences for the abstract type implementation?

7.3.2   Arrays as abstract types—alternative implementations

The following example demonstrates the usefulness of concealing a particular representation of an abstract type from the programmer. The first implementation of `array` could be replaced by an implementation as a list of tuples, without altering its public interface.

An array as a list of lists

This implementation shows an abstract type representation of a two-dimensional array, where an array may be defined as a fixed size aggregate data structure whose elements may be changed or retrieved by reference to an index.

A two-dimensional array data structure can very easily be represented as a list of lists (where the innermost lists represent the rows of the array). The function definitions are fairly straightforward but rely upon the existence of some of the list handling functions introduced in Chapter 3 and some of the higher order functions of Chapter 4. As recommended for larger programs, the implementation is presented as a literate script:

```
>|| List of lists array representation.   (Page 1 of 2)

> abstype array *
> with
>    num_rows    ::  array * -> num
>    num_cols    ::  array * -> num
>    init_array  ::  num -> num -> * -> array *
>    change_item ::  array * -> num -> num -> * -> array *
>    get_item    ::  array * -> num -> num -> *

> array * == [[*]]

> num_rows anarray = # anarray

> num_cols [] = 0
> num_cols anarray = # (hd anarray)

replace applies a function ff to a item in a list
giving an identical list except that the item is
replaced by the result of the function application

> replace ::  num -> (*->*) -> [*] -> [*]
> replace pos ff anylist
>    = error "replace:  illegal position",
>         if (pos > # anylist) \/ (pos <= 0)
>    = (take (pos - 1) anylist)
>         ++ [ff (get_nth pos anylist)]
>         ++ (drop pos anylist), otherwise

>get_nth ::  num -> [*] -> *
>get_nth n anylist
>       = anylist !  (n - 1)
```

```
>|| List of lists array representation continued (Page 2)

init_array produces an initial array from:
   i.  how many rows and columns the array should have
  ii.  and a starting value for all the elements.

repeat creates a list of the right length to represent
a row, and also constructs an array of many such rows.

> init_array nrows ncols first_val
>    = error "init_array:  negative rows",
>        if nrows < 0
>    = error "init_array:  negative columns",
>        if ncols < 0
>    = hd [a | b<-[take nrows (repeat x)];
>           a<-[take ncols (repeat b)]], otherwise


change_item returns the input array with an altered item.
replace's outer application finds the appropriate row and
its inner application is applied to that row to replace
the item in the column position with a new value using the
built-in combinator const (cf cancel as shown in Chapter 4).
The inner use of replace is a partial application, it is
not fully evaluated until the appropriate row has been
selected.

> change_item anarray row column newvalue
>    = error "change_item:  illegal position",
>        if (row <= 0) \/ (column <= 0)
>            \/ (row > num_rows anarray)
>            \/ (column > num_cols anarray)
>    = replace row (replace column (const newvalue)) anarray,
>        otherwise

> get_item anarray row column
>    = error "get_item:  illegal position",
>        if (row <= 0) \/ (column <= 0)
>            \/ (row > num_rows anarray)
>            \/ (column > num_cols anarray)
>    = get_nth column (get_nth row anarray), otherwise
```

The **array** primitives can now be used directly in programs and also to build more complex utilities:

```
> get_col ::   array * -> num -> [*]
> get_col anarray column
>    = error "get_col:  illegal column number",
>        if (column <= 0) \/ (column > num_cols anarray)
>    = map (converse (get_item anarray) column)
>            [1..(num_rows x)], otherwise

> get_row ::   array * -> num -> [*]
> get_row anarray row
>    = error "get_row:  illegal row number",
>        if (row <= 0) \/ (row > num_rows anarray)
>    = map (get_item anarray row)
>            [1..(num_cols x)], otherwise
```

An array as a list of tuples

The first implementation of the *array* can now be replaced with an implementation as a list of tuples, without changing the interface function signatures and therefore without the need to change any part of any program that uses such an *array* type.

```
>|| list of tuples array representation.   (Page 1 of 2)

> abstype array *
> with
>    num_rows    ::  array * -> num
>    num_cols    ::  array * -> num
>    init_array  ::  num -> num -> * -> array *
>    change_item ::  array * -> num -> num -> * -> array *
>    get_item    ::  array * -> num -> num -> *

> array * == (num,num,*,[(num,num,*)])

The array is represented by its dimensions (nrows * ncols),
a value (default) for all items that have not been updated,
together with a list of tuples representing the row and
column position and new value of any updated item "changes"

> num_rows (nrows, ncols, default, changes) = nrows

> num_cols (nrows, ncols, default, changes) = ncols
```

```
>|| list of tuples array representation.    (Page 2)

> init_array nrows ncols default
>       = error "init_array:  inappropriate dimensions",
>           if (nrows < 0) \/ (ncols < 0)
>               \/ anyfractional [nrows,ncols]
>       = (nrows, ncols, default, []), otherwise
```

Changing an item involves removing the changes list entry and
appending the new entry. There is no check whether the new
value differs from the existing entry or the default value

```
> change_item (nrows,ncols,default,changes) row col newvalue
>       = error "change_item:  inappropriate dimensions",
>           if invalid nrows ncols row col
>       = (nrows,ncols,default,newchanges), otherwise
>         where
>         newchanges
>             = (filter ((~) .  (compare row col)) changes)
>                 ++ [(row,col,newvalue)]
```

Getting an item involves filtering it from the changes list;
if there is no entry then the default entry becomes the head
of the items list otherwise it is ignored.

```
> get_item (nrows,ncols,default,changes) row col
>       = error "get_item:  inappropriate dimensions",
>           if invalid nrows ncols row col
>       = (third .  hd) items, otherwise
>         where
>         third (row, col,value) = value
>         items = (filter (compare row col) changes)
>                 ++ [(row,col,default)]

> compare row1 col1 (row2, col2, item)
>     = (row1 = row2) & (col1 = col2)

> anyfractional nlist = and (map ((~) .  integer) nlist)

> invalid nrows ncols row col
>     = (row > nrows) \/ (row <= 0) \/ (col > ncols) \/
>         (col <= 0) \/ anyfractional [nrows,nrows,col,ncols]
```

The functions `get_col` and `get_row` defined using the first (list of lists) version of **array** can now be substituted with the second (list of tuples) version *without modification of the existing code*; all that is necessary is to recompile the program, to ensure that the new representation is used throughout (recompilation will be done automatically on exit from the editor).

Exercise 7.7

  A *queue* aggregate data structure (Standish, 1980) can be defined as either being empty or as consisting of a queue followed by an element; operations include creating a new queue, inserting an element at the end of a queue and removing the first element in a queue. The following declares a set of primitives for a polymorphic abstract type queue:

```
abstype queue *
with
    qisempty    = queue * -> bool
    qtop        = queue * -> *
    qinsert     = queue * -> * -> queue *
    qcreate     = queue *
```

Provide an implementation for this abstract type.

7.4   Guidelines for abstract type primitive selection

Apart from the criterion that an **abstype** must provide all the operations that are necessary and sufficient to manipulate the underlying type, there are no other rigid rules to determine which functions should be provided to make the abstract type easy to use. Two of the necessary primitives for all abstract types are *creation* and *inspection*. Many abstract types will also have *initialization* and *modification* primitives, the former sometimes being incorporated into the *creation* primitive (as with the **abstree** definition). A useful set is an initialization primitive to create an "empty" object, together with a modification primitive to change the underlying value and an inspection primitive to view that value—this works particularly well when the underlying type is a recursive algebraic type. Furthermore, it is often useful to provide the equivalents of **map** and **reduce** for the abstract type. It is however unwise to provide too large a set of primitive functions, because this will tend to reinforce the current underlying representation and make it difficult to make future changes to this representation.

  For example, the above **array** implementation provided primitives for creating a new array, together with those for inspecting and changing one element. It can be shown that these three are sufficient for array manipulation, but in practice an *equality* primitive and functions to extract the contents of a row or column would probably be provided. Indeed, for many abstract types it will often be the case that additional functions, which build on the basic primitives, should be offered by the abstract type implementor. The rationale for this is threefold:

1. To eliminate programmer effort and potential error, by writing these "non-essential" primitives once only.
2. To provide efficient implementations based on a knowledge of the underlying algebraic type representation.
3. There is sometimes a choice of which primitives comprise a necessary and sufficient set of operations. For example, an abstract type for binary Boolean algebra could be represented by a unary *not* operator, together with a dyadic *and* operator; or by *not*, together with the dyadic *or* operator. In this case, it is obvious that both dyadic operators should be provided to reflect different programmers' views of the data.

Notice that it is always safe to change an abstract type's underlying representation in order to *extend* the functionality of the type; however it is *not* safe to decrease the number of interface functions without potentially affecting parts of the program already written.

Finally, there are many instances of general purpose types (such as the **coords** algebraic type) for which it is not possible to predict an adequate and easy to use set of primitives. For these types it does not make sense to force them into an abstract type.[5]

7.5 Summary

This chapter has extended the principle of strong typing introduced in Chapter 1 and emphasized throughout this book. The use of *abstract types* helps to ensure that values of a certain type (a basic type or a new type) are only operated on by appropriately defined functions. Not only does this help to detect errors, it also serves to document the program and helps to keep the program structure clear.

This mechanism also extends the principle of structured programming discussed in Chapter 5 to show how a programmer can have safer and more reusable code. The **abstype** code is generally code that will be used by many programmers for different applications and can be provided in a library with the underlying implementation hidden from the application programmers.

Large-scale programming benefits enormously from the rigorous application of the concepts of closure, modularity, encapsulation and self-documentation, as described and recommended throughout this book.

---

[5]However, it may be reasonable to encapsulate a "library" of related operations in a file, as shown in Chapter 9

Chapter 8

Files and Interaction

8.1 Introduction

This chapter introduces Miranda's mechanisms for the input of data into a program and for the output of data from a program. Data may be transferred between the program and one or more files, or may be transferred between the program and the user. For data transfer to and from the user, the program must take the form of a dialogue; the user must be prompted for information and the program must respond to the user's input. This dialogue between the program and the user is termed *interaction*.

Input and output ("i/o") between programs and files is considered first, starting with simple i/o mechanisms and proceeding to formatted i/o. This is followed by a discussion of interaction with the user via the keyboard and the screen, and finally the mechanisms for interaction with the operating system.[1]

8.2 File input

8.2.1 Simple input

In previous chapters, functions have mainly been applied to data entered at the keyboard; however, this is both tedious and prone to error if large data volumes must be processed. An alternative approach is to store the data as part of the program in the script file, but this entails editing the script file every time there is a change in the data. It is often preferable to put the data into separate files and access these files from within the Miranda system; if the data changes, only the data file need be edited, thereby reducing the chance of introducing an error

---

[1]The current version of Miranda is only available for the UNIX operating system (or UNIX clones), and so discussion of operating system interaction will be specific to UNIX.

into the program code. Data can be read from a file by using the built-in **read** function, which is of type [char]->[char]. The parameter to **read** is a string (that is, a list of characters) representing a UNIX file.[2] The return value is a string containing the contents of the file; if the file does not exist or cannot be read, Miranda halts its evaluation and gives an error message.

The example below shows how the *grep* program, developed throughout this book, can be adapted to work for file input. It uses the built-in function **read** together with the predefined function lines which splits a flat string into a list of strings using the newline as a delimiter:

```
in_grep ::  [char] -> [char] -> [[char]]
in_grep regexp filename
    = grep regexp ((lines .  read) filename)
```

Another demonstration of the use of **read** is the following *wordcount* program. This is similar to the standard UNIX facility *wc*, which counts the total number of characters, words and lines in a given file.

In this program the expression **read infile** evaluates (lazily) to a string (a list of char) representing the entire content of the specified input file; this list is used as the input to the auxiliary function xwc, which is initialized with zero values in the three accumulators representing the number of lines, words and characters in the input file. Notice that xwc does not need to check for any special "end-of-file" marker—the end of the data is represented by the empty list.

```
wordcount ::  [char] -> (num, num, num)
wordcount infile
    = xwc (read infile) 0 0 0
      where
      xwc [] nlines nwords nchars
       = (nline, nwords, nchars)
      xwc (first :  second :  rest) nlines nwords nchars
       = xwc rest nlines (nwords + 1) (nchars + 2),
           if member [' ','\t'] second
       = xwc rest (nlines + 1) (nwords + 1) (nchars + 2),
           if second = '\n'
       = xwc (second :  rest) nlines nwords (nchars + 1),
           otherwise
      xwc (first :  rest) nlines nwords nchars
       = xwc rest nlines nwords (nchars + 1),
           if member [' ','\t'] first
       = xwc rest (nlines + 1) nwords (nchars + 1),
           if first = '\n'
       = (nlines, nwords + 1, nchars + 1),
           otherwise
```

---

[2]Strictly speaking, it represents a UNIX pathname indicating a file or device.

The characters in the file are read lazily (a character at a time) and are discarded as soon as they have been scanned (this is evident from the fact that none of the alternative return values for xwc contain the name first).[3]

8.2.2   Formatted input—readvals

The built-in function **read** only returns a list of characters, yet programs often require values of other types. To this end, Miranda provides the **readvals** function, which takes a string representing a file and returns a list of values of a specified type (and so the type of **readvals** is [char] -> [*]). Each value in the input file must appear on a separate line and will be returned as a separate item in the list; blank lines and Miranda || comments may be embedded in the input file and are *not* read into the resultant list.

UNIX represents the user's screen and keyboard as a file,[4] so that it is possible to read from the keyboard in the same manner as reading from a file (similarly, it is possible to write to a file and have the data appear on the screen). In recognition of this fact, Miranda's **readvals** function checks with the operating system to determine whether the input is actually coming from a file or is coming from a keyboard; if the input comes from a keyboard, **readvals** checks for errors and reacts to bad data by prompting the user to repeat the line (the bad values are omitted from the result list). If the input file is not connected to a keyboard, bad data will cause the program to terminate with an error message.

The following example shows how an input file could be treated as a list of numbers:

```
numberlist ::   [num]
numberlist = readvals "data"
```

Note that Miranda must be able to determine the type of input file used by **readvals**. Thus, despite the polymorphic type of **readvals**, the programmer must specify a monomorphic (non-polymorphic) type each time it is used. To omit the type leads to a compile-time error:

```
numberlist = readvals "data"
```

```
compiling script.m
checking types in script.m
type error - readvals or $+ used at polymorphic type :: [*]
(line 1 of "script.m")
```

---

[3]In principle, the program should be able to deal with any size of file; unfortunately, with the current implementation, Miranda runs out of space for very large input files.

[4]For example, the file */dev/tty* represents the screen and keyboard currently being operated by the user.

Exercise 8.1

Adapt the *wordcount* program so that it will work for more than one input file.

Exercise 8.2

Explain why the following code is incorrect:

```
wrongsplit infile
            = first second
              where first = hd inlist
                    second = tl inlist
                    inlist = readvals infile
```

User-defined formatting

The **readvals** function operates on the whole file at once and expects all items in
the file to be the same type. However, the data file might contain items of different
type, in which case it is necessary to treat the file as a list of characters and then
to define a collection of functions which will translate a part of the file into data
of a different type. The following examples illustrate how to translate data from
a list of characters to whatever type is required by the rest of the program. Each
user-defined formatting function translates a small portion of data from the start of
the file. For each function there is also a data-discarding mirror, which is required
in order to access the remainder of the file's data. These functions operate in pairs,
much like **hd** and **tl** or **takewhile** and **dropwhile**.

```
>|| user-defined formatting (Page 1 of 2)

read first integer from input file

> readint ::  [char] -> num
> readint infile
>    = string_to_int (takewhile digit (read infile))
>       || where
>       || string_to_int was defined in Chapter 2

drop first integer from input file

> dropint ::  [char] -> [char]
> dropint infile
>    = (dropwhile notdigit (dropwhile digit (read infile)))
```

```
>|| user-defined formatting continued (Page 2)

read first word from input file

> readword ::  [char] -> [char]
> readword infile
>    = (takewhile notspace (read infile))

drop first word from input file

> dropword ::  [char] -> [char]
> dropword infile
>    = (dropwhile isspace (dropwhile notspace (read infile)))

general-purpose character handlers:

> isspace x = member [' ', '\t', '\n'] x
> notspace = (~) .  isspace
> notdigit = (~) .  digit

 digit is built-in:  digit x = '0' <= x <= '9'

readN will read up to a specified number of characters from
its given input file, and result in a tuple containing
a count of the number of characters actually read together
with those characters

> readN ::  [char] -> ([char],num)
> readN infile nchars
>       = (instringLength, instring),
>            if instringLength < nchars
>       = (nchars, take nchars instring), otherwise
>         where
>          instringLength = # instring
>          instring = read infile

> dropN ::  [char] -> ([char],num)
> dropN infile nchars
>       = (instringLength, []),
>            if instringLength < nchars
>       = (nchars, drop nchars instring), otherwise
>         where
>          instringLength = # instring
>          instring = read infile
```

Exercise 8.3

Provide the functions `readbool` and `dropbool` which, respectively, will read and discard a Boolean value from the start of an input file.

8.2.3   Safe input—filemode

So far, the discussion of file input has assumed that the desired input file exists and that the user is entitled to access it. This is clearly not a safe assumption in anything other than a development context. It is possible to check the status of a given file using the built-in **filemode** function, which is of type `[char]->[char]`. The parameter represents a file and the return value represents its UNIX user access permissions.[5]

If the result string is empty then the file does not exist. Otherwise it will contain four characters:

1. The first position will be the character `'d'` if the file is a directory or `'-'` if it is not.
2. The second position will be the character `'r'` if the file is readable or `'-'` if it is not readable.
3. The third position will be the character `'w'` if the file is writable or `'-'` if it is not writable.
4. The final position will be the character `'x'` if the file is executable or `'-'` if it is not executable.

Making use of this information, the *wordcount* program can now be made safe by checking the file status before applying `xwc`:

```
wordcount ::   [char] -> (num, num, num)
wordcount infile
     = error "can't open" ++ infile,
         if cantopen (filemode infile)
            where
              cantopen [] = True
              cantopen ('d' :   rest) = True
              cantopen (any :   '-' :   rest) = True
              cantopen anyother = False
     = xwc (read infile) 0 0 0, otherwise
        || etc
```

---

[5]The UNIX "group" and "other" access permissions are not available.

8.3   Input and referential transparency

In earlier chapters it has been stressed that the functional programming view of computation is that a name is bound to a value which never changes. This is in direct contrast to the imperative view of programming, where a name is bound to a memory location—the memory location never changes, but the value stored in the memory location can change.

A name in a functional program might be bound to an expression to be calculated, and that expression might be different each time the program is run (because it depends on data entered at run-time); however, once a value has been calculated for that name, it cannot change. This is called "referential transparency".

As a result of referential transparency, the following two definitions must always be equivalent:

```
shared_def g x = y ++ y
                  where
                  y = g x

unshared_def g x = (g x) ++ (g x)
```

Unfortunately, both **read** and **filemode** may exhibit a lack of referential transparency, such that if either were substituted for **g** in the above definitions, and if **x** were the name of a file, the above definitions might not give equivalent results. This is because in a multi-tasking system, such as UNIX, the file contents and the permissions on a file might change at the same time as the Miranda program is running.

In the following example, the function **samecopy** takes a copy of the input file and duplicates it, whereas the function **diffcopy** reads the input file twice. It is just feasible that someone may have edited this file between the first and second evaluations of **read infile**:

```
samecopy infile = instring ++ instring
                  where
                  instring = read infile

diffcopy infile = read infile ++ read infile
```

8.4   File output

Just as it is necessary to take data from the files and the keyboard, it is also necessary to output data to files and the user's screen. In Miranda, all program *output* occurs as part of the value returned by the topmost function, that is, the function whose name is invoked at the Miranda prompt in order to run the program The Miranda on-line manual calls this a "command-level expression".

The following section introduces the concept of *system messages*, which provide mechanisms for a program to control where data is saved and in which format.

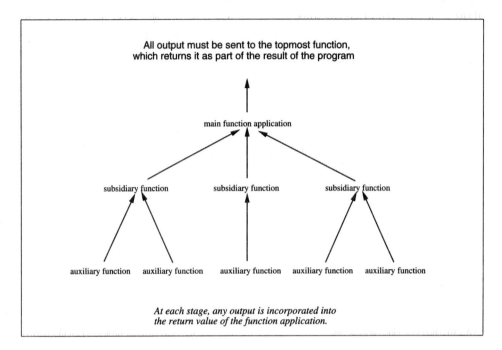

Figure 8.1 File output.

8.4.1   System messages

The value of a command-level expression is always a list of system messages, that is, it has result type [sys_message]. A system message is defined as an algebraic type, where each constructor corresponds to a different output action:

```
sys_message ::= Stdout [char] | Stderr [char] |
                Tofile [char] [char] | Closefile [char] |
                Appendfile [char] | System [char] | Exit num
```

For example, a program might produce the result:

```
[ Stdout "twinkle", Tofile "myfile" "twinkle little star" ]
```

The above list of system messages is a sequence of commands to the Miranda system; these commands are obeyed in left-to-right order. Thus, in the above example, the Miranda system will first send the string "twinkle" to the standard output (usually the user's screen), then send the string "twinkle little star" to the file myfile. The actions of each of the sys_message constructors will be explained in detail in the following subsections.

The default message wrapper

The above discussion may seem somewhat disconcerting, since none of the example programs in the preceding chapters have required the top-level function of a program to produce a value of type [sys_message]. This is because they have all operated under a "default wrapper", which converts simple program output into a value of type [sys_message]. The default wrapper assumes that the output is meant to be displayed as a string on the screen. If the program produces the value x then it will silently be translated into [Stdout (show x)]. This works for a value of any type recognized by **show**.

This feature is particularly useful to enable rapid prototyping and separate module testing.

8.4.2   Writing to a file

So far, all the functions in this book have output their results to other functions or to the screen; hence the output data has not survived the Miranda session. It is easy to save this output data in a file using the sys_message constructor Tofile which takes a string representing the name of the output file (or device, such as a printer) and a string consisting of the output data.

The first time an element of the form *Tofile file data* appears in the sys_message list, the *file* is opened for writing and *data* is written to it: subsequent use of the same Tofile expression (most likely with new data) will cause the new data to be *appended* to the *file*. Note that, in keeping with the spirit of UNIX, if the *file* already exists then its old contents will be deleted before the new data is first written.

The following example copies the contents of a named input file to a named output file, discarding all "white space" characters. This is achieved by reading the entire input file, then removing all white space characters and then writing the result:

```
compresscopy ::   [char] -> [char] -> [sys_message]

compresscopy infile outfile
     = [Tofile outfile (xcompress (read infile))]
        where
         xcompress = filter (( ) .  isspace)
         isspace x = (x = ' ') \/ (x = '\t') \/ (x = '\n')
```

Appending to files

Sometimes, it is necessary to add to an existing file rather than write a new file.
This can be achieved using the constructor Appendfile, which takes a string representing the name of a file that will have data concatenated to it. This element
must appear in the sys_message *before* any Tofile element that writes to file.

```
add_to_diary ::   [char] -> [sys_message]

add_to_diary message
            = [Appendfile "diary", Tofile "diary" message]
```

8.4.3   Formatted output

Data values other than character lists, can be written to output files using **show**.
For example:

```
writeint ::   [char] -> num -> [sys_message]

writeint outfile n = [Tofile outfile (show n)]
```

Two restrictions apply:

1. Infinite data values cannot be written to a file.
2. The **show** keyword only works for known types. It will not work for functions,
   and abstract types require the special treatment described in Chapter 7.

If **show** did not exist then it would be necessary to write separate functions to
convert values to character lists; thus the above example could be written as:

```
writeint ::   [char] -> num -> [sys_message]

writeint outfile n
     = [Tofile outfile (int_to_string n)]
         || using int_to_string as shown in Chapter 2
```

Notice that any data written to a file using **show** is stored in a form that is appropriate for subsequent reading by using **readvals**. However, it is generally considered bad style to have the same file open for both reading and writing during a program. This is because of the danger of accidentally overwriting data that has not yet been read.

Closing files

The constructor `Closefile` takes a string giving the name of a file and, assuming the file has previously been opened by a `Tofile` message, it will close that file.

In practice, explicit file closing is normally unnecessary because all files are normally closed on exit from the Miranda prompt. Nonetheless, there are three situations where it is necessary:

1. Where it is required to read from and write to the same file within a single program; it is normally necessary and advisable to close the file after writing and before reading (or vice versa).

2. Where the number of files open exceeds the operating system limits.

3. Where it is required to flush the output to the file, to ensure all data has been written.

8.5   Special streams

Miranda i/o was designed with the UNIX operating system in mind, and follows the UNIX approach of having three "special" files, the standard input (normally representing the user's keyboard), the standard output (normally the user's screen) and the standard error output (also normally the user's screen). These special files are automatically opened at the start of any UNIX process which has been started from the standard UNIX command interpreter (the "shell") and provide convenient communication with the terminal. Thus, a Miranda session will always start with these three files already open: the standard input is open for reading, the standard output and standard error output are both open for writing.

These three special files are sometimes called "streams" and are primarily used for *interactive* programming, as will be discussed later in this chapter. They may however also be redirected (at the UNIX command line), so that they are connected to files instead of being connected to the user's terminal; they may therefore be used to prototype file processing programs (input and output can initially be with the keyboard and screen, and then redirected to files once the program is working correctly).

8.5.1   Standard input

The special form $- is a list of characters representing the contents of the standard input. Multiple occurrences of $- always represent the same input. Hence $-++ $- reads data from the keyboard and duplicates it. Keyboard data entry is terminated by entering <control-D> *at the start of a new line.*

Formatted standard input

The use of $+ is the equivalent of using **readvals** with the name of a file denoting the standard input. For example:

```
Miranda foldr (+) 0 $+
```

will take a a sequence of numbers from the keyboard (one per line) up to the next <control-D> and then return their sum.

8.5.2   Standard output and standard error output

To send data to the standard output stream, the program should include the system message Stdout x as part of its result, where x is a value of type [char]. Similarly, data can be sent to the standard error output, using the system message Stderr x. If it is necessary to send a number to the standard output or standard error output streams, it should first be formatted as a string:

```
Miranda [Stdout "hello"]
hello

Miranda [Stderr (show (300 + 45))]
345
```

In each of the above examples the result will appear on the user's screen. Sometimes it is necessary to clear the screen before displaying messages, this will be explained in the next subsection.

The "System" message

It is possible to send commands to the UNIX operating system by using System messages as part of the output of the program. This message takes a string argument which is interpreted and evaluated by the UNIX command interpreter. For example, the program can clear the user's screen by using the message System "clear" as part of its sys_message list. Any valid UNIX command can be given:

```
Miranda [System "date"]
Sat May 14 14:51:07 BST 1994
```

```
Miranda [Stdout "The date is: ", System "date", Stdout " A.D."]
The date is: Sat May 14 14:51:07 BST 1994
A.D.
```

Note that in the last example the date printed by the system includes a newline: thus, the characters " A.D." appear on the next line.[6] Finally, notice that the command evaluated by the operating system might not produce any visible output:

```
Miranda [Stdout "Start:", System "mv a b", Stdout ":End"]
Start::End
```

The "Exit" message

When a UNIX process terminates it may return an exit status number to the operating system. This can be achieved with the system message `Exit x` where x is a number between 0 and 127. As soon as `Exit` is detected in the output of the program, the program is terminated. Thus, any system messages following `Exit` will be ignored. An exit value of zero usually indicates that the program has terminated with no errors.

If a program ends without using the `Exit` system message, Miranda will generate an exit value of 0 for normal exit and 1 for program exit due to an error.

8.6   Interaction

Interactive programs must interact with the user's terminal—to accept input from the keyboard and to print output to the screen. Most terminals provide a character-based interface to the program; that is, the keyboard produces characters and the screen will accept characters. Since there is no way to tell in advance how many characters a user will type at the keyboard, Miranda treats the data coming from the keyboard as a (potentially infinite) list of characters; output is treated similarly. Thus, an interactive Miranda program should have the type `[char] -> [char]`.

The `[char] -> [char]` paradigm is simple and convenient. However, it is necessary to keep in mind the following two points:

1. As explained previously with regard to file output, *all* output must be channelled through the topmost function.
2. It is necessary for the programmer to specify the precise order in which user interaction should take place.

---

[6]If it is required to format the output from a UNIX command then the program should use the `system` function discussed in Section 7 of this chapter.

8.6.1   Specifying a dialogue sequence

The user dialogue is one of the few places[7] in a Miranda program where the specification of evaluation order is necessary; in the rest of the program it is normally sufficient merely to specify how results will be combined to produce a new value and leave the evaluation sequence to Miranda.

Miranda determines the evaluation order by inspecting the data dependencies implied by the program. For example, in the expression ((3 * 4) + 5) the addition operator cannot proceed until the values of both of its operands are known and so the multiplication must take place before the addition. In the example (2 + (fst ((3 * 4), (5 / 6)))), the function fst does not need to know the result of the division and so the division is never done (this is lazy evaluation); however, the addition needs to know the result of the multiplication and so the multiplication is done before the addition. Finally, note that the Miranda system is free to choose an evaluation order at random where there are alternatives. For example, in the expression ((4 * 5) + (6 * 7)) both multiplications must be done before the addition, but which multiplication happens first is not defined. Normally, the Miranda programmer need never be concerned about such operational issues, but it becomes important when dealing with the interactive part of a program, as shown in the rest of this section.

There are two simple ways in which a programmer can force Miranda to evaluate one expression before another:

1. Use function composition. For example, in the expression ((f . g . h) 45) the application of the function h will be evaluated first, followed by the application of g to the intermediate result, followed by f. Lazy evaluation will still mean that only the necessary parts of the data will be evaluated, but now the programmer has some control over the order in which function applications are considered.
2. Use pattern matching, since if an argument must be checked against any pattern other than a formal parameter name then it must be evaluated at least enough to determine whether it matches, and furthermore this evaluation must happen *before* the function body is evaluated.

Simple interaction example

The following simple example demonstrates a dialogue with the user where the program waits for the user to type a line and then prints the date; it does this repeatedly until the user types <control-D>. The correct sequence of question and response is guaranteed by the use of pattern matching:

---

[7]Control of evaluation order may be necessary for advanced program optimisation (which is beyond the scope of this book) and perhaps where the program interacts with the outside world using read or system—see Section 8.7.

```
prompt = "Please enter something:   "
msg = "Here is the date:   "

loop [] = [Stdout "\nGoodbye"]
loop (any:rest) = Stdout msg :   System "date"
                        :   Stdout prompt :   (loop rest)

main = Stdout prompt :   (loop $-)
```

By contrast, the following example gets the sequencing wrong and prints the first date before it is requested:

```
prompt = "Please enter something:   "
msg = "Here is the date:   "

wrongloop ip
        = Stdout msg :   System "date"
              :   Stdout prompt :   wrongloop (tl ip)

main = Stdout prompt :   (wrongloop $-)
```

The above error is quite understandable, since the output of the program does not depend on the value of the data entered by the user. This highlights the difference between programming the interactive part of a program (where the correct sequence of operations is of primary importance) and the body of the program (where values are of primary importance).

8.6.2   Using a menu

A common user interface is to present the user with a menu of items and ask the user to choose one item (perhaps an action) by entering a number. A simple example of this behaviour is illustrated in the following program which mimics a drink-vending machine. Of course, there are no real drinks on offer; it is a "virtual" vending machine. This program will be presented as four different versions: the first two will illustrate two equivalent ways to implement a single menu and the second two will illustrate two equivalent ways to implement a more complex program with three menus.

The user interface for the program with just one menu is simple:

1. First, the user is presented with a choice of either Tea, Coffee, Soup or Quit. The user makes a choice by entering a number (1, 2, 3 or 4) and the computer prints an acknowledgement on the screen.
2. If the choice was 4 (for Quit) the program stops. Otherwise, it loops and prints the menu again.

The above interaction between human and computer will be the same in both of the following two examples. The common code shared between the two examples is now presented:

```
Screen messages for first two vending program examples:

> welcome ::  [char]
> welcome
>   = "Welcome to the Virtual Vending Machine\n\n"
>       ++ "You may choose from the following menu:\n\n"
>       ++ "1.  Tea\n2.  Coffee\n3.  Soup\n"
>       ++ "4.  Quit\n" ++ request

> request ::  [char]
> request
>   = "Please enter the number of your choice:  "

Message to confirm the user's choice:

> confirm ::  [char] -> [sys_message]
> confirm choice
>   = Stdout [("\nThank you for choosing "
>                ++ choice ++ ".\n")]

Leave the program, with ok exit status:

> quit ::  [sys_message]
> quit = [Stdout "End of program\n", Exit 0]
```

Preformatted menu input

If it is clear that the user will always enter values of the same type (for example, if the user can only enter numbers in response to menus) then it is appropriate to use the $+ special form to represent the input. Miranda will automatically interpret the characters typed at the keyboard and translate them into values of the correct type. Remember that the user must always press the Return key to send the input to the program and if the user enters a value that cannot be interpreted then Miranda will issue a warning and wait for input of the correct type.

```
>|| version 1 of vending program

> vend ::  [sys_message]
> vend = (System "clear" ) :   dialogue $+

> dialogue ::   [num] -> [sys_message]
> dialogue ip
>    = [Stdout welcome] ++ (next sel)
>      where
>      (sel :  rest) = ip
>        next 1 = confirm "tea" ++ dialogue rest
>        next 2 = confirm "coffee" ++ dialogue rest
>        next 3 = confirm "soup" ++ dialogue rest
>        next 4 = quit
```

In the above example, pattern matching on the input is done inside the **where**
block rather than in the formal parameter list for the function; this ensures that
the welcome message is printed *before* the program interrogates the keyboard. It
is instructive to run the following (wrong) version which will wait for user input
before printing the menu:

```
> vend = (System "clear") :   wrongdialogue $+

> wrongdialogue (sel :  rest)
>    = [Stdout welcome] ++ (next sel)
>      where
>        next 1 = confirm "tea" ++ wrongdialogue rest
>        next 2 = confirm "coffee" ++ wrongdialogue rest
>        next 3 = confirm "soup" ++ wrongdialogue rest
>        next 4 = quit
```

Exercise 8.4

Explain why the following attempt at vend is incorrect:

```
vend = (System "clear") : wrongdialogue $+
wrongdialogue ip = [Stdout welcome] ++ quit, if sel = 4
                 = [Stdout welcome] ++ (next sel), otherwise
                   where
                   (sel : rest) = ip
                   next 1 = confirm "tea" ++ wrongdialogue rest
                   next 2 = confirm "coffee" ++ wrongdialogue rest
                   next 3 = confirm "soup" ++ wrongdialogue rest
                   next 4 = quit
```

Program-formatted menu input

If the program expects the user to enter values of differing type in any order, then it is necessary to use the $- special form to represent the input. The user input will be available to the program as a list of characters which can then be interpreted according to the types of values expected. Remember that the user must always press the Return key to send the input to the program. When using $-, the end-of-line character representing the Return key will also be part of the input list of characters, and so the program must interpret this Return character.

The following version of **vend** employs $- to allow the user to enter words representing the desired drinks or to enter numbers representing the menu option. Notice that the **split** function discards the end of line character.

```
>|| version 2 of vending program

> vend ::   [sys_message]
> vend = (System "clear") :   dialogue $-

> dialogue ::   [char] -> [sys_message]
> dialogue ip
>    = [Stdout welcome] ++ (next sel)
>      where
>      (sel,rest) = split ip
>      next "1" = confirm "tea" ++ dialogue rest
>      next "tea" = confirm "tea" ++ dialogue rest
>      next "2" = confirm "coffee" ++ dialogue rest
>      next "coffee" = confirm "coffee" ++ dialogue rest
>      next "3" = confirm "soup" ++ dialogue rest
>      next "soup" = confirm "soup" ++ dialogue rest
>      next anyother = quit
>
>      split [] = ([],[])
>      split ('\n' :   rest) = ([],rest)
>      split (x :   rest) = (x :   a, b)
>      where
>         (a,b) = split rest
```

Plumbing multiple menus together

This third version of the vending machine program and the final version both have more than one menu. It will be seen that the correct sequencing of the dialogue between multiple menus requires the careful "plumbing" of both the user's input and the program's output.

These programs share an interface consisting of three menus:

1. Initially, the user is presented with a choice of either Tea, Coffee or Soup. The user makes a choice by entering a number (1, 2 or 3) and Miranda prints an acknowledgement on the screen.

2. If the user has chosen Tea or Coffee (but not if the user has chosen Soup), a second menu allows the user to choose Milk, Sugar, Milk and Sugar, or None. The user makes this choice by entering a number (1, 2, 3 or 4) and Miranda prints an acknowledgement on the screen.

3. Finally, the computer displays a message on the screen, followed by a menu which allows the user to choose either to exit the program or to choose another drink.

```
Screen messages for third & fourth vending programs:

> welcome :: [char]
> welcome = "Welcome to the Virtual Vending Machine\n\n"
>           ++ "You may choose from the following menu:\n\n"
>           ++ "1.  Tea\n2.  Coffee\n3.  Soup\n"
>           ++ "4.  Quit\n" ++ request


> request :: [char]
> request = "Please enter the number of your choice:  "


> menu2 :: [char]
> menu2 = "You may also choose from:\n" ++
>         "1.  Milk and Sugar\n" ++
>         "2.  Milk only\n" ++
>         "3.  Sugar only\n" ++
>         "4.  None of the above\n" ++ request


> menu3 :: [char]
> menu3 = "Enjoy your virtual drink!\n\n" ++
>         "Please enter 1 to exit or 2 for another drink\n"


Message to confirm the user's choice:

> confirm :: [char] -> [sys_message]
> confirm choice = [Stdout ("\nThank you for choosing "
>                  ++ choice ++ ".\n")]


Leave program with ok exit status, discarding surplus input

> quit :: [num] -> [sys_message]
> quit x = Stdout "End of program.\n" :  [Exit 0]
```

The rest of the program for version three is now presented. The `dialogue` function prints the first menu to the screen as before, and inspects the user's response by pattern matching on the input; this is done inside the **where** block in order to achieve the correct sequencing. However, if the user has chosen Tea or Coffee then a second menu must be displayed and the input must be further interrogated. Once this has been achieved, the `dialogue` function must present the user with a third menu and, according to the user's response, either terminate or recurse.

The third menu interaction is achieved in a straightforward manner by the function `check` inside the **where** block. The second menu interaction is, however, more complex because it involves the action of functions which are *not* part of the `dialogue` function. In general, it is not possible to know how much of the user input will be consumed by these separate functions and so the entire user input data must be transferred explicitly *into* the subsidiary function (this is sometimes called "downward plumbing"). Subsequently, the input data which has not been consumed must be transferred *out of* the subsidiary function as part of its result for further inspection by the `dialogue` function (this is sometimes called "upward plumbing").

In this example, the functions for tea, coffee and soup return the remainder of the input as part of their result tuple and the other part is the output to be sent to the user. This is another example of "upward plumbing", and it is important that the `dialogue` function should correctly sequence this data as part of the overall output of the program.

```
>|| version 3 of vending program (Page 1 of 2)

> vend ::   [sys_message]
> vend = (System "clear") :   dialogue $+

> dialogue ::   [num] -> [sys_message]
> dialogue ip
>    = [Stdout welcome] ++ next ++ (check rest2)
>      where
>      (sel :  rest) = ip
>      (next, rest2)
>           = ([tea, coffee, soup] !  (sel - 1)) rest
>      check xip = [Stdout menu3] ++ xcheck xip
>                  where
>                  xcheck (1:rest3) = quit rest3
>                  xcheck (2:rest3) = dialogue rest3
>                  xcheck any       = quit any
```

```
>|| version 3 of vending program continued (Page 2)

> tea ::   [num] -> ([sys_message], [num])
> tea ip
>   = (confirm "Tea" ++ [Stdout menu2] ++ next, rest)
>     where
>       (sel :  rest) = ip
>       next = acknowledge "Tea" sel

> coffee ::   [num] -> ([sys_message], [num])
> coffee ip
>   = (confirm "Coffee" ++ [Stdout menu2] ++ next, rest)
>     where
>       (sel :  rest) = ip
>       next = acknowledge "Coffee" sel

> soup ::   [num] -> ([sys_message], [num])
> soup ip = (confirm "Soup", ip)

> acknowledge ::   [char] -> num -> [sys_message]
> acknowledge d 1 = confirm (d ++ " with Milk & Sugar")
> acknowledge d 2 = confirm (d ++ " with Milk")
> acknowledge d 3 = confirm (d ++ " with Sugar")
> acknowledge d 4 = confirm d
```

Exercise 8.5
   Why is it necessary for check to have a **where** block, and why is confirm repeatedly
applied within acknowledge?

Menus using continuation functions

The final version of the vending machine program uses a general-purpose function
which takes the input stream, a message and a list of functions; it prints the message and reads the user's input (which must be a number), and then applies one of
the functions to the remainder of the input stream. The function which is applied
(often called a "continuation function", because it determines how the program will
continue) is chosen according to the number returned by the user. Note that the
whole user interface is mutually recursive; it is not easy to reason about and is difficult to test, since individual functions cannot be tested in isolation from the other

functions.[8] However, this style of programming user interfaces is enthusiastically promoted and supported by some other functional programming languages; it can also be generalized to encompass interaction with the operating system, with different continuation functions provided for successful and unsuccessful operations. This style of programming is sometimes known as "continuation-passing style", or just "CPS".

```
>|| version 4 of vending program

>vend ::   [sys_message]
>vend = (System "clear") :   dialogue $+

>dialogue ::   [num] -> [sys_message]
>dialogue ip
>   = gendialogue ip welcome [tea, coffee, soup]
>     where
>       tea newip = xdial "Tea" newip
>       coffee newip = xdial "Coffee" newip
>       xdial d newip
>         = confirm d ++ gendialogue newip menu2 (extras d)
>       extras d = map option [(d," with Milk & Sugar"),
>                              (d," with Milk"),
>                              (d," with Sugar"), (d,"")]
>       soup newip = confirm "Soup" ++ continue newip

>option ::   ([char],[char]) -> [num] -> [sys_message]
>option (drink, extra) ip
>     = confirm (drink ++ extra) ++ continue ip

>continue ::   [num] -> [sys_message]
>continue ip = gendialogue ip menu3 [quit, dialogue]

>gendialogue ::   [num] -> [char] -> [[num]->[sys_message]]
>                 -> [sys_message]
>gendialogue ip msg fns
>     = Stdout msg :   xdial ip fns
>       where
>         xdial [] fns = quit []
>         xdial (x :   rest) fns = (fns ! (x - 1)) rest
```

---

[8]The reader might notice that it implements a finite state machine (Minsky, 1967).

8.7   Advanced features

This section brings together various advanced Miranda features which either facilitate interaction with the operating system or provide greater control over the evaluation mechanism. Because all current implementations of Miranda are designed to run on the UNIX operating system (or a UNIX equivalent such as LINUX), the operating-system features discussed in this section are specific to UNIX.

8.7.1   Interaction with the Miranda evaluation mechanism

The Miranda lazy-evaluation mechanism provides a powerful computational model. However, it is sometimes useful to be able to encourage Miranda either to evaluate two expressions in a certain order, or to evaluate an expression more fully than it would otherwise. This manipulation of the evaluation mechanism is necessary either in the user-interface part of a program, in order to achieve a desired sequencing effect, or in the main body of a program, in order to optimize the efficiency of the code.[9]

In addition to function composition and pattern matching, Miranda offers two built-in functions:

1. The built-in function **seq**. This function has type:

   ```
   seq:: * -> ** -> **
   ```

   The **seq** function takes two arguments. It checks that the first argument is not completely undefined, which requires some evaluation of the first argument, but not full evaluation. It then returns the second argument as its result, so that the extent to which the second argument is evaluated depends on the context in which **seq** has been applied.
   The phrase "not completely undefined" means that if the first argument is a list then it will be evaluated to the extent that its length is known but its elements may still be undefined.

2. If the **seq** function does not provide sufficient evaluation of the first argument, it can be combined with the built-in function **force**. This function has type:

   ```
   force:: * -> *
   ```

   The **force** function forcibly evaluates all of its argument and then returns that argument's value as its result. Thus, **force** cannot be used on its own to enforce order of evaluation of one thing before another, but it can be used in conjunction with **seq**:

   ```
   fullseq x y = seq (force x) y
   ```

---

[9]However, issues of efficiency are beyond the scope of this book.

The functions `seq` and `force` evaluate their arguments to differing extents: `force` will return an error (or an undefined result) if evaluation any part of its argument returns an error (or is undefined), whereas `seq` can sometimes return a result which contains undefined parts. For example:

```
Miranda seq [(3 div 0)] 45
45
```

```
Miranda force [(3 div 0)]
[
program error: attempt to divide by zero
```

It is possible to get correct dialogue sequencing using `seq` instead of pattern matching. In the following example, the use of `seq` ensures that the first item of the standard input is evaluated before the program produces the next date:

```
prompt = "Please enter something:   "
msg = "Here is the date:   "

loop [] = [Stdout "\nGoodbye"]
loop ip
    = seq (hd ip) (Stdout msg :   System "date"
                        :   Stdout prompt :   (loop (tl ip)))

main = Stdout prompt :   (loop $-)
```

8.7.2   Interaction with UNIX

Subsection 8.5.2 showed how the *System* message could be utilized to ask the operating system to evaluate a command; any output from that command is printed to the standard output. This subsection shows how the output from an operating system command can be manipulated *inside* a Miranda program.

The built-in function `system` takes a string argument which is a command to be evaluated by the UNIX command interpreter. A new UNIX process is created[10] in order to run this command and the result of the `system` function is a three-tuple containing:

1. A string containing whatever data the program wrote to its standard output. This list of characters is created lazily—each character is available as soon as it is output by the program.
2. A string containing whatever data the program wrote to its standard error output. Each character in the list is available as soon as it is output by the program.

---

[10] The new process has its standard input closed, so that it cannot interfere with input to the Miranda program.

3. A number containing the exit status of the program (0 means that the program terminated correctly; any other value indicates that an error occurred). The number will always be an integer between 0 and 127. The number is only available after the program has finished.

The type of this function is therefore:

```
system :: [char]->([char],[char],num)
```

Note that Miranda's lazy evaluation of the first two elements of the above tuple means that it is possible for the Miranda program and the called program to run concurrently, with synchronizing pauses only necessary if the Miranda program tries to read data faster than the called program can generate that data.

If UNIX cannot evaluate the given command, the result returned by `system` will be (`[]`, `error_message`, `-1`), where `error_message` is some error message, indicating why the command failed.

Referential transparency and system

The function `system` provides a general mechanism for interfacing with the operating system. It is perhaps rather too powerful than is appropriate for a functional language. Recall that in a functional language one attempts to "program by value" rather than "program by effect", and it is precisely this value-oriented discipline that gives functional programs enormous advantages over imperative programs; functional programs tend to be shorter, more modular and easier to understand.

With the `system` function it is possible to introduce the "program by effect" style into a Miranda program; *this should be avoided!* The `system` function should only be used to gain information from the operating system, and never as a mechanism to cause some effect on the system outside of the Miranda program. It should be remembered that a functional program should only effect the rest of the system by means of system messages in the result of the program. Thus, to have an effect on the operating system, one should use the *System* message. By contrast, to gain information from the operating system one should use the `system` built-in function.

Despite the above discussion, some UNIX commands will by their very nature introduce a degree of referential opacity (the opposite of referential transparency) to a Miranda program. For example:

```
shared_def g x = y ++ y
                    where
                    y = g x

unshared_def g x = (g x) ++ (g x)

main = shared_def system "date"
```

The program above will read the date (which includes the current time) once and print out that value twice. However, if the program were changed so that the `main` function called the function `unshared_def` instead of `shared_def` then the date would be read twice and it is quite likely that the second reading would be different from the first. This demonstrates that `system` is not referentially transparent and should be used with great care!

8.7.3 Modifying UNIX interactive behaviour

In all the previous examples, the user has been required to press the Return key in order to send input to the computer program. Furthermore, every time the user presses a key on the keyboard this is displayed on the screen; this is done by UNIX, not by the computer program.

UNIX allows these two behavourial features (and many others) to be controlled by the program. This permits the programmer to develop a more direct interaction between the program and the user, as illustrated by the following simple program which provides a square board on the screen within which the user can manoeuvre. This simple form of interaction is the basis of many computer games, though issues of optimized screen control, the use of bit-mapped graphics and windowing systems are beyond the scope of this book.

In the following example, the system message `System "stty cbreak -echo"` contains the two instructions to UNIX:[11]

1. Allow each keyboard character to be input to the program when it is pressed (that is, do *not* wait for the Return key to be pressed before sending characters to the program).
2. Do not echo the keyboard character to the screen. In this example, this is just an aesthetic decision concerning screen display; however this feature is required for many applications, such as full-screen editors and to conceal password entry.

Note that at the end of the program, UNIX is instructed to return to "normal" behaviour by use of the system message `System "stty -cbreak echo"`. Also note that the modification of UNIX behaviour in this way is not suitable for the user once the program has finished and so the programmer must be sure that the program resets this behaviour *whenever the program terminates, for whatever reason.* The programmer should be particularly careful of the following causes of program termination:

1. Normal termination due to the end of input.
2. Normal termination due to some other reason (for example, the end of the game, if the program implements a game).

---

[11]This `stty` command will not necessarily work correctly for all versions of UNIX; readers are recommended to consult their local system documentation.

3. Termination due to a program-detected error (thus, use of the **error** function becomes more complex, as demonstrated in the example below).

4. Termination due to an error in the program being detected by Miranda (thus, the program should be thoroughly tested, especially for missing cases and the possibility of list indexes exceeding the bounds of the list, before being released to the user).

```
>|| Boardgame program:  places 'X' onto board (Page 1 of 2)

> main = [System "stty cbreak -echo"]
>           ++ (display board) ++ (dialogue board startpos $-)

> board = Board (rep 10 " ")
> startpos = (5,5)

> dialogue bd (x,y) ip
>  = xdial bd ip
>    where
>      xdial Error any = dialogue_over "Game error\n" 1
>      xdial b ('n' :  rest) = newpos (0,-1) rest
>      xdial b ('e' :  rest) = newpos (1,0) rest
>      xdial b ('w' :  rest) = newpos (-1,0) rest
>      xdial b ('s' :  rest) = newpos (0,1) rest
>      xdial b ('q' :  rest) = dialogue_over "Game over\n" 0
>      xdial b any = dialogue_over "Game error\n" 1
>
>      newpos (p,q) ip
>        = (display (setboard bd (x+p,y+q)))
>            ++ dialogue (setboard bd (x+p,y+q)) (x+p,y+q) ip

> dialogue_over m s
>      = [Stdout m, System "stty -cbreak echo", Exit s]

> abstype game_board
> with
>   board    ::  game_board
>   setboard ::  game_board -> (num,num) -> game_board
>   display  ::  game_board -> [sys_message]
>   dialogue ::  game_board -> (num,num) -> [char]
>                   -> [sys_message]

> board_type ::= Error | Board [[char]]
> game_board == board_type
```

```
>|| Boardgame program continued (Page 2)

> setboard Error (x,y) = Error
> setboard (Board bd) (x,y)
>    = Error, if (x<0) \/ (x>9) \/ (y<0) \/ (y>9)
>    = Board (take y bd ++ [setrow (bd!y) x]
>              ++ drop (y+1) bd), otherwise
>    where
>      setrow row x
>          = (take x row) ++ "X" ++ (drop (x+1) row)

> display Error = [System "clear",Stdout "ERROR\n"]
> display (Board bd)
>    = [System "clear",Stdout (lay newbd)]
>    where
>      newbd = [rep 12 '-'] ++
>              (map (++ "|") (map ('|' :)  bd))
>              ++ [rep 12 '-']
```

Exercise 8.6

Use the above board as the basis for a simple game of noughts and crosses (tic-tac-toe).

8.8 Summary

This chapter introduced tools to facilitate communication between the programmer and the world outside of the Miranda system. File input makes it possible to have programs that work on different data values, without artificially amending the script file; whilst file output allows the results of Miranda programs to be saved outside of a Miranda session. The chapter continued by introducing special files or streams for communicating with the keyboard and the screen, hence allowing for interaction with another user. The process of interaction requires careful consideration of the sequencing of function application via pattern matching or the use of continuation functions. Finally, some mechanisms for interacting with the operating system were discussed.

Chapter 9

Programming in the Large

This chapter introduces three mechanisms that extend the principles of modularity and abstraction discussed in previous chapters to facilitate large-scale program development. The first of these mechanisms is the (**%include**) directive, which allows a number of definitions to be grouped together in a script file as a single program block and then to be incorporated into another script file—thereby encouraging the reuse of existing software components. The second mechanism, the (**%export**) directive gives the programmer the option of making visible only those definitions that may be useful to other program blocks, and so hiding those definitions that are used solely within that particular block. It will be seen that this builds on Miranda's **where** facility by allowing an auxiliary function to be bound to many specified functions. Finally the (**%free**) directive enables the generalization of script files into program *templates*. Here, the full definition of certain identifiers is left unbound within the template and only completed when the template is included in another file. This has the major advantage of allowing different specializations of the template to cope with different problems.

9.1   The %include directive

A simple **%include** directive has the format:

>   *%include "filename"*

This will make available (that is, put into scope) the definitions that appear in the file *filename*, as long as all the definitions within *filename* are both *correct* and *closed*—that is, there are no unbound identifiers.[1]

---

[1] By convention, *filename* should have the suffix *.m*; otherwise Miranda will create an equivalent *.m* anyway. Note that, within the UNIX context, files can be included from the current directory, a named pathway or the default Miranda system directory. The reader is referred to Section 27 of the On-line Manual for further details.

This facility means that the various components of a large program can be developed separately (perhaps by different programmers) as separate scripts. These separate scripts can then be linked as and when necessary, rather than having one monolithic program. Furthermore, identifiable "libraries" of related objects (for example, a graphics-handling suite) can be developed and made available to other programmers.

%include usage

A number of points about **%include** usage are worth noting:

1. A script file can contain any number of **%include** directives; they can appear anywhere in the file, but a good policy is to place them at the start of the file.
2. **%include** directives cannot appear within **where** constructs; they are top-level objects, like type declarations.
3. Nested **%include** directives are permitted to a reasonable depth of nesting. In other words, an included file can include other **%include** directives, which themselves may include others and so on—as long as no inclusion circularity exists.
4. The definitions of an included file are restricted in scope to the file that *directly* includes them. They are not inherited by a file that includes the includer. Hence, if *file1* is included by *file2* which is, in turn, included by *file3* then the definitions of *file1* are visible to *file2* but not to *file3*. This has the advantage of allowing the whole of *file1*'s definitions to be local to *file2*, without causing name clashes within *file3*.

9.1.1 Avoiding name clashes

Miranda allows two qualifications to the **%include** directive in order to avoid potential name clashes between the *included* file and the *including* file (or indeed any other included file).

Firstly, an *alias* can be used to rename an included identifier (which can be a type name or a constructor). The general format is:

%include "filename" newname1/oldname1 newname2/oldname2 ...

Thus, the identifier *oldname1* within the file *filename* is renamed *newname1*. If a constructor is aliased and the associated **show** function for its type is included, then the definition of the **show** function will automatically be modified to work with the new alias for the constructor name.

Secondly, it is possible to drop any unwanted definition from the include file, the general format is:

> *%include "filename" -dropped1 -dropped2 ...*

This guarantees that the definitions within *filename* for *dropped1* and *dropped2* etc., are not included within the current script file and hence they can have alternative definitions. Note that, although it is permitted to alias type names and constructors (see above), they cannot be dropped.

Incorporating the Standard Environment

The Standard Environment is included into *every* script file, and it is currently *not* possible to include it explicitly, nor to rename or drop any of its components.

9.2   The %export directive

By default, a **%include** directive will incorporate *all* the top-level contents of the included file. The **%export** directive can be used in the included file to modify this default to specify which components are made visible to the including file.

A script file may have just one **%export** directive, which may take a number of optional qualifiers:

1. To export all definitions.
2. To export selected definitions.
3. To export included files.
4. To not export specified objects.

Exporting all definitions

For any script file, the default is that all of its top-level definitions will be visible to an including file. This can be made explicit by the following directive:

```
%export +
```

Exporting selected definitions

In order to restrict the scope of auxiliary definitions (that are only relevant within the exporting file), if the **%export** directive is followed by an export list of identifiers (which may be type names and constructor names) then only these will be visible within the including file.

The general format for the **%export** directive is:

> *%export function1 function2 type1 ...*

All other definitions within the exporting file become local to that file. This facility has the advantage over the **where** construct, in that a function or identifier can be made local to *several* other functions rather than just one.

Exporting included files

In order to override the safeguard that definitions from a **%include** file are only visible within the file that has included them, it is possible to export that included file. The following extract shows the advantages of this facility to combine existing modules into a new module:

```
%include "graphicslib"
%include "matrixlib"
%export "graphicslib" "matrixlib"
|| etc
```

Not exporting specific objects

Sometimes it may be more elegant to exclude certain functions from being exported, rather than provide an export list. The following program extract first directs that all the definitions within the current file and *otherfile* be exported, and then directs that **f1** and **f2** should *not* be exported. Note that the excluded identifiers could be from the current file and/or *otherfile*.

> *%export + "otherfile" -f1 -f2*

9.2.1   Exporting types

The following subsection, provides a brief outline of the safeguards that Miranda provides for exporting types; the reader is referred to Section 27 of the On-line Manual for further details.

Type abstraction

Exporting an algebraic type name will *automatically* export all of its constructors. There is no way to override this mechanism; it is necessary to use the **abstype** mechanism (described in Chapter 7) in the exporting file to achieve the equivalent of data hiding.

Type orphans

It is illegal to export an identifier to a place where its type, or any part of its type, is unknown; this prevents "type orphans". Thus, if a script file *tree.m* provides definitions for an algebraic type *tree* * and a function *flatten_tree* :: *tree* * -> *[char]* then *tree* * *must* be exported if *flatten_tree* is exported.

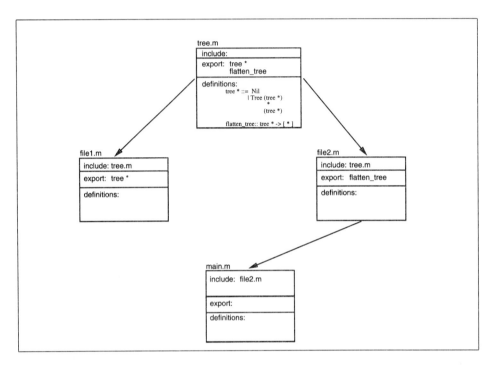

Figure 9.1 An illegal inclusion produces a type orphan.

If a function is exported without its type then the unbound type expression is known as a "type orphan". Figure 9.1 illustrates an illegal inclusion which causes Miranda to issue the following error message:

```
Miranda /f main
compiling main.m
checking types in main.m
MISSING TYPENAME
the following type is needed but has no name in this scope:
'tree' of file "tree.m", needed by: flatten;
typecheck cannot proceed - compilation abandoned
Miranda
```

Re-adoption of type orphans

If there are several levels of inclusion (recall that **%include** works transitively), then it would be possible for the above type *tree* * to be included into the main script from a different file to that which exported *flatten_tree*. Thus, the main script can "re-adopt" type orphans that would otherwise be without a parent from the most immediately included file. However, the file which exported the function *flatten_tree* must have had the type definition for *tree* * in scope: *and both the main script file and the file which exported the function must derive the type definition from the same source file.* Miranda always recognizes when the same file has been included, however indirectly. Figure 9.2 illustrates a re-adoption of the type *tree.m*, thus solving the type orphan problem seen in Figure 9.1.

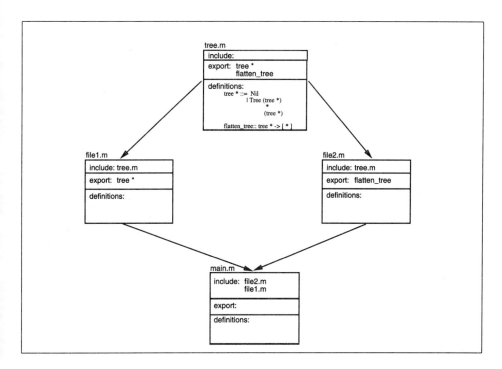

Figure 9.2 Re-adoption of a type orphan.

Type clashes

Two types with identical textual definitions but different source files will always be considered as different types and so give rise to a type clash. Furthermore, it is illegal for the same original type to be included twice into the same scope, even under different aliases.

9.2.2   Example: text justification

The example in the rest of this section discusses the design of a formatting module *justify*, to perform text justification. This module may be exported to become part of a text editor, and itself will include a number of tried and tested general-purpose functions that have already been collected into a library file.

Specification

The `justify` program will take a string of characters and a desired line width and transform it into a left and right justified text with lines of the desired line width. The last line will not be right justified. It is assumed that the selected line width is long enough to hold the longest word in the input string.

Target signature requirements

The first stage in the design of `justify` is to choose which objects will be shown to the outside world; this is simply the `justify` function itself; no other functions should be in scope outside of `justify`'s script file. This is achieved by the following directive:

```
%export justify
```

Now there will be no accidental name clashes or confusion with the other top-level functions within the including file.

Program design overview

The program follows a divide and conquer principle. The input text is considered as an unformatted paragraph with possible multiple spaces, blank lines (two consecutive newline characters) and lines of different width from the desired line width. The final output will have a fixed line width and regular spacing between each word.

The first step is to compress the "white space" characters (this has already been discussed in Section 5.2). Subsequently the text is split into lines, which are then split into words, which are output with at least one space between them.

Extra spaces must be added if a word straddles a line divide. In this situation, the word is shunted to the next line and the current line must be padded out with extra spaces to fill the gap. The program will evenly distribute extra spaces from the left; this is perhaps simplistic but the design makes a more elegant distribution quite easy to implement later.

Implementation

The script file (*justify.m*) for the justify program is now presented—it makes use of several functions to manipulate lists which are assumed to be contained within a general-purpose list manipulation library *listtools.m*. To avoid potential name clashes, the definitions within the *justify.m* file will be explicitly dropped from *listtools.m*.

The file *listtools.m:* contains functions which have not been given elsewhere in this text; these functions are now presented, followed by the main script file *justify.m*:

```
>|| Literate Script:  part of listtools.m

Contains:  a library of list manipulation functions


> isspace c = c = ' '

> occurs []      x = False
> occurs (front :  rest) front = True
> occurs (front :  rest) x = occurs rest x

> replicate n x = take n (repeat x)

note:  replicate is the equivalent
       of the built-in function ''rep''

> takeafter f []     = []
> takeafter f (front :  rest)
>          = rest, if (f front)
>          = takeafter f rest, otherwise


     etc
```

```
>|| justify.m (Page 1 of 2)

> %export justify
> %include "listtools.m"
>           -justify -compress -justifytext
>           -justifyline -splittext -splitline
>
> string == [char]
>
> justify :: num -> string -> string
> justify width text = justifytext width (compress text)

Warning:  it is assumed that each word in the text
is not greater than the specified width

Reduce multiple white space to a single space
and delete all leading and trailing white space

> compress :: string -> string
> compress line
> = (notrailing . xcompress . noleading) line
>   where
>     xcompress [] = []
>     xcompress (front : rest)
>       = ' ' : (xcompress (dropwhile isspace rest)),
>         if isspace front
>       = front : (xcompress rest), otherwise
>     notrailing = reverse . (dropwhile isspace) . reverse
>     noleading = dropwhile isspace

Split text and justify a line at a time, it passes
the number of gaps between words and the number of
leftover spaces

> justifytext :: num -> string -> string
> justifytext width text
>   = text ++ "\n", if (# text) <= width
>             || last line in paragraph
>   = (justifyline line gaps leftover)
>     ++ (justifytext width restoftext), otherwise
>     where
>       (line, leftover, restoftext) = splittext width text
>       gaps = occurs line ' '
```

```
justify.m continued (Page 2)

No extra padding needed if no more words or extra spaces
at least 1 space between words, otherwise

> justifyline ::  string -> num -> num -> string
> justifyline line gaps 0 = line ++ "\n"
> justifyline line 0 leftover = line ++ "\n"
> justifyline line gaps leftover
>   = word ++ (replicate (extraspaces + 1) ' ') ++
>       justifyline rest (gaps - 1) (leftover - extraspaces)
>       where
>         (word, extraspaces, rest)
>           = splitline line gaps leftover

Split the text and calculate the number of left over spaces
necessary to pad out line

> splittext ::  num -> string -> (string,num,string)
> splittext width text
>   = (line, leftover, restoftext)
>       where
>         revline = reverse (take (width + 1) text)
>         leftover = # (takewhile ((~) . isspace) revline)
>         line = take (width - leftover) text
>         restoftext = drop (width - leftover + 1) text

Split line and calculate extra spaces between words

> splitline ::  string -> num -> num -> (string,num,string)
> splitline line gaps leftover
>   = (word, extraspaces, restofline)
>       where
>         word = takewhile ((~) . isspace) line
>         restofline = takeafter isspace line
>         extraspaces = leftover div gaps,
>                     if leftover mod gaps = 0
>                   = (leftover div gaps) + 1, otherwise
```

9.2.3 Constraining include files

In the above program, *justify.m* dropped definitions from the included *listtools.m* file in order to avoid potential name clashes. An alternative approach is to set up an intermediate "header file" *header.m* which includes all of *listtools.m* and only exports those definitions needed by *justify.m*. The entire contents of *header.m* would be:

```
%include "listtools.m"
%export takeafter isspace replicate occurs
```

The directives at the top of *justify.m* would now read:

```
%include "header.m"
%export justify
```

Although this approach is slightly more complex, it has two major benefits:

1. The programmer only needs to know as much about the contents of the original included file as is required for their own program.
2. If the original included file is later modified to incorporate further definitions then there is no danger of any name clashes between these additions and the current program.

9.3 The %free directive

A Miranda script file may contain one **%free** directive to be used in conjunction with an **%export** directive (and an extended **%include** directive), which gives the programmer the opportunity to write a "template" containing incomplete definitions to be completed by an including file. This can be thought of as parameterizing the exporting file.

The general format used within the exporting file is:

%free signature

where *signature* is a sequence of specifications for identifiers which will be fully defined within an including file. In other words, these identifiers are "free" or unbound within the exporting file. For example:[2]

---

[2]Notice that the syntax of the free type declarations is the same as that of placeholder types, and indeed the two concepts are similar, in that they allow the program designer to defer implementation decisions. For placeholder types, Miranda expects just one final type definition: for free types, Miranda will accept different files with different definitions as long as they meet the free type template.

```
|| File:   queue.m

%free {
        queue * ::  type
        qmax ::  num
        }
        || etc
```

The general format for the including file is:

   %include "filename" bindings

where *bindings* is a semicolon-delimited sequence of definitions for the free identifiers in the included file. It may contain definitions for the free types using the type synonym mechanism (==), and definitions for other identifiers, using the token =.

   Hence, the above *queue.m* file, could have a corresponding including file with directives such as:

```
|| File:   receiver.m

%include "queue.m" {queue * == [num]; qmax = thismax;}

    || etc

thismax = 100
```

Here the free objects in *queue.m* are bound by the *receiver.m* file. In this case, the free type **queue** obtains a binding as a number list, and the identifier **qmax** is bound to **thismax**.

   The important advantage of a script which has been parameterized by a **%free** directive is that different bindings may be given for its free identifiers on different occasions. Thus a program, using the file *another_receiver*, might need **queue** to be a polytype and the value of **qmax** within *queue.m* to be the same as the value of **qmax** within *another_receiver*:

```
|| File:   another_receiver.m

%include "queue.m" {queue * == [*]; qmax = qmax;}

    || etc

qmax = 9000
```

The benefits of this approach are more fully apparent in Section 9.4, which presents an expanded version of the *grep* program, modularized into five files. The use of the **%free** directive and its associated **%include** directive will be seen in the two files *grep.m* and *main.m*. The program is then modified to deal with different meta-characters but, because of the parameterization, it is only necessary to modify the main file and the file dealing with these different meta-characters.

Rules for %free directives

The following rules hold when using **%free** directives:

1. All free types and identifiers must be exported; either explicitly in a **%export** directive or as the default behaviour of any included file.
2. The identifiers declared within a **%free** directive may denote types as well as values. When the file is included by another, bindings must be provided for *all* free identifiers. The bindings are given in braces following the pathname in the **%include** directive (before the aliases, if any), and each binding must be terminated by a semicolon.
3. The bindings for a parameterized script's free identifiers must be *explicitly* stated, even if the new name being bound is the same as the name formally defined to be "free" in the included file, as shown above with qmax. Another example of this explicit binding is given in Section 9.4.5, where the free type regexplist in the included file is bound to the type regexplist, which is in scope in the including file.
4. When a parameterized script exports a locally created type (other than a synonym type), each instantiation of the script by a **%include** is deemed to create a *new* type. This is relevant when deciding whether two types are the same for the purpose of re-adopting a type orphan.

9.4   Reusable software—grep revisited

The *grep* utility presented throughout the text is now extended as a comprehensive example of program construction using template files. The sublist and lex activities are separated and the primary grep function is parameterized on them. In addition to giving the program greater modularity, it has the advantage of making the sublist code *reusable*. It is now possible to change the "lexical analyser" so that it will recognize different representations of the meta-characters (for example, to deal with the UNIX Bourne Shell file-generation codes) without changing the sublist code.

The rest of this section continues the design shown in Chapter 3 to incorporate the other *grep* meta-characters. The inclusion of Range meta-characters leads to a slight revision in the way that regular expressions are represented and how any particular regular expression element is compared with its corresponding searched line character. However, the original search *strategy* remains essentially unaltered.

9.4.1   Program structure

The overall structure of this *grep* program is that of five interconnected files, as illustrated in Figure 9.3. These files communicate with each other as follows:

1. The file *types.m* exports definitions for common types and exports definitions for the functions `equal` and `notequal`.
2. The file *sublist.m* exports a definition for the function `sublist` but keeps the function `startswith` private.
3. The file *stdlex.m* exports a definition for the function `lex` but keeps many other functions private.
4. The file *grep.m* exports the function `xgrep`, which relies on the definitions of `sublist` and `lex`.
5. The file *main.m* is used to combine all the other files, to create the function `grep`.

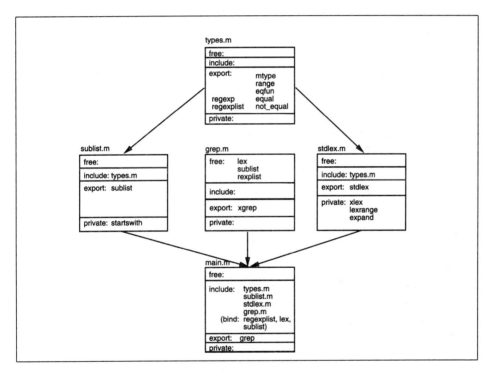

Figure 9.3 A large program divided into five files.

9.4.2 Incorporating "End of Line" and "Start of Line"

As shown in Section 3.9.2, the regular expression can be expressed as a list of pairs; the first component representing the type of match (zero or more, or one

BIRKBECK
LIBRARY
COLLEGE

only) and the second component the actual value to be matched. This principle can be extended to cater for the meta-characters to anchor a search to the start of a line (`^`) or to the end of a line (`$`). To anchor a match from the start of the line means that the **sublist** function is only applied once (that is, it does not recurse). Matching the end of the line can only succeed if the searched line is empty when the end of line meta-character is encountered (as the last element) in the regular expression list. These considerations give rise to an extended **mtype** algebraic type, with SOL for start of line and EOL for end of line:

mtype ::= ZERO_MORE | ONCE | SOL | EOL

The existing *grep* program must be changed in three places:

1. **lex**: to recognize the new meta-characters.
2. **sublist**: to anchor the regular expression match to the start of the search line.
3. **startswith**: to succeed in a match, if the search line is empty when EOL is met in the regular expression.

The actual code is presented in Section 9.4.5, after discussion of the other meta-characters.

9.4.3   Incorporating "Any" and "Range"

The final stage of the initial design is to incorporate the meta-characters for *any* and a *range* of characters. An initial case analysis shows all the possible combinations:[3]

Number of occurrences	Object affected
One Only	a given single character
Zero or More	a given single character
One Only	any single character
Zero or More	any single character
One Only	any single character from the range [...]
Zero or More	any single character from the range [...]
One Only	any single character not in the range [...]
Zero or More	any single character not in the range [...]

---

[3]Notice that "Zero or More of any single character in a range" does not constrain the pattern to be a number of occurrences of the *same* character from the range; rather, for each new occurrence, a different character may be chosen from the range.

Such an inspection reveals that the matching requirements of the new meta-characters are in fact quite similar to that of matching a single character.

Ranges

One method of treating a ranged regular expression element is to expand it into a list of valid characters, then check whether the current line position matches any of the characters in the list by using the function **member** (introduced in Chapter 3). For example the range "[b-e]" can be expanded into the range list "bcde" and "[a-d_1-3]" can be expanded to "abcd_123".

With this approach, a single actual value has the same representation as a single item range, for example "a" and "[a]" will both be represented as "a".

Negative ranges

Negative ranged regular expression elements such as "[^a-d]" (which imply that a single character should be chosen which may be any character *except* those in the range) can be treated in one of two ways:

1. A range list could be generated with all the values that are not in [a-d], that is ['e','f',...], and **member** can be used as a test for equality.

2. The range list [a-d] could be expanded to "abcd" and the truth value returned by **member** subsequently inverted.

Both options are equally valid. The first option probably requires extra initial work to construct the range list. The latter requires either additional match types NOT_ONCE and NOT_ZERO_MORE or an additional component to the regular expression tuple that indicates what to do with the result of **member**. The design followed here is the second option (using an additional tuple element) for reasons now discussed.

Any

On inspection it can be seen that the "." meta-character is really a convenient shorthand for the range "[\0 - \127]", which could be expanded accordingly. An alternative approach is to consider it in terms of *"not matching nothing"*, that is given **member** returns **False** for the empty list ([]) then "." really corresponds to the test ((~) . (member [])).

Type requirements

The latter method using `member` implies that a consistent treatment of all the wild cards and actual values can be achieved by representing a regular expression element as the triple (`mtype`, `eqfun`, `range`) with the predefinitions:

```
mtype ::= ZERO_MORE | ONCE | SOL | EOL
range == [char]
eqfun == range -> char -> bool
```

The equality functional type `eqfun` will either be `equal` or `notequal`, based on a membership function that maps a `range` and a `char` to a Boolean value. If `range` is a `[char]` then the built-in `member` function will suffice:

```
equal::eqfun
equal = member

notequal ::  eqfun
notequal r = ((~) .  (member r))
```

9.4.4   The program libraries

Figure 9.3 illustrates the division of the *grep* program into separate files. One of these files (*main.m*) combines the other files to form the program; the others are called "library" files.

The structure presented in Figure 9.3 demonstrates that the overall program need only export the `grep` function; this function will take a string (of type `[char]`) representing the raw regular expression and another string to be searched and returns a list of strings (of type `[[char]]`) that have been matched. Hence the file *main.m* need only export the following:

```
%export grep
```

The file *grep.m* holds the definitions of `xgrep` and `xgrep_pred`; only the former is exported to *main.m*. The code in *grep.m* requires definitions for `lex` and `sublist` and for the type `regexp`; these are defined in other files and must therefore be declared *free* in *grep.m*. Bindings for these names are given in *main.m* as part of the **%include** directive for *grep.m*.

The file *sublist.m* exports the function `sublist` and must include the file *types.m*, so that it may know details of the `regexplist` type, including:

1. The underlying `mtype` enumeration to enable meta-character pattern matching.
2. The `eqfun` datatype to deconstruct the embedded membership function.

The file *stdlex.m* similarly must include *types.m* and exports the function `stdlex`. The implementation of each of the five files is presented in the following section.

9.4.5   Implementation of the grep program

The *grep* program consists of four library files and one main file which combines the exported definitions from the library files and provides appropriate bindings. The implementation of these files is now presented.

The file types.m

```
>|| types.m:  contains type definitions for grep

> %export regexp regexplist mtype range eqfun equal notequal

A regular expression is held as a list of regexp triples
with an enumeration type for meta-character pattern matching
and range types a list of characters

> regexp == (mtype, eqfun, range)
> regexplist == [regexp]

> mtype ::= ZERO_MORE | ONCE | SOL | EOL

> range == [char]

Equality functions are derived from
the built-in member function:

> eqfun ::= Eqfun (range -> char -> bool)

> equal ::  eqfun
> equal = Eqfun member

> notequal ::  eqfun
> notequal = Eqfun f
>            where
>              f r = ((~) .  (member r))
```

The file sublist.m

The new versions of **startswith** and **sublist** are both held in the file *sublist.m*. The actual code is remarkably similar to the previous version (shown in Chapter 3) because the basic search strategy has not been altered:

```
>|| sublist.m

Contains:  definitions for sublist and startswith

> %include "types"
> %export sublist

Sublist determines whether a regular expression occurs
within a given text line.  It uses startswith.

> sublist ::  regexplist -> [char] -> bool
> sublist ((SOL, x, y) :   rest) line
>      = (startswith rest line)
> sublist expr line
>      = (startswith expr line) \/ xsublist line
>         where
>           xsublist [] = False
>           xsublist ( x :   lrest)
>               = (startswith expr lrest) \/
>                   (xsublist lrest)

Startswith determines whether a regular expression
occurs at the beginning of a given line of text:

> startswith ::  regexplist -> [char] -> bool
> startswith [] line = True
> startswith ((ZERO_MORE, x , y) :   regrest) []
>      = startswith regrest []
> startswith [(EOL, x , y)] line = (line = [])
> startswith rexp [] = False
> startswith ((ZERO_MORE,
>                 (Eqfun ismatch), chrange) :   regrest)
>                 (lfront :   lrest)
>      = startswith regrest (lfront :   lrest) \/
>          (ismatch chrange lfront &
>           startswith ((ZERO_MORE,
>                        (Eqfun ismatch), chrange) :   regrest)
>                        lrest
>          )
> startswith ((x, (Eqfun ismatch), chrange) :   regrest)
>                 (lfront :   lrest)
>      = ismatch chrange lfront &
>          startswith regrest lrest
```

The file grep.m

```
>|| grep.m

Contains:  definition for xgrep

> %free { regexplist ::  type
>          sublist ::  regexplist -> [char] -> bool
>          lex ::  [char] -> regexplist
>          }

> %export xgrep

The grep function returns those lines from text
which contain a match for the given regular expression:

> xgrep ::  [char] -> [[char]] -> [[char]]
> xgrep x text = filter (sublist (lex x)) text
```

The file stdlex.m

The code for the extended lexical analyser is a straightforward matter of listing which patterns have special meanings for *grep* and converting them to the appropriate format for the matching algorithms to manipulate. In problems of this nature, the technique of case analysis (discussed in Chapter 3) is of particular importance:

```
>|| stdlex.m (Page 1 of 3)

Contains:  definitions for stdlex, xlex, lexrange & expand

> %include "types.m"
> %export stdlex

This is the "standard" lexical analyser for grep.
The top-level function stdlex first checks
for the start-of-line pattern and then applies xlex:

> stdlex ::  [char] -> regexplist
> stdlex ('^' :  rest) = (SOL, equal, []) :  xlex rest
> stdlex p = xlex p
```

```
stdlex.m continued (Page 2 of 3)

xlex does most of the conversion from the meta-patterns
to their underlying representation based on
(mtype, eqfun, range) triples:

> xlex ::  [char] -> regexplist

> xlex []
>    = []
> xlex ('\\' :  ch :   '*' :  rest)
>    = (ZERO_MORE, equal, [ch]) :  xlex rest
> xlex ('\\' :  ch :  rest)
>    = (ONCE, equal, [ch]) :  xlex rest
> xlex ('\\' :  [])
>    = [(ONCE, equal, ['\\'])]
> xlex ('.'  :   '*' :  rest)
>    = (ZERO_MORE, notequal, []) :  xlex rest
>
> xlex ('[' :   '^' :  rest)
>    = rangepart :  (xlex exprest)
>      where
>       (rangepart, exprest)
>         = lexrange (notequal, []) rest
>
> xlex ('[' :  rest)
>    = rangepart :  (xlex exprest)
>      where
>       (rangepart, exprest)
>         = lexrange (equal, []) rest
>
> xlex ('.'  :  rest)
>    = (ONCE, notequal, []) :  xlex rest
> xlex (ch :   '*' :  rest)
>    = (ZERO_MORE, equal, [ch]) :  xlex rest
> xlex ('$' :  [])
>    = [(EOL, equal, [])]
> xlex (ch :  rest)
>    = (ONCE, equal, [ch]) :  xlex rest
```

```
stdlex.m continued (Page 3)

lexrange is called by xlex when a range pattern
(in square brackets) must be deciphered.
It evaluates to the underlying representation
for the deciphered range, plus the rest of the input
which is then scanned in a recursive application of xlex:

> lexrange ::  (eqfun,range) -> [char] -> (regexp,[char])
>
> lexrange (x,y) []
>   = error "lexrange error"
> lexrange (mfunc, chrange) ('\\' :  ch :  rest)
>   = lexrange (mfunc, ch :  chrange) rest
> lexrange (x, []) (']' :  rest)
>   = error "empty range"
> lexrange (mfunc, chrange) (']' :  '*' :  rest)
>   = ((ZERO_MORE, mfunc, chrange), rest)
> lexrange (mfunc, chrange) (']' :  rest)
>   = ((ONCE, mfunc, chrange), rest)
>
> lexrange (mfunc, chrange) (start :  '-' :  stop :  rest)
>   = error "bad range",
>       if (start > stop)
>   = lexrange (mfunc,(expand chrange start stop)) rest,
>       otherwise
>
> lexrange (mfunc, chrange) (ch :  rest)
>   = lexrange (mfunc, ch :  chrange) rest


expand is used by lexrange in order to create
all the characters in a range:

>expand ::  range -> char -> char -> [char]
>
>expand chrange start stop
>   = chrange ++ (map decode [(code start)..(code stop)])
```

The file main.m

A usable instance of *grep* program can now be created by including both the
sublist.m file and the *stdlex.m* file into an application file called *main.m*:

```
>|| main.m

Contains:  definition for grep

> %include "types"
> %include "sublist"
> %include "stdlex"
> %include "grep" {regexplist == regexplist;
>                          lex = stdlex; sublist = sublist;}

> %export grep

> grep ::  [char] -> [[char]] -> [[char]]
> grep = xgrep
```

Notice that the above binding `regexplist == regexplist` is obligatory. It is not
redundant, nor is it cyclic; the `regexplist` on the left of the `==` refers to the current
file and that on the right to the definition within the file that has been included.

The following session illustrates how the grep function might be used (the output
line has been broken for clarity):

```
Miranda grep "[a-d]c*h"  (lines (read "/etc/passwd"))
["bsmith::1033:30::/usr/users/bsmith:/bin/csh"]
```

9.4.6   Using a different lexical analyser

The UNIX Bourne Shell[4] has a number of meta-characters for file name expansion
that are similar but not identical to the *grep* meta-characters. The following table
can be compared to Table 3.9 for their differences. For example, it can be seen
that the wild card for a single character is different and there is no point in looking
for a file name anchored at the start of a line. Otherwise the ZERO_MORE, ONCE and
RANGE requirements are semantically the same, and so the `sublist` and `startswith`
functions can work equally well for a program that meets the Bourne Shell parsing
requirements as for the *grep* requirements.

---

[4]This is a job control language which provides an interface between the user and the UNIX
Operating System.

Table 9.1 Options for the UNIX *Bourne shell*

Character	Meaning
c	any non-special character c matches itself
\c	turn off any special meaning of character c
?	any single character
[...]	any one of characters in ...
	(e.g. 1-9 covers all ASCII values between 1 and 9)
[!...]	any one of characters not in ...
	matches any string (including the empty string)
New line	is not matched by anything

The above meta-characters can be emulated simply by writing another lexical analyser (called *bournelex.m*) and changing the **%include** directive and the bindings in *main.m*.

The new file bournelex.m

```
>|| bournelex.m:   (Page 1 of 2)


Contains:   bournelex, xlex, lexrange and expand

> %include "types.m"
> %export bournelex

This is the "Bourne" lexical analyser for grep.
It uses a meta-level syntax that is similar to
the filename generation syntax of the UNIX Bourne shell.
The top-level function bournelex just applies xlex

> bournelex ::  [char] -> regexplist
> bournelex p = xlex p

The functions xlex and lexrange behave similarly
to their grep equivalents, expand is identical
```

```
bournelex.m (Page 2)

> xlex ::   [char] -> regexplist
> xlex [] = []
> xlex ('\\' :   ch :   rest)
>    = (ONCE, equal, [ch]) :   xlex rest
> xlex ('\\' :   [])
>    = [(ONCE, equal, ['\\'])]
> xlex ('*' :   rest)
>    = (ZERO_MORE, notequal, []) :   xlex rest
> xlex ('[' :   '!' :   rest)
>    = rangepart :   (xlex exprest)
>      where
>        (rangepart, exprest) = lexrange (notequal, []) rest
> xlex ('[' :   rest)
>    = rangepart :   (xlex exprest)
>      where
>        (rangepart, exprest) = lexrange (equal, []) rest
> xlex ('?' :   rest)
>    = (ONCE, notequal, []) :   xlex rest
> xlex (ch :   rest)
>    = (ONCE, equal, [ch]) :   xlex rest

> lexrange ::   (eqfun,range) -> [char] -> (regexp,[char])
> lexrange (x,y) [] = error "lexrange error"
> lexrange (mfunc, chrange) ('\\' :   ch :   rest)
>      = lexrange (mfunc, ch :   chrange) rest
> lexrange (x, []) (']' :   rest)
>      = error "empty range"
> lexrange (mfunc, chrange) (']' :   rest)
>      = ((ONCE, mfunc, chrange), rest)
> lexrange (mfunc, chrange) (start :   '-' :   stop :   rest)
>      = error "bad range", if (start > stop)
>      = lexrange (mfunc, (expand chrange start stop))
>                  rest, otherwise
> lexrange (mfunc, chrange) (ch :   rest)
>      = lexrange (mfunc, ch :   chrange) rest

> expand ::   range -> char -> char -> [char]
> expand chrange start stop
>    = chrange ++ (map decode [(code start)..(code stop)])
```

The new file main.m

```
>|| main.m:  Contains definition for grep

> %include "types"
> %include "sublist"
> %include "bournelex"
> %include "grep" {regexplist == regexplist;
>                         lex = bournelex; sublist = sublist;}

> %export grep

> grep ::  [char] -> [[char]] -> [[char]]
> grep = xgrep
```

The new *grep* program now interprets the meta-level patterns in a different way:

```
Miranda grep "[a-d]c*h"  (lines (read "/etc/passwd"))
["adm:*:5:3:SGI Accounting Files Owner:/usr/adm:/bin/sh",
 "don:1h/87cnH8JbxH:16:10::/usr/users/don:/bin/csh",
 "SGIguest::998:998:SGI Guest account:/usr/people/guest:/bin/csh",
 "clack:3H/BFyMrLgGxM:1021:500::/usr/users/clack:/bin/csh",
 "macstuff:2J%Gh9xHnvBMh:1025:500::/usr/users/macstuff:/bin/csh"]
```

9.5   Summary

When "programming in the large", it is normally desirable to break the problem into manageable sub-problems, which themselves may be split further. This division should be reflected by encapsulating each sub-solution into its own script file. The communication between the files can be co-ordinated, using the features introduced into this chapter:

1. **%include**—to control the interface between files.
2. **%export**—to control the visibility of identifiers.
3. **%free**—to provide program templates.

By adopting this approach, large programs will be easier to code, test and modify, as shown in the development of the *justify* and *grep* programs. Furthermore, libraries of general purpose software components can be developed separately and then confidently reused as part of many other programs. This was demonstrated in the reuse of components from *grep* program to develop a Bourne shell filename expansion program.

Appendix A

The Initial Miranda Environment

This appendix provides information on three topics:

1. What names are allowable as identifiers.
2. Those names that are reserved and predefined.
3. The use of functions and type constructors in infix form.

A.1 Identifiers

An *Identifier* is a sequence of alphanumeric characters: including letters (A–Z, a–z), digits (0–9), underscores (_) or single quotes (') but *starting with a letter*. If the starting letter is *lower case* then the Identifier is used to name constants, functions and types (and is known as an *identifier*). If the starting letter is *Upper case* then the Identifier can only name a constructor (and is known as an *IDENTIFIER*).

A.2 Reserved and predefined names

Reserved names

The following names are reserved for use by the Miranda system and cannot be used as identifiers. They cannot be the names of formal parameters and they cannot be redefined within **where** blocks.

> **abstype div if mod otherwise**
> **readvals show type where with**

Predefined names

The following identifiers are predefined, and thus always in scope. They are available at the start of all Miranda sessions and constitute the *standard environment* of Miranda (release 2). For details of their functionality and possible implementation the reader is referred to the Miranda On-line Manual (Research Software, 1990).

In contrast to reserved names, these identifiers may be the names of formal parameters and may be redefined within **where** blocks. However, this practice is *not* recommended.

Predefined typenames
```
bool char num sys_message
```

Predefined constructors
```
False, True ::  bool

Appendfile, Closefile, Exit,
Stderr, Stdout, System, Tofile ::  sys_message
```

The undefined value
undef names the completely undefined value. Any attempt to access it results in an error message. Note that undef belongs to every type. It may be defined as:

```
undef ::  *
undef = error "undefined"
```

Predefined functions
```
abs and arctan cjustify code concat const converse cos decode

digit drop dropwhile e entier error exp filemode filter foldl

foldl1 foldr foldr1 force fst getenv hd hugenum id index init

integer iterate last lay layn letter limit lines ljustify log

log10 map map2 max max2 member merge min min2 mkset neg numval

or pi postfix product read rep repeat reverse rjustify scan

seq showfloat shownum showscaled sin snd sort spaces sqrt
subtract sum system take takewhile tinynum tl transpose until

zip2 zip3 zip4 zip5 zip6 zip
```

A.3   Functions as operators

The Miranda **$** token is the complement of the Miranda *section* facility, in that it is
possible to use functions or algebraic type constructors in an *infix* manner. For example, given the prefix function `implies`, which corresponds to *logical implication*,
then it may be used as an *infix* operator by preceding it with a **$**:

```
implies ::  bool -> bool -> bool

implies True False = False
implies any1 any2 = True
```

```
    Miranda False $implies False = False
    True
```

Notice that it is *not* possible to use the **$** token to create an infix function or
constructor:

```
not_infix_implies = $implies
```

```
    Miranda True not_infix_implies False
    type error in expression
    cannot apply bool to bool->bool->bool
```

Solutions to Exercises

Solutions for Chapter 2

Exercise 2.1

Provide a function to check if a character is alphanumeric, that is lower case, upper case or numeric.

One solution is to follow the same approach as in the function isupper for each of the three possibilities and link them with the special operator \/ :

```
isalpha c = (c >= 'A' & c <= 'Z')
            \/
            (c >= 'a' & c <= 'z')
            \/
            (c >= '0' & c <= '9')
```

An second approach is to use continued relations:

```
isalpha c = ('A' <= c <= 'Z')
            \/
            ('a' <= c <= 'z')
            \/
            ('0' <= c <= '9')
```

A final approach is to define the functions isupper, islower and isdigit and combine them:

```
isalpha c = (isupper c) \/ (islower c) \/ (isdigit c)
```

This approach shows the advantage of reusing existing simple functions to build more complex functions.

Exercise 2.2

What happens in the following application and why?

```
myfst (3, (4 div 0))
```

The function evaluates to 3, the potential divide by zero error is ignored because Miranda only evaluates as much of its parameter as it needs.

Exercise 2.3

Define a function dup which takes a single element of any type and returns a tuple with the element duplicated.

The answer is just a direct translation of the specification into Miranda:

```
dup :: * -> (*,*)
dup x = (x, x)
```

Exercise 2.4

Modify both versions of the function solomonGrundy so that Thursday and Friday may be treated with special significance.

The pattern matching version is easily modified; all that is needed is to insert the extra cases somewhere before the default pattern:

```
solomonGrundy "Monday"   = "Born"
solomonGrundy "Thursday" = "Ill"
solomonGrundy "Friday"   = "Worse"
solomonGrundy "Sunday"   = "Buried"
solomonGrundy anyday     = "Did something else"
```

By contrast, the guarded conditional version is rather messy:

```
solomonGrundy day = "Born", if day = "Monday"
solomonGrundy day = "Ill", if day = "Thursday"
solomonGrundy day = "Worse", if day = "Friday"
solomonGrundy day = "Buried", if day = "Sunday"
solomonGrundy day = "Did something else", otherwise
```

Exercise 2.5

Define a function intmax which takes a number pair and returns the greater of its two components.

```
intmax :: (num,num) -> num
intmax (x, y) = x, if x > y
              = y, otherwise
```

Exercise 2.6

Define a recursive function to add up all the integers from 1 to a given upper limit.

```
addints :: num -> num
addints 1  = 1
addints n  = n + addints (n - 1)
```

The terminating condition is the first pattern (the integer 1) and the parameter of recursion is n, which converges towards 1 by repeated subtraction. Note that `addints` fails if it is applied to a number less than 1. See also Chapter 2.9.

Exercise 2.7

Write `printdots` in an accumulative recursive style. This will require more than one function.

The accumulator will hold the growing sequence of dots; since the number n cannot be used for this purpose, another parameter is needed. This involves the definition of an auxiliary function to incorporate the accumulator:

```
printdots :: num -> [char]
printdots n = xprintdots (n, "")

xprintdots :: (num, [char]) -> [char]
xprintdots (0, dotstring) = dotstring
xprintdots (n, dotstring)
    = xprintdots (n - 1,  dotstring ++ ".")
```

Notice that the function `printdots` initializes the accumulator `dotstring` with an empty string.

Exercise 2.8

Write the function `plus` in a stack recursive style.

The parameter of recursion is y and the terminating condition is when y is 0. In this version, x no longer serves as an accumulator, but as the second operand to the final addition:

```
plus :: (num,num) -> num
plus (x, 0) = x
plus (x, y) = 1 + plus (x, y - 1)
```

Exercise 2.9

Write the function int_divide using only integer subtraction and addition.

The division is straightforward: what requires some thought is the handling of positive and negative values of the operands. Not every problem has an elegant pattern matching solution!

```
int_divide :: (num,num) -> num
int_divide (n, 0) = error "Division by zero"
int_divide (n, m) = error "Division: operands must be integers",
                    if ~ ((integer n) & (integer m))
               = posdiv (-n, -m),    if (n < 0) & (m < 0)
               = - (posdiv (n, -m)), if m < 0
               = - (posdiv (-n, -m)),if n < 0
               = posdiv (n,m), otherwise


posdiv :: (num,num) -> num
posdiv (n, m) = 0, if n < m
              = 1 + posdiv (n - m, m), otherwise
```

Note that the applications -(posdiv (n, -m)) and -(posdiv (-n, m)) must be bracketed to evaluate to a numeric result for the unary negation operator -. If the brackets were omitted then Miranda would attempt to apply - to the function posdiv rather than to its result.

Solutions for Chapter 3

Exercise 3.1

Give the two possible correct versions of wrong_y.

Either the first operand should be an integer or the second operand should be a list of integer lists:

```
correct_y1 = 1 : [2,3]
correct_y2 = [1] : [[2,3]]
```

Exercise 3.2

Which of the following are legal list constructions?

```
list1 = 1 : []
list2 = 1 : [] : []
list3 = 1 : [1]
list4 = [] : [1]
list5 = [1] : [1] : []
```

The correct constructions are list1, list3 and list5.

The construction list2 fails because : is right-associative. Thus, list2 is defined to be (1 : ([] : [])), which is the same as (1 : [[]]), which in turn is a type error because it attempts to join an integer to a list of lists.

The construction list4 fails because it attempts to add a list (in this case the empty list) to a list of integers, which causes a type error.

Exercise 3.3

Miranda adopts the view that it is meaningless to attempt to extract something from nothing; generating an error seems a reasonable treatment for such an attempt. What would be the consequences if hd and tl were to evaluate to [] when applied to an empty list?

The following equality would no longer hold for all values of alist:

```
alist = hd alist : tl alist
```

The equality would not hold when alist was [], since the right-hand side would evaluate to [[]].

Furthermore, such definitions for hd and tl would be totally incompatible with the Miranda type system; for example, any function which applied hd to a list of integers could not be sure whether the value returned was going to be an integer or a list!

Exercise 3.4

At first sight it would appear that show can be bypassed by defining a function that quotes its numeric parameter:

```
numbertostring :: num -> [char]
numbertostring n = "n"
```

Explain what the above function *actually* does.

All it does is produce the string "n". The quotation marks are *not* constructors, unlike the square brackets which denote the list aggregate format.

Exercise 3.5

Write a stack recursive function to add all numbers less than 3 which appear in a list of numbers.

```
addlessthanthree :: [num] -> num
addlessthanthree [] = 0
addlessthanthree (front : rest)
    = front + addlessthanthree rest, if (front < 3)
    = addlessthanthree rest, otherwise
```

BIRKBECK
LIBRARY
COLLEGE

Exercise 3.6

The following function listmax is accumulative recursive. Rather than using an explicit accumulator, it uses the front of the list to hold the current maximum value.

```
numlist == [num]

listmax :: numlist -> num
listmax [] = error "listmax: empty list"
listmax (front : []) = front
listmax (front : next : rest)
    = listmax (front : rest), if front > rest
    = listmax (next : rest), otherwise
```

Rewrite listmax so that it uses an auxiliary function and an explicit accumulator to store the current largest item in the list.

The explicit accumulator is initialized with the front of a non-empty list; the rest of the code is remarkably similar:

```
numlist == [num]

listmax :: numlist -> num
listmax [] = error "listmax: empty list"
listmax (front : rest) = xlistmax (rest, front)

xlistmax :: (numlist, num) -> num
xlistmax ([], maxvalue) = maxvalue
xlistmax (front : rest, maxvalue)
        = xlistmax (rest, front), if  front > maxvalue
        = xlistmax (rest, maxvalue), otherwise
```

Exercise 3.7

What happens if a negative value of n is supplied to the first version of mydrop ?

Eventually (front :   rest) will converge to [] and an error will be reported.

Exercise 3.8

Write the function shorterthan used by the final version of mydrop.

The approach taken is similar to that in defining the function **startswith** in Chapter 3.7.2. Both the number and the list converge towards terminating conditions, respectively, by the integer one and by an element at a time. Hence, zero indicates that there may still be items in the list, in which case the list cannot be shorter than the specified number. Conversely, [] indicates that the list is shorter than the number of items to be discarded.

```
shorterthan :: (num, [*]) -> bool

shorterthan (0, alist) = False
shorterthan (n, []) = True
shorterthan (n, front : rest) = shorterthan (n - 1, rest)
```

Exercise 3.9

Use structural induction to design the function mytake, which works similarly to mydrop but takes the first n items in a list and discards the rest.

The type of the function is:

```
(num, [*] -> [*])
```

The general case is:

```
mytake (n, front : rest) = ??
```

There are two parameters of recursion; the inductive hypothesis must therefore assume that take (n - 1, rest) evaluates to an appropriate list. The inductive step is to construct a list of the front value (which must be retained) with that list:

```
mytake (n, front : rest)
    = front : mytake (n - 1, rest)
```

The terminating cases are:

1. Taking no elements; this must just give an empty list:

```
mytake (0, alist) = []
```

2. Attempting to take some items from an empty list; this is an error:

```
mytake (n, []) = error "take: list too small"
```

Notice that asking for zero items from an empty list is covered by mytake (0, alist) and therefore this pattern must appear first.

The final code is:

```
mytake :: (num, [*] -> [*]

mytake (0, alist) = []
mytake (n, []) = error "mytake: list too small"
mytake (n, front : rest)
    = front : mytake (n - 1, rest)
```

This approach deals with negative numbers in the same manner as the first definition of mydrop.

Exercise 3.10

Write a function `fromto` which takes two numbers and a list and outputs all the elements in the list starting from the position indicated by the first integer up to the position indicated by the second integer. For example:

```
Miranda fromto (3, 5, ['a','b','c','d','e','f'])
['d','e','f']
```

To meet this specification, it is necessary to assume that it is possible to extract the first n elements from a list and that it is also possible to drop the first m elements from a list. Of course, it is quite feasible to write this function from first principles but a lot easier to reuse existing code:

```
fromto :: (num,num,[*]) -> [*]
fromto (m, n, alist) = mydrop (m, mytake (n,alist))
```

Exercise 3.11

Modify the `skipbrackets` program to cater for nested brackets.

```
stringtostring == [char] -> [char]

skipbrackets :: stringtostring
skipbrackets [] = []
skipbrackets ('(' : rest) = skipbrackets (inbrackets rest)
skipbrackets (front : rest) = front : skipbrackets rest

inbrackets :: stringtostring
inbrackets (')' : rest) = rest
inbrackets ('(' : rest) = inbrackets (inbrackets rest)
inbrackets (front : rest) = inbrackets rest
```

Notice the adjustment is minor; the nesting of brackets is a recursive requirement and its treatment is recursively achieved by matching the start of a nested bracket within `inbrackets`, which itself ignores brackets.

An alternative solution, though not recommended, would have been to use mutual recursion within `skipbrackets`, without changing the original definition of `inbrackets`:

```
notrecommended_skipbrackets [] = []
notrecommended_skipbrackets ('(' : rest)
    = inbrackets (notrecommended_skipbrackets rest)
notrecommended_skipbrackets (front : rest)
    = front : notrecommended_skipbrackets rest
```

As with mutually defined functions, it is quite difficult to reason how and why this function succeeds.

Exercise 3.12

It would appear that sublist no longer needs its first function pattern because this is checked as the first pattern in startswith. Explain why this is incorrect, and also whether the second pattern of sublist can safely be removed.

It is not safe to remove the first pattern because matching the empty regular expression with an empty line to be searched would now be met by the second pattern and incorrectly evaluate to **False**. The second pattern cannot be removed because it serves as the terminating condition for recursion along the line to be searched.

Exercise 3.13

An incorrect attempt to optimize the startswith program would combine startswith and sublist in one function:

```
stringpair = ([char], [char])

sublist :: stringpair -> bool
sublist ([], alist) = True
sublist (alist, []) = False
sublist ((regfront : regrest), (lfront : lrest))
    = ((regfront = lfront) & sublist (regrest, lrest))
      \/ sublist ((regfront : regrest), lrest)
```

This follows the general inductive case that the result is True if the front two items of the lists are equal and the result of a sublist search of the rest of the two lists is also True. Alternatively the entire regular expression matches the rest of the search line. Show why this approach is wrong.

The following application would erroneously evaluate to True:

```
sublist ("abc", "ab_this_will_be_ignored_c")
```

Exercise 3.14

Explain the presence of the final pattern in the function startswith, even though it should never be encountered.

The type **regtype** could have any number of possible strings, rather than just the strings "ONCE" and "ZERO_MORE"; the final pattern is intended to suppress the system warning message. A safer solution is presented in Chapter 6.2.4.

Exercise 3.15

What would happen if the second and third pattern in startswith were swapped?

The function would still produce the same results; the two patterns are mutually exclusive and it does not matter which appears first.

Exercise 3.16

Alter the sublist function so that "A*" matches the empty string.

The naive solution is to introduce an extra pattern as the new first pattern:

```
sublist ([("ZERO_MORE", alist)], []) = True
    ...
```

However, this does not cater for regular expressions of the form "A*B*". An easy solution is to ensure that **startswith** is always applied at least once; this solution is presented in Chapter 9.

Solutions for Chapter 4

Exercise 4.1

Give the types of the following compositions:

```
tl . (++ [])
abs . fst
code . code
show . tl
```

The first composition has the type: [*] -> [*] which shows that it is legitimate to compose partially applied functions. The second expression has the type (num,*) -> num, which shows that it is valid to compose functions which have tupled parameters. Notice also that **fst** is now only polymorphic in the second component of its parameter because **abs** expects a **num** parameter. The third composition is invalid because the **code** that will be applied second expects its input parameter to be a **char** but the **code** that is applied first produces a value of type **num**.

The final composition is interesting in that the expression could be used at the Miranda prompt:

```
Miranda  (show . tl) "abc"
bc
```

However, it would be illegal to attempt to use the expression on its own, as the right-hand side of a script file definition:

```
wrongshowtail = show . tl
```

This will result in an error because Miranda could not resolve the type of the overloaded **show** function.

Exercise 4.2

Theoreticians claim that all of the combinators (and consequently all functions) can be written in terms of the combinator K (cancel) and the following combinator S (distribute):

    distribute f g x = f x (g x)

Define the combinator identity (which returns its argument unaltered) using only the functions distribute and cancel in the function body. Provide a similar definition for a curried version of snd.

    identity = distribute cancel cancel
    || I = SKK

    curried_snd = distribute cancel
    || curried_snd = SK

Whilst the above are relatively straightforward, it is not always so easy to provide combinator expressions; for example compose, (B) is defined as:

    compose = distribute (cancel distribute) cancel
    || B = S (KS) K

and the simplest combinator expression for swap, (C) is:

    swap = distribute (compose compose distribute) (cancel cancel)
    || C = S (BBS) (KK)

Exercise 4.3

Explain why make_curried cannot be generalized to work for functions with an arbitrary number of tuple components.

This is because all functions must have a well-defined source type and therefore must have either a fixed number of curried arguments or a tuple of fixed size. A separate conversion function is therefore necessary for all the uncurried functions with two arguments, another for all the uncurried functions of three arguments, and so on.

Exercise 4.4

Write the function make_uncurried which will allow a curried, dyadic function to accept a tuple as its argument.

This is the mirror of make_curried:

    make_uncurried :: (* -> ** -> ***) -> (*,**) -> ***

    make_uncurried ff (x,y) = ff x y

Exercise 4.5

The built-in function `fst` can be written using `make_uncurried` and the `cancel` combinator:

```
myfst = make_uncurried cancel
```

Provide a similar definition for the built-in function `snd`.

The function `snd` can be thought of as `fst` with its parameters swapped, that is:

```
mysnd = make_uncurried (swap cancel)
```

A hand evaluation reveals:

```
mysnd (1,2)
==> make_uncurried (swap cancel) (1,2)
==> (swap cancel) 1 2
==> swap cancel 1 2
==> cancel 2 1
==> 2
```

Exercise 4.6

Explain why `myiterate` is non-robust and provide a robust version.

The function should check that n is a *positive integer*; the best way to achieve this is to separate the validation from the processing:

```
myiterate :: num -> (* -> *) -> * -> *
myiterate n ff result
    = error "myiterate", if  n < 0  \/ not (integer n)
    = xmyiterate n ff result, otherwise
```

where the auxiliary function `xmyiterate` is the same as the original version of `myiterate`. Chapter 5 shows how the auxiliary function can be tightly coupled to the new version of `myiterate`.

Exercise 4.7

Imperative programming languages generally have a general-purpose iterative control structure known as a "while" loop. This construct will repeatedly apply a function to a variable whilst the variable satisfies some predefined condition. Define an equivalent function in Miranda.

This function can be written directly from its informal specification:

```
whiletrue :: (* -> bool) -> (* -> *) -> * -> *
whiletrue pred ff state
    = whiletrue pred ff (ff state), if pred state
    = state, otherwise
```

Here the predefined condition is the guard **pred state**, the repeated application is the recursive application of **while**, with the application **ff state** representing the change in the variable.

Note that there is no guarantee that the condition (**pred state**) will ever be satisfied. This is a general problem of computing, known as the *halting problem*. Stated briefly, it is impossible to write a program that will infallibly determine whether an arbitrary function (given some arbitrary input) will terminate or loop forever. One consequence is that there is no point in attempting excessive and unnecessary validation of such general-purpose iterative constructs as **whiletrue**.

Exercise 4.8

In the definition of map_two, source lists of unequal length have been treated as an error. It is an equally valid design decision to truncate the longer list; amend the definition to meet this revised specification.

This is a trivial task; the last error-handling pattern can be converted to have an action that returns the empty list. This pattern also caters for the case of both lists being empty.

```
map_two (* -> ** -> ***) -> [*] -> [**] -> [***]
map_two ff (front1 : rest1) (front2 : rest2)
      = (ff front1 front2) : map_two ff rest1 rest2
map_two ff alist blist = []
```

Note that this function has the same behaviour as the Standard Environment function **zip2**.

Exercise 4.9

Write a function applylist which takes a list of functions (each of type *->**) and an item (of type *) and returns a list of the results of applying each function to the item. For example: applylist [(+ 10),(* 3)] 2 will evaluate to [12,6].

This function has a similar shape to **map**, only here it is the head of the list that is applied to the first parameter rather than vice versa:

```
applylist :: [* -> **] -> * -> [**]
applylist [] item = []
applylist (ffront : frest) item
          = (ffront item) : applylist frest item
```

Exercise 4.10

Explain why the following definitions are equivalent:

```
f1 x alist = map (plus x) alist
f2 x = map (plus x)
f3 = (map . plus)
```

The definition of f2 is that of a partially applied function; Miranda can infer that it requires an extra list parameter from the type of map.

The definition of f3 makes use of the following equivalence:

$$(f \ . \ g) \ x = f \ (g \ x)$$

In this case f is map and g is plus and the x can be discarded for the same reason as in the definition of f2.

To a certain extent, it is a matter of taste which function should be used; f1 has the advantage that *all* of its arguments are visible at the function definition, whilst f3 has the advantage of brevity and perhaps the fact that the programmer can concentrate on what the function does rather than what it does it to. There are no absolute guidelines, but it is important to be able to read all three kinds of definitions. Finally, notice that the type of each function is the same, that is:

```
num -> [num] -> [num]
```

Exercise 4.11

Rewrite the function map in terms of reduce.

This is simply done by generalizing the code in the text:

```
map_inc = reduce ((:) . inc) [])
```

That is, by replacing the specific function inc with a polymorphic parameter:

```
reduce_map :: (*->**) -> [*] -> [**]
reduce_map ff = reduce ((:) . ff) []
```

Now reduce_map can be used in exactly the same way as map:

```
map_inc :: (num->num)->[num]->[num]
map_inc = reduce_map inc
```

Exercise 4.12

Some functions cannot be generalized over lists, as they have no obvious default value for the empty list; for example, it does not make sense to take the maximum value of an empty list. Write the function reduce1 to cater for functions that require at least one list item.

It is clear from the specification that an empty list must be considered an error, otherwise the first item in the list can be used as the default value to reduce. This is a good example of reusing code.

```
reduce1 :: (* -> * -> *) -> [*] -> [*]
reduce1 ff [] = error "reduce1"
reduce1 ff (front : rest) = reduce ff front rest
```

Exercise 4.13

Write two curried versions of mymember (as specified in Chapter 3.6), using reduce and accumulate, respectively, and discuss their types and differences.

The **reduce** version is straightforward and uses the prefix, curried functions defined in Chapter 4.1.2:

```
reduce_member alist item
      = reduce (either . (equal item)) False alist
```

A hand evaluation of (reduce_member [1,2,3] 1) shows:

```
reduce_member [1,2,3] 1
==> reduce (either . (equal 1)) False [1,2,3]
==> ((either . (equal 1)) 1) (reduce (either . (equal 1)) False [2,3])
==> (either (equal 1 1)) (reduce (either . (equal 1)) False [2,3])
==> either True (reduce (either . (equal 1)) False [2,3])
==> True \/ (reduce (either . (equal 1)) False [2,3])
==> True
```

The **accumulate** version is less straightforward; this is not an example where **accumulate** can be safely substituted for **reduce**. An attempt to define member as:

```
accumulate_member alist item
      = accumulate (either . equal item) False alist
```

will only work if item and the elements of alist are of type bool. This is easily verified by checking the type of the above function:

```
Miranda accumulate_member ::
[bool] -> bool -> bool
```

For example, a hand evaluation of accumulate_member to a list [a,b,c] (where the list elements are of arbitrary type) shows:

```
accumulate_member [a,b] item
==> accumulate (either . equal item) False [a,b]
==> accumulate (either . equal item) ((either . equal item) False a) [b]
==> accumulate (either . equal item) (either (equal item False) a) [b]
==> error or item must be of type bool, since equal
    expects both its arguments to be of the same type
```

In order to make the function more general, the default value **False** must become the second of the parameters to the functional argument. This is easily achieved using the **swap** combinator:

```
accumulate_member :: [*] -> * -> bool
accumulate_member alist item
      = accumulate (swap (either . (equal item))) False alist
```

A hand evaluation of (accumulate_member [1,2,3] 1) now shows:

```
accumulate_member [1,2,3] item
==> accumulate (swap (either . (equal 1))) False [1,2,3]
==> accumulate (swap (either . (equal 1)))
               (swap (either . (equal 1)) False 1) [2,3]
==> accumulate (swap (either . (equal 1)))
               ((either . (equal 1)) 1 False) [2,3]
==> accumulate (swap (either . (equal 1)))
               (either (equal 1 1) False) [2,3]
==> accumulate (swap (either . (equal 1))) (True \/ False) [2,3]
==> accumulate (swap (either . (equal 1))) True [2,3]
==> ...
```

Exercise 4.14

Define the function `mydropwhile` which takes a list and a predicate as arguments and returns the list without the initial sublist of members which satisfy the predicate.

This function has same behaviour as the Standard Environment `dropwhile` and can be written using the same approach as the function `takewhile`:

```
mydropwhile :: (* -> bool) -> [*] -> [*]
mydropwhile pred  [] = []
mydropwhile pred (front : rest)
    = mydropwhile pred rest, if pred front
    = (front : rest), otherwise
```

Exercise 4.15

The *set* data structure may be considered as an unordered list of unique items. Using the built-in functions `filter` and `member`, the following function will yield a list of all the items common to two sets:

```
intersection :: [*] -> [*] -> [*]
intersection aset bset = filter (member aset) bset
```

Write a function `union` to create a set of all the items in two sets.

The union of two sets can be considered as all the members of the first set that are *not* in the second set, together with that second set. The answer makes use of the design for `intersection`, but inverts the truth value of the predicate to `filter` in order to exclude common members (by means of the composition of ~with `member`):

```
union :: [*] -> [*] -> [*]
union aset bset = aset ++ filter ((~) . (member aset)) bset
```

An alternative specification is to remove the duplicates from the result of appending the two sets.

Exercise 4.16

An equivalent version of `stringsort` using `accumulate` would require that the arguments to (`insert lessthan`) be reversed. Why is this the case?

For the same reasons as discussed with the accumulative version of member. The default value [] becomes the first argument to the (`insert lessthan`) and an attempt would be made to compare it with an actual value. This will only work if that value is also an empty list.

Exercise 4.17

A function `foldiftrue` which reduces only those elements of a list which satisfy a given predicate could be defined as:

```
foldiftrue :: (* -> bool) -> (* -> ** -> **) -> ** -> [*]
foldiftrue pred ff default [] = default
foldiftrue pred ff default (front : rest)
     = (ff front (foldiftrue pred ff default rest)), if pred front
     = foldiftrue pred ff default rest, otherwise
```

Write this function in terms of a composition of `reduce` and `filter`.

```
foldiftrue :: (* -> bool) -> (* -> ** -> **) -> ** -> [*]
foldiftrue pred ff default = (reduce ff default) . (filter pred)
```

The composed style is probably easier to read; the explicit recursion may appear algorithmically more efficient, but this really depends upon the underlying implementation (which might automatically convert function compositions to their equivalent explicit recursive form (Darlington *et al.*, 1982)).

Exercise 4.18

What is the purpose of the function `guesswhat`?

The function is a rather convoluted method of writing the built-in operator # in terms of itself.

Solutions for Chapter 5

Exercise 5.1

Write a function, using **where** definitions, to return the string that appears before a given sublist in a string. For example, `beforestring "and" "Miranda"` will return the string "Mir".

This is yet another example where it makes sense to reuse existing code, in this case the `startswith` function designed in Chapter 3:

```
beforestring :: [char] -> [char] -> [char]

beforestring any []
    = error "Beforestring: empty string to search"
beforestring bstring (front : rest)
    = [], if  startswith (bstring, front : rest)
      where
        startswith ([], any) = True
        startswith (any, []) = False
        startswith (front1 : rest1,  front2 : rest2)
            = (front1 = front2)
              & startswith (rest1, rest2)
    = front : beforestring bstring rest, otherwise
```

Note that it is not permitted to incorporate **type** declarations within a **where** clause.

Exercise 5.2

The Standard Environment function lines translates a list of characters containing new-lines into a list of character lists, by splitting the original at the newline characters, which are deleted from the result. For example, lines applied to:

```
"Programming with Miranda\nby\nClack\nMyers\nand Poon"
```

evaluates to:

```
["Programming with Miranda","by","Clack","Myers","and Poon"]
```

Write this function using a **where** definition.

```
mylines :: [char]->[[char]]
mylines [] = []
mylines ('\n' : rest) = [] : mylines rest
mylines (front : rest)
  = (front : thisline) : otherlines
    where
      (thisline : otherlines)
          = mylines rest, if rest ~= []
          = [[]], otherwise
          || handle missing '\n' on last line
```

The above code uses the induction hypothesis that mylines rest will correctly return a list of strings as required. Thus, in order to return the correct result, all that is necessary is to cons the **front** element onto the start of the first string returned by the recursive call. There are two base cases, the first of which deals with an empty list (this is the terminating condition), and the second of which returns an appropriate result if the front character in the input string is a newline.

Exercise 5.3

Define a list comprehension which has the same behaviour as the built-in function `filter`.

```
filter :: (* -> bool) -> [*] -> [*]
filter pred anylist = [x <- anylist | pred x]
```

This can be read as the list of all elements x, **where** x is sequentially from the list anylist **such that** pred x evaluates to True.

Exercise 5.4

Rewrite *quicksort* using list comprehensions.

```
qsort :: (* -> * -> bool) -> [*] -> [*]
qsort order = xqsort
              where
               xqsort [] = []
               xqsort (front : rest)
                  = xqsort [x | x <- rest; order x front]
                  ++ [front] ++
                  xqsort [x | x <- rest; ~ (order x front)]
```

The algorithm is the same as shown earlier in this chapter, but the `split` function has been replaced by two list comprehensions. The first generates all values from the `rest` of the list such that, for each value x, the `order` predicate on x and the `front` evaluates to `True`; the second where it does not. Notice also that the auxiliary function does not need to carry around `order`, which is in scope.

Exercise 5.5

Use a list comprehension to write a function that generates a list of the squares of all the even numbers from a given lower limit to upper limit. Change this function to generate an infinite list of even numbers and their squares.

One approach is to generate all the possible integers between `low` and `high` and create a list of the squares of only those integers that satisfy the constraint mod 2 - 0:

```
gensquares low high
        = [x * x | x <- [low .. high] ; x mod 2 = 0]
```

This is readily adapted to cater for infinite lists:

```
infinite_squares
        = [(x, x * x) | x <- [2..]; x mod 2 = 0]
```

Alternatively, it is possible to utilize the list comprehension's ability to recognize integer intervals:

```
infinite_squares = [(x, x * x) | x <- [2,4..]]
```

Solutions for Chapter 6

Exercise 6.1
Write a function to calculate the distance between a pair of coords.

The hardest part of this solution is to remember the geometry!

```
coords ::= Coords (num,num,num)


distance :: coords -> coords -> num
distance (Coords (x1,y1,z1)) (Coords (x2,y2,z2))
    = sqrt (square (x2 - x1) + square (y2 - y1) + square (z2 - z1))
      where
        square n = n * n
```

Exercise 6.2
Given the algebraic type:

```
action ::= Stop | No_change | Start
         | Slow_down | Prepare_to_start
```

write a function to take the appropriate action at each possible change in state for traffic_light.

```
drive :: traffic_light -> traffic_light -> action
drive Green Amber       = Slow_down
drive Amber Red         = Stop
drive Red Red_amber     = Prepare_to_start
drive Red_amber Green   = Start
drive x x               = No_change
drive x y               = error "broken lights"
```

Exercise 6.3
A Bochvar three-state logic has constants to indicate whether an expression is true, false or meaningless. Provide an algebraic type definition for this logic together with functions to perform the equivalent three-state versions of &, \/ and logical *implication*. Note that, if any part of an expression is meaningless then the entire expression should be considered meaningless.

```
bochvar ::= TRUE | FALSE | MEANINGLESS


andB :: bochvar -> bochvar -> bochvar
andB TRUE TRUE = TRUE
andB MEANINGLESS any = MEANINGLESS
andB any MEANINGLESS = MEANINGLESS
andB avalue bvalue = FALSE
```

```
orB :: bochvar -> bochvar -> bochvar
orB FALSE FALSE = FALSE
orB MEANINGLESS any = MEANINGLESS
orB any MEANINGLESS = MEANINGLESS
orB avalue bvalue = TRUE

impB :: bochvar -> bochvar -> bochvar
impB TRUE FALSE = FALSE
impB MEANINGLESS any = MEANINGLESS
impB any MEANINGLESS = MEANINGLESS
impB avalue bvalue = TRUE
```

Exercise 6.4

Explain why it is not sensible to attempt to mirror the tree data structure using nested lists.

It is necessary to know the depth of the tree before the correct level of list nesting can be determined. This is because Miranda does not allow lists to contain elements of mixed types and, for example, a double-nested list is of a different type than a triple-nested list. If the depth of the tree is known then each nested list can have the same depth; but this defeats the purpose of the tree data structure, which is designed to be of arbitrary depth.

Exercise 6.5

A number of useful tree manipulation functions follow naturally from the specification of a binary tree. Write functions to parallel the list manipulation functions map and # (in terms of the number of nodes in the tree).

The equivalent of map just traverses the tree, applying the parameter function to each non-empty node:

```
maptree :: (* -> **) -> tree * -> tree **

maptree ff Tnil = Tnil
maptree ff (Tree (ltree, node, rtree))
    = Tree (maptree ff ltree, ff node, maptree ff rtree)
```

The equivalent of # could be written by traversing the tree and adding 1 for each non-empty node, although an easier method is to reuse some existing code:

```
nodecount = (#) . tree_to_list
```

Exercise 6.6

What would have been the consequence of writing the function `list_to_tree` as:

```
list_to_tree order = reduce (insertleaf order) Tnil
```

This will fail because **reduce** expects its first argument to be a function of the form:

```
* -> ** -> **
```

whereas (`insertleaf order`) has the type:

```
tree * -> * -> tree *
```

which has the general form:

```
* -> ** -> *
```

It is always worth looking at a function's type for program design and debugging purposes.

Exercise 6.7

Write a function to remove an element from a sorted tree and return a tree that is still sorted.

The base cases are: deleting terminal nodes (for example, node 0 and node 7), which leaves the rest of the tree unaltered, and attempting to delete a node from an empty tree, which is an error.

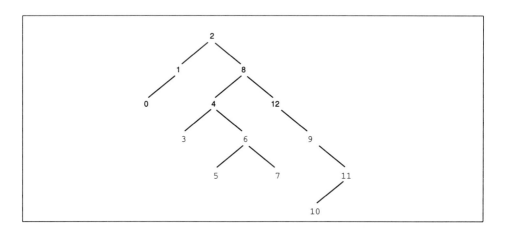

Figure A.1 A sample tree.

The general case is that of deleting non-terminal nodes. Here, only the subtree below the deleted node needs to be re-sorted. One method is to replace the deleted value with the highest value in the left subtree below the deleted node. Thus, given the sample tree in Figure A.1, deleting node 8 will require the value 8 to be replaced with the value 7. The node which contained the replacement value must now be deleted; this may cause yet another re-sorting of the tree.

For example, to delete node 12 will require the value 11 to take the place of 12; this means that node 11 must next be deleted from its original position, thus causing the value 10 to take its place; this means that node 10 must next be deleted from its original position, which can be achieved with a simple deletion and with no need to consider further subtrees.

Following the above informal specification:

```
delnode :: (* -> * -> bool) -> * -> tree * -> tree *

delnode ff item Tnil
    = error "delnode: item not in tree"
delnode order item (Tree(Tnil, item, rtree))
    = rtree    || 'promote' right subtree
delnode order item (Tree(ltree, item, rtree))
    =  || replace deleted node with new root and
       || delete new root from left subtree
      Tree (delnode order newroot ltree, newroot, rtree)
      where
       newroot
          = findhighest ltree
       findhighest (Tree (ltree, node, Tnil))
          = node
       findhighest (Tree (ltree, node, rtree))
          = findhighest rtree
delnode order item (Tree(ltree, node, rtree))
    = || look for item in rest of tree
      Tree (delnode order item ltree, node, rtree),
          if order item node
    = Tree (ltree, node, delnode order item rtree),
          otherwise
```

Note that when the condition item = node is true, the method proceeds by chosing a new root from the left subtree; hence there is no need to check if the right subtree is empty.

There is a simpler approach which merely flattens the tree, then deletes the item from the resultant list, and then turns the list back into a tree using list_to_tree. However, this approach immediately leads to a pathologically unbalanced tree, because the list argument to list_to_tree is totally sorted and therefore all tree nodes will have only one branch.

Solutions for Chapter 7

Exercise 7.1

Provide function definitions for the nat primitives if a recursive underlying data representation is used as follows: algnat ::= Zero | Succ algnat.

The solution to this exercise shows that the natural numbers can be modelled using only the constructors Succ and Zero; there is no need for any underlying built-in type. The abstype body provides a sample of the arithmetic and relational operators, as well as makeNat and show interfaces.

```
abstype nat
with
    makeNat :: num -> nat
    plusNat :: nat -> nat -> nat
    timesNat :: nat -> nat -> nat
    equalNat :: nat -> nat -> bool
    shownat :: nat -> [char]
    || etc
nat_type ::= Zero | Succ nat_type
nat == nat_type

makeNat x = error "makeNat: non-negative integer expected\n",
            if (x < 0) \/ (~ (integer x))
          = xmakeNat x, otherwise
            where
              xmakeNat 0 = Zero
              xmakeNat x = Succ (xmakeNat (x - 1))

plusNat x Zero = x
plusNat x (Succ y) = plusNat (Succ x) y

timesNat x Zero = Zero
timesNat x (Succ Zero) = x
timesNat x (Succ y) = plusNat x (timesNat x y)

equalNat (Zero) (Zero) = True
equalNat (Succ x) (Succ y) = x = y
equalNat (Succ x) (Zero) = False
equalNat (Zero) (Succ x) = False

shownat Zero = "Zero"
shownat (Succ x) = "(Succ " ++ (shownat x) ++ ")"
```

Note that the definition of plusNat is remarkably similar to the accumulative recursive definition of plus shown in Chapter 2.

Exercise 7.2

A *date* consists of a day, month and year. Legitimate operations on a date include: creating a date, checking whether a date is earlier or later than another date, adding a day to a date to give a new date, subtracting two dates to give a number of days, and checking if the date is within a leap year. Provide an abstract type declaration for a date.

The fact that the **date** abstract type can be declared on its own, demonstrates that a programmer does not necessarily have to worry about *implementation* at the same time as determining requirements. Coding the interface functions can be deferred or left to another programmer. Notice in this case, the declaration assumes that the date will be converted from a three number tuple, but makes no assumption concerning the type of a **day** or of a **date** itself.

```
abstype date
with
    makeDate :: (num,num,num) -> date
    lessDate :: date -> date -> bool
    greaterDate :: date -> date -> bool
    addday :: day -> date -> date
    diffDate :: date -> date -> day
    isleapyear :: date -> bool
```

Exercise 7.3

Complete the implementation for the sequence abstract type.

The completed implementation requires some code reuse for the left-to-right operations, and employing the built-in function **reverse** to cater for right-to-left operations:

```
seqHdL =  hd
seqHdR =  hd . reverse
seqTlL =  tl
seqTlR =  reverse . tl . reverse
seqAppend = (++)
```

Exercise 7.4

Provide a *show* function for the sequence abstract type.

Because **sequence** is a polymorphic abstract type, its corresponding **show** function requires a 'dummy' parameter. The **showsequence** implementation takes the first element in the underlying list, applies the dummy function **f** to it, and then concatenates the result to the recursive application on the rest of the list. The identity element is the empty list.

BIRKBECK
LIBRARY
COLLEGE

```
abstype sequence *
with

   ...
   seqDisplay :: (sequence *) -> [*]
   showsequence :: (* -> [char]) -> sequence * -> [char]

sequence * == [*]
   ...
seqDisplay s = s
   ...
showsequence f s = foldr ((++) . f) [] s
```

Notice that it is not possible to take the following approach:

```
showsequence f s = s
```

It is necessary to apply the dummy function to *every* component of the data structure. However, the definition for `seqDisplay` is perfectly acceptable because `seqDisplay` is not a *show* function.

Exercise 7.5

Assuming that the underlying type for an abstract date type is a three number tuple (day, month, year), provide functions to display the day and month in US format (month, day), UK format (day, month) and to display the month as a string such as "Jan" or "Feb".

This exercise demonstrates that "showing" an abstract type is rather arbitrary. More often than not, what is needed is to show some property of the type:

```
abstype date
with
   makeDate :: (num,num,num) -> date
   ...
   displayUK :: date -> (num,num)
   displayUS :: date -> (num,num)
   displayMonth :: date -> [char]

date = (num,num,num)

displayUK (day, month, year) = (month, day)
displayUS (day, month, year) = (day, month)
displayMonth (day, month, year)
   = ["Jan",Feb","March","April","May","June",
      "July","Aug","Sept","Oct","Nov","Dec"] ! (month - 1)
      || remember list indexing starts at 0
```

Exercise 7.6

An alternative representation of the `Atree` would be:

```
abstype other_tree *
with
    || declarations

    ordering * == * -> * -> bool
    other_tree * ::= Anil (ordering *)
                   | ATree (ordering *) (other_tree *) * (other_tree *)
```

What would be the consequences for the abstract type implementation?

The ordering function would be contained at each node in the `other_tree` rather than just once at the highest root in the tree.

Exercise 7.7

A *queue* aggregate data structure (Standish, 1980) can be defined as either being empty or as consisting of a queue followed by an element; operations include creating a new queue, inserting an element at the end of a queue and removing the first element in a queue. The following declares a set of primitives for a polymorphic abstract type queue:

```
abstype queue *
with
    qisempty = queue * -> bool
    qtop     = queue * -> *
    qinsert  = queue * -> * -> queue *
    qcreate  = queue *
```

Provide an implementation for this abstract type.

Just as with the *array* examples, there are many possible implementations and, as far as the meaning of a program is concerned, it should not matter which is chosen. The implementation rationale is often determined by algorithmic complexity, based on assumptions about the pattern of accesses and updates; however, this subject is beyond the scope of this book. For this **abstype**, it is possible to use a simple list as the underlying type, however the following construction shows an equally valid alternative:

```
queue_type * ::= Qnil | Queue (queue *, *)
queue * == queue_type *

qtop Qnil = error "Queue: empty queue"
qtop (Queue (Qnil, qfirst)) = qfirst
qtop (Queue (qrest, qfirst))  = qtop qrest

qisempty aq = (aq = Qnil)
qinsert queue item = Queue (queue, item)
qcreate = Qnil
```

Solutions for Chapter 8

Exercise 8.1

Adapt the *wordcount* program so that it will work for more than one input file.

```
manywordcount :: [[char]] -> [char]
manywordcount filenames
   = lay (map f filenames)
     where
       f name = name ++ ":\t" ++ show (wordcount name)
```

This simple solution invokes `wordcount` for each of the given filenames; each result is formatted so that it is transformed from a three-tuple to a string using `show` and then appears after the name of the file, a colon and a tab. The result of `map` is a list of strings, which `lay` (a function from the Standard Environment) concatenates as a single string using newline delimiters.

The above example does not give the total for all the files, nor does it return the result numerically. A different solution might only return a three-tuple giving the totals across all the files:

```
manywordcount2 :: [[char]] -> [char]
manywordcount2 filenames
   = foldr totals (0,0,0) (map f filenames)
     where
         f name = (wordcount name)
         totals (a,b,c) (t1,t2,t3) = (a+t1, b+t2, c+t3)
```

Exercise 8.2

Explain why the following code is incorrect:

```
wrongsplit infile
             = first second
               where first = hd inlist
                     second = tl inlist
                     inlist = readvals infile
```

The code is wrong because Miranda does not know the type of the contents of `infile`, and so `readvals` cannot work. Furthermore, because there is no concrete representation of a function, there is no possible way that `readvals` could create a list of values such that the first item could be treated as a function.

Exercise 8.3

Provide the functions readbool and dropbool which, respectively, will read and discard a Boolean value from the start of an input file.

These answers use the function **readword** as defined in the text of Chapter 8. They expect the input to be a string representing a Boolean; this is checked and either the appropriate action is taken or an error message is given:

```
readbool :: [char] -> bool
readbool infile
   = check (readword infile)
     where
       check "True" = True
       check "False" = False
       check other = error "readbool"

dropbool :: [char] -> [char]
dropbool infile
   = check (readword infile)
     where
       check "True" = dropword infile
       check "False" = dropword infile
       check other = error "dropbool"
```

Exercise 8.4

Explain why the following attempt at vend is incorrect:

```
vend = (System "clear") : wrongdialogue $+
wrongdialogue ip = [Stdout welcome] ++ quit, if sel = 4
                 = [Stdout welcome] ++ (next sel), otherwise
                   where
                   (sel : rest) = ip
                   next 1 = confirm "tea" ++ wrongdialogue rest
                   next 2 = confirm "coffee" ++ wrongdialogue rest
                   next 3 = confirm "soup" ++ wrongdialogue rest
                   next 4 = quit
```

In the above code, the guard if sel = 4 requires the value of sel and therefore causes the input to be scanned **before** the welcome message is printed to the screen.

Exercise 8.5

Why is it necessary for check to have a **where** block, and why is confirm repeatedly applied within acknowledge?

The definition of dialogue is given as:

```
dialogue :: [num] -> [sys_message]
dialogue ip
  = [Stdout welcome] ++ next ++ (check rest2)
    where
    (sel : rest) = ip
    (next, rest2)
        = (([tea, coffee, soup] ! (sel - 1)) rest
    check xip = [Stdout menu3] ++ xcheck xip
                where
                xcheck (1:rest3) = quit rest3
                xcheck (2:rest3) = dialogue rest3
                xcheck any       = quit any
```

The function **check** must have a **where** block because menu3 must be output to the screen before the user's response xip is evaluated. In the expression [Stdout menu3] ++ xcheck xip, the evaluation of xcheck only occurs after the left operand of ++ has been output.

The definition of acknowledge is given as:

```
acknowledge :: [char] -> num -> [sys_message]
acknowledge d 1 = confirm (d ++ " with Milk & Sugar")
acknowledge d 2 = confirm (d ++ " with Milk")
acknowledge d 3 = confirm (d ++ " with Sugar")
acknowledge d 4 = confirm d
```

An alternative definition does not use confirm repeatedly:

```
wrongacknowledge :: [char] -> num -> [sys_message]
wrongacknowledge d x = confirm (d ++ (mesg x))
                       where
                       mesg 1 = " with Milk & Sugar"
                       mesg 2 = " with Milk"
                       mesg 3 = " with Sugar"
                       mesg 4 = []
```

Unfortunately, this (wrong) version has the undesirable effect that the the phrase "Thank you for choosing" is printed *before* the user has entered a number. This becomes obvious when the definition for confirm is given:

```
confirm :: [char] -> [sys_message]
confirm choice = Stdout [("\nThank you for choosing "
                 ++ choice ++ ".\n")]
```

Exercise 8.6
   Use the above board, as the basis for a simple game of noughts and crosses (tic-tac-toe).

```
>|| Noughts and crosses (tic-tac-toe) game: (Page 1 of 4)

Controlling program - main:
    This makes use of Miranda's keyboard input directive $+
    Start the game by entering 'main' at the Miranda prompt.

> move==(num,num)

> main = [System "stty cbreak"] ++
>        [Stdout greeting] ++
>        [Stdout (game $+)] ++
>        [System "stty sane"]

> greeting
> = "\nWelcome to the Noughts and Crosses game\n\n" ++
>    "Please enter moves in the form (x,y) followed by a newline\n" ++
>    "Each number should be either 0, 1 or 2; for example: (1,2)\n\n" ++
>    "Enter your first move now, and further moves after the display:\n"

> game:: [move]->[char]
> game ip = xgame ip empty_board

> xgame [] brd = []
> xgame ((x,y) : rest) brd
>    = prompt ++ m1, if ss1
>      ||
>      || don't test s2 here because it will delay printout
>      || of the user's move until the computer move is done
>      ||
>    = prompt ++ m1 ++ xgame rest brd, if (~s1)
>    = prompt ++ "Computer's move:\n" ++ nextmove, otherwise
>      where
>      prompt = clearscreen ++ "Player's move:\n"
>                ++ print_board newboard1
>      clearscreen = "\f"
>      nextmove = print_board newboard2 ++ m2 , if ss2
>               = print_board newboard2 ++ m2
>                 ++ xgame rest newboard2, if (~s2)
>               = print_board newboard2
>                 ++ xgame rest newboard2, otherwise
>      (newboard1,s1,ss1,m1) = user_move brd (x,y)
>      (newboard2,s2,ss2,m2) = comp_move newboard1
```

```
>|| Noughts and crosses game continued (Page 2 of 4)
```

State:

```
> state == (board, bool, bool, [char])
```

Board:

```
> abstype board
> with
>    empty_board   :: board     || in order to start the game
>    print_board   :: board -> [char]
>    game_over     :: board -> state
>    user_move     :: board -> (num,num) -> state
>    computer_move :: board -> state
```

Represent the board as a list of lists of cells,
where a cell is either Empty or contains a Nought or a Cross:

```
> cell ::= Empty | Nought | Cross
> board == [[cell]]
```

An empty board has 9 empty cells

```
> empty_board = [ [Empty,Empty,Empty],
>                  [Empty,Empty,Empty],
>                  [Empty,Empty,Empty]
>                ]
```

Print the board:

```
> print_board [row1,row2,row3]
>        = edge ++ printrow1 ++ edge ++ printrow2 ++ edge
>          ++ printrow3 ++ edge
>          where
>          edge = "-------------" ++ "\n"
>          printrow1 = (concat (map showcell row1)) ++ "|\n"
>          printrow2 = (concat (map showcell row2)) ++ "|\n"
>          printrow3 = (concat (map showcell row3)) ++ "|\n"
>          showcell Empty  = "|   "
>          showcell Nought = "| O "
>          showcell Cross  = "| X "
```

>|| Noughts and crosses game continued (Page 3 of 4)

Check for "game over".
  Find three Noughts or Crosses in a row, column or diagonal
  and then indicate who won (computer plays crosses).

```
> game_over brd
>       = (brd,over,over,msg)
>         where
>           over = cross_wins \/ nought_wins \/ board_full
>           cross_wins  = finished Cross
>           nought_wins = finished Nought
>           board_full  = ~(member (concat brd) Empty)
>
>           finished token = or (map (isline token) (rows ++ cols ++ diags))
>           isline x [x,x,x] = True
>           isline x [a,b,c] = False
>
>           rows = brd
>           cols = transpose brd
>           diags = [ [brd!0!0,brd!1!1,brd!2!2], [brd!0!2,brd!1!1,brd!2!0] ]
>
>           msg = "Computer won!\n", if cross_wins
>               = "Player won!\n",   if nought_wins
>               = "Board Full\n",    if board_full
>               = "",                otherwise
```

Add the user's move to the board.
  But first check if the new cell is on or off the board
      then check if the new cell is already occupied.
  Then return a four-tuple indicating:
    (i)   the new board after the change has been made
    (ii) a boolean to say whether the change was successful
    (iii) a boolean to say whether the program should terminate
    (iv) a string containing an error message if the change failed.

```
> user_move brd (x,y)
>     = (newb,False,True,message2),    if over
>     = (newb,success,False,message1), otherwise
>       where
>         (newb,success,message1) = do_move brd (x,y) Nought
>         (b1,over,s2,message2) = game_over newb
```

```
>|| Noughts and crosses game continued (Page 4)

> do_move :: [[cell]]->(num,num)->cell->([[cell]],bool,[char])
> do_move brd (x,y) token
>       = (brd,False,"illegal move - off the board\n"),
>           if ~((0 <= x <= 2) & (0 <= y <= 2))
>       = (brd,False,"cell not empty\n"),
>           if (brd!y)!x ~= Empty
>       = (newb,True,""), otherwise
>         where
>           newb = simple_move brd (x,y)
>           simple_move [d,e,f] (x,0) = (newcol d x):[e,f]
>           simple_move [d,e,f] (x,1) = d:(newcol e x):[f]
>           simple_move [d,e,f] (x,2) = d:e:[newcol f x]
>           simple_move [d,e,f] (x,n)
>               = error (seq (force (system "stty sane"))
>                                 "out of bounds\n")
>           newcol [cell1,cell2,cell3] 0 = [token,cell2,cell3]
>           newcol [cell1,cell2,cell3] 1 = [cell1,token,cell3]
>           newcol [cell1,cell2,cell3] 2 = [cell1,cell2,token]
>           newcol [cell1,cell2,cell3] n
>               = error (seq (force (system "stty sane"))
>                                 "out of bounds\n")
```

Computer move:
    first check whether all positions are full,
    then choose where to put a cross:
    note: there is no attempt to win, just to play honestly!

```
> comp_move b  = (newb,False,True,message2),    if over
>               = (newb,success,False,message1),otherwise
>                   where
>                     (newb,success,x,message1) = computer_move b
>                     (b1,over,s2,message2) = game_over newb
>
> computer_move brd
>     = (brd,False,True,"Board full\n"),
>         if ~(member (concat brd) Empty)
>     = hd [ (newb,success,False,m) | i,j <- [0..2];
>           (newb,success,m) <- [do_move brd (i,j) Cross];
>           (success = True) ], otherwise
```

draw successful moves from a list containing
the results of moves for all values of i and j

Bibliography

Annotated bibliography

Miranda

Turner D. *Miranda: A Non-Strict Functional Language with Polymorphic Types*

Turner D. *An Overview of Miranda*
  The first papers to describe the Miranda system, written by its creator.

Research Software Limited, *Miranda On-line Reference Manual* On-line documentation, available with all Miranda implementations; this also contains details of additional features and built-in library functions.

Holyer I. *Functional Programming with Miranda* Presents an overview of Miranda and some theoretical and implementation issues.

Bird R. & Wadler P. *Introduction to Functional Programming* This book uses a notation similar to Miranda. Its emphasis is on mathematical examples and the algebraic manipulation of functions. It is suitable for a range of abilities from the mathematically-oriented beginner to the more advanced programmer.

History and future of functional programming

Backus J. *Can programming be liberated from the von Neumann style* A seminal paper which discusses the problems of basing programming languages on the Turing computational model; it then outlines a functional language known as FP.

Landin P. *The next 700 programming languages* Apart from having a great title, this paper is important for highlighting the relation between a language's written representation and its meaning. The proposed language ISWIM (*If you See What I Mean*) deals with expressions rather than procedural statements. As such it probably shares with LISP the genesis of modern functional programming languages.

Hudak P. *Conception, Evolution and Application of Functional Programming Languages* This excellent reference has a self-explanatory title!

Functional programming in general

Burge W. *Recursive Programming Techniques* Probably the first book to discuss the functional style of programming and still relevant. It also has several very useful parsing and sorting algorithms which demonstrate the functional programming style.

Darlington J., Henderson P. & Turner D. *Functional Programming and its applications* Contains a number of interesting articles from theoretical background to practical applications.

Eisenbach S. (ed.) *Functional Programming, languages, tools and architectures* A collection of introductory articles covering other Functional programming languages (HOPE and FP), practice, theory and implementation. Chapter 4 is of particular interest in that it shows that the functional style of programming can be used to good effect with a procedural language.

Field A. & Harrison P. *Functional Programming* An intermediate to advanced level book which uses Hope as the base functional language. It has a modern approach and covers a lot of ground, from an introduction to functional programming through to implementation techniques.

Glaser H., Hankin C. & Till D. *Principles of Functional Programming* One of the first general textbooks in this area; it also gives a gentle introduction to the lambda calculus and some related topics. The first chapter gives a language-independent example of functional program development.

Henson M. *Elements of Functional Languages* A general-purpose text with a treatment of program transformation.

MacLennan B. *Functional Programming Theory and Practice* This book introduces the practice and theory of functional language by using mathematical notation in preference to a particular Functional programming language. Discusses performance and implementation issues.

Myers C., Clack C. & Poon E. *Programming with Standard ML* Standard ML is a strict functional programming language, which contrasts to the lazy evaluation of Miranda. The book serves as a companion volume to this text, and should be useful to anyone wishing to learn the strict functional programming style.

Reade C. *Elements of Functional Programming* A relatively advanced textbook, using a language similar to SML. It has the purpose of covering functional programming in general; Chapters 4 and 6 give some extended examples of functional software. The book also introduces more theoretical issues, including: denotational semantics, type systems, lambda calculus and combinators and a discussion of implementation considerations.

Implementation of functional languages

Diller A. *Compiling Functional Languages* An advanced book, providing an overview of a wide range of techniques used in Functional language compilers. Uses LispKit LISP as the base language.

Henderson P. *Functional Programming Application and Implementation* One of the first books dealing with functional programming. It has some good examples of programming using higher order functions based on a purely functional subset of LISP (called LispKit). The book discusses how LispKit might be isolated from LISP. Since LISP is still widely used in the world of Artificial Intelligence, the use of a good functional style of programming in LISP is to be encouraged.

Peyton Jones S. *The Implementation of Functional Programming Languages* Apart from dealing with the implementation of functional programming languages, this book also gives an overview of the lambda calculus and some other theoretical issues required for an understanding of implementations.

Peyton Jones S. & Lester D. *Implementing Functional Languages* A very good practical book showing different implementation approaches using Miranda as the target language.

Functional programming and formal methods

Barendregt H. *The Lambda Calculus: Its Syntax and Semantics*

Michaelson G. *Functional Programming through Lambda Calculus*

Revesz G. *Lambda-Calculus, Combinators and Functional Programming*
The lambda calculus is a small but important mathematical language which forms the basis of understanding many of the theoretical issues of functional programming languages and of programming language theory in general.
The first of these books is the standard reference book for the lambda calculus; it is more of a mathematical interest rather than being essential for a computer scientist. The second text is a gentle guide, whilst the third takes a more rigorous approach which leads to techniques for functional programming implementation.

Thompson S. *Type Theory and Functional Programming* Constructive type theory is a formal system which covers both logic and functional programming. It can be used a programming language in its own right, a tool to develop functional programs and to reason about their correctness.

References

Aho A., Hopcroft J. & Ullman J. (1974), *The Design and Analysis of Computer Algorithms*, Addison-Wesley.

Backus J. (1978), *Can programming be liberated from the von Neumann style?*, Communications of the ACM, vol 21 no 8 pp 613-641.

Barendregt H. (1984), *The Lambda Calculus: Its Syntax and Semantics*, North Holland.

Bird R. & Wadler P. (1988), *Introduction to Functional Programming*, Prentice Hall.

Brooks F. (1975), *The Mythical Man-month*, Addison-Wesley.

Burge W. (1975), *Recursive Programming Techniques*, Addison-Wesley.

Darlington J., Henderson P. & Turner D. (1982), *Functional Programming and its Applications*, Cambridge University Press.

Diller A. (1988), *Compiling Functional Languages*, Wiley.

Eisenbach S. (ed.), (1987) *Functional Programming, languages, tools and architectures*, Ellis-Horwood.

Field A. & Harrison P. (1988), *Functional Programming*, Addison-Wesley.

Glaser H., Hankin C. & Till D. (1984), *Principles of Functional Programming*, Prentice Hall.

Gordon M. (1979), *The Denotational Description of Programming Languages*, Springer.

Henderson P. (1980), *Functional Programming, Application and Implementation*, Prentice Hall.

Henson M. (1987), *Elements of Functional Languages*, Blackwell Scientific Publications.

Holyer I. (1991), *Programming with Miranda*, Pitman.

Hudak P. (1989), *Conception, Evolution and Application of Functional Programming Languages*, ACM Computing Surveys, vol 21 no 3 pp 359-411.

Hughes J. (1984), *Why Functional Programming Matters*, Report 16, Programming Methodology Group, University of Göteborg and Chalmers University of Technology.

Kelley P. (1989), *Functional Programming for Loosely-coupled Multiprocessors*, Pitman.

Kernighan B. & Pike R. (1984), *The UNIX Programming Environment*, Prentice Hall.

Landin P. (1966), *The next 700 programming languages*, Communications of the ACM, vol 9 no 3 pp 157-164.

MacLennan B. (1990), *Functional Programming Theory and Practice*, Addison Wesley.

Michaelson G. (1989), *Functional Programming through Lambda Calculus*, Addison-Wesley.

Minsky, M. (1967), *Computation: Finite and Infinite Machines*, Prentice Hall.

Myers C., Clack C. & Poon E. (1993), *Programming with Standard ML*, Prentice Hall.

Park S. & Miller K. (1988), *Random number generators: good ones are hard to find,* Communications ACM 31, pp 1192-1201.

Peyton Jones S. (1987), *The Implementation of Functional Programming Languages,* Prentice Hall.

Peyton Jones S. & Lester D. (1991), *Implementing Functional Languages,* Prentice Hall.

Reade C. (1989), *Elements of Functional Programming,* Addison-Wesley.

Revesz G. (1988), *Lambda-Calculus, Combinators and Functional Programming,* Cambridge University Press.

Research Software Limited (1990), *Miranda On-line Reference Manual.*

Standish T. (1980), *Data Structure Techniques,* Addison-Wesley.

Thompson S. (1991), *Type Theory and Functional Programming,* Addison-Wesley.

Turner D. (1976), *SASL Language Manual,* St. Andrews University, Technical Report.

Turner D. (1979), *A New Implementation Technique for Applicative Languages,* Software Practice and Experience, vol 9, pp 31-49

Turner D. (1982), *Recursion equations as a programming language,* in (Darlington *et al.,* 1982).

Turner D. (1985a), *Functional Programs as Executable Specifications,* in Hoare C. & Shepherdson (eds), *Mathematical Logic and Programming Languages* Prentice Hall.

Turner D. (1985b), *Miranda: A Non-Strict Functional Language with Polymorphic Types,* in Proceedings IFIP Conference on Functional Programming Languages and Computer Architecture, Springer Lecture Notes in Computer Science, vol 201.

Turner D. (1986), *An Overview of Miranda,* in ACM SIGPLAN Notices, vol 21 no 12.

Index

005.
133
CLA

BIRKBECK COLLEGE

19 0275797 X